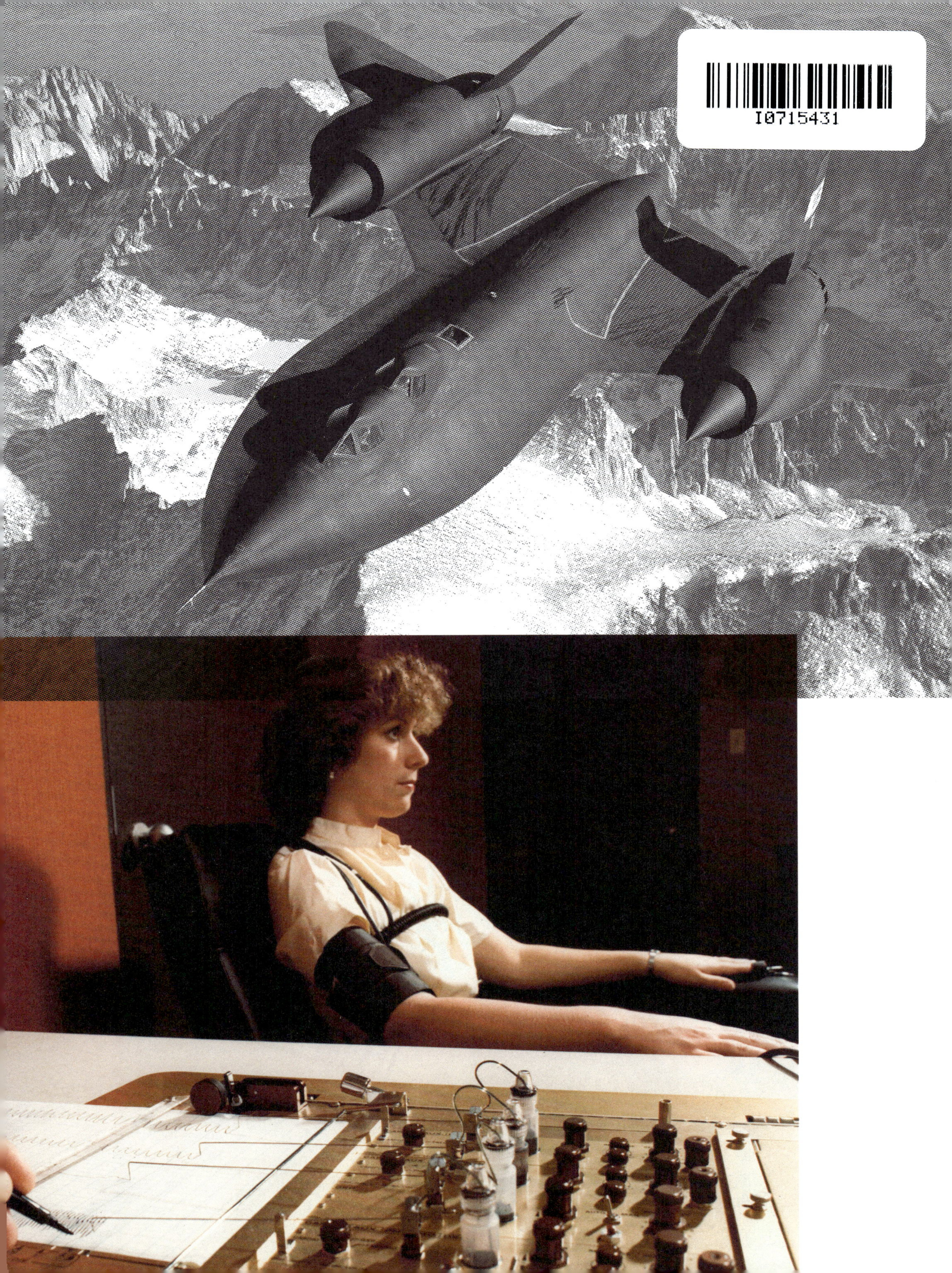

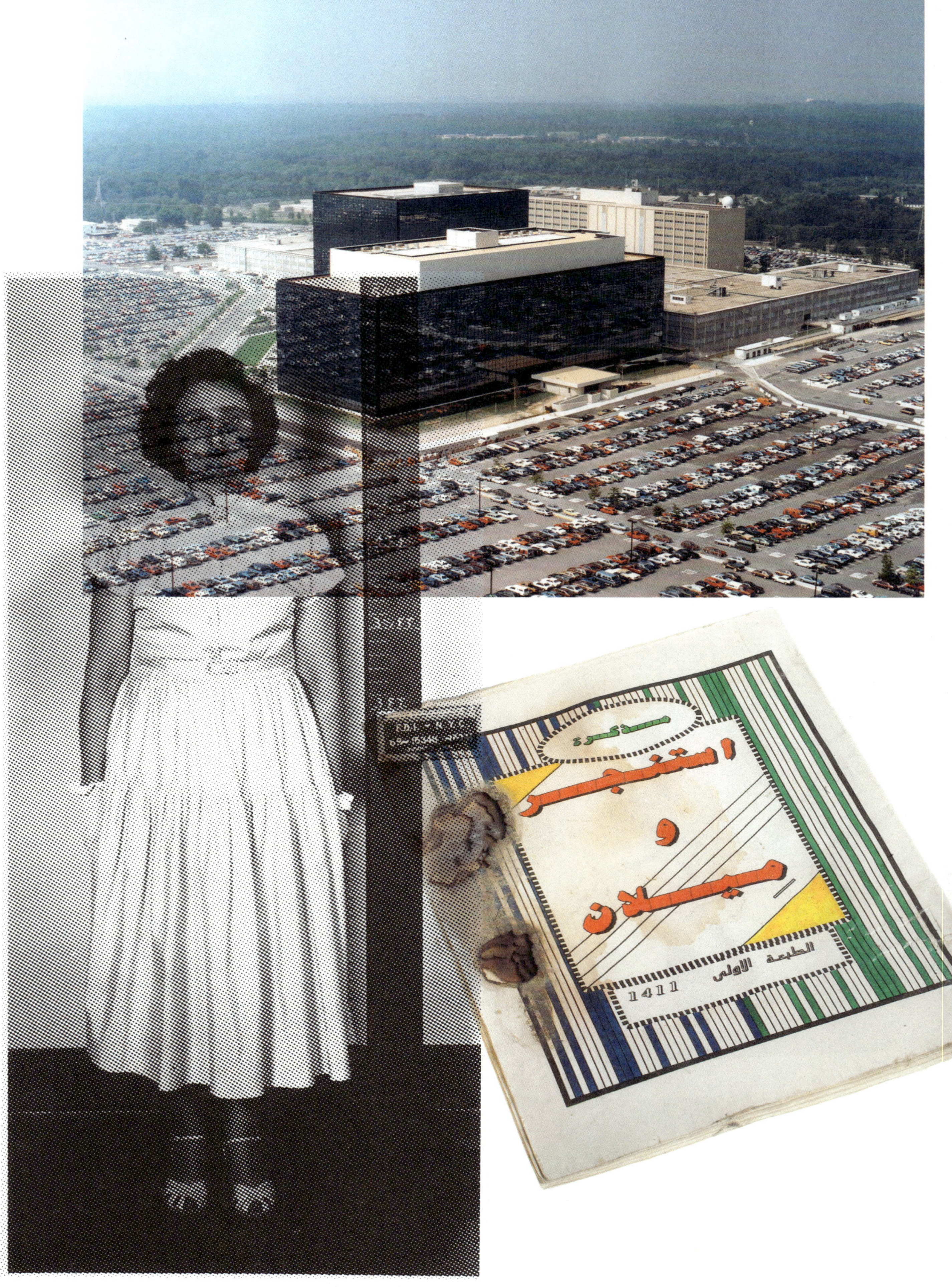
مذكرة
استنجر
و
ميلان
الطبعة الأولى
1411

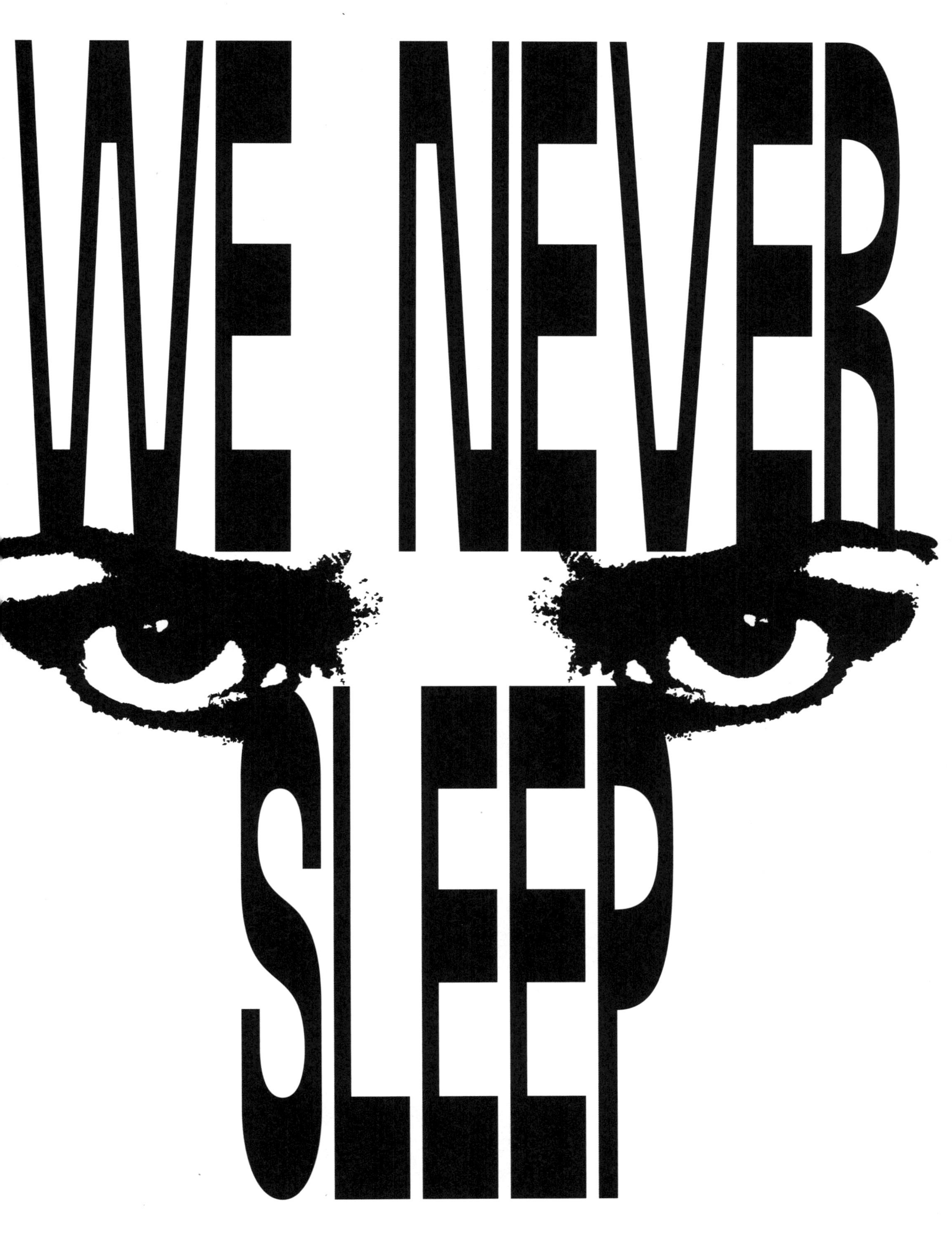

WE NEVER
SLEEP

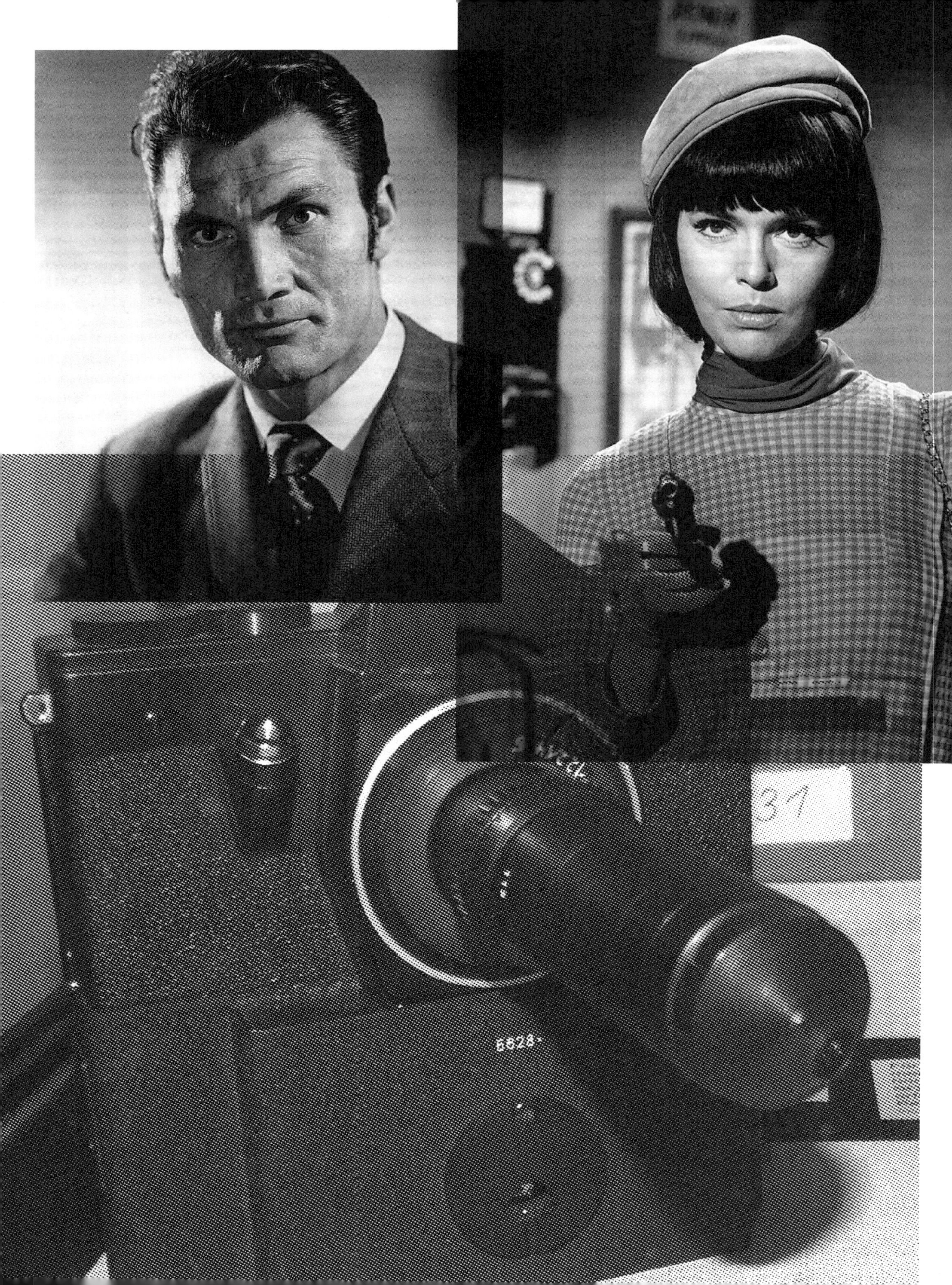

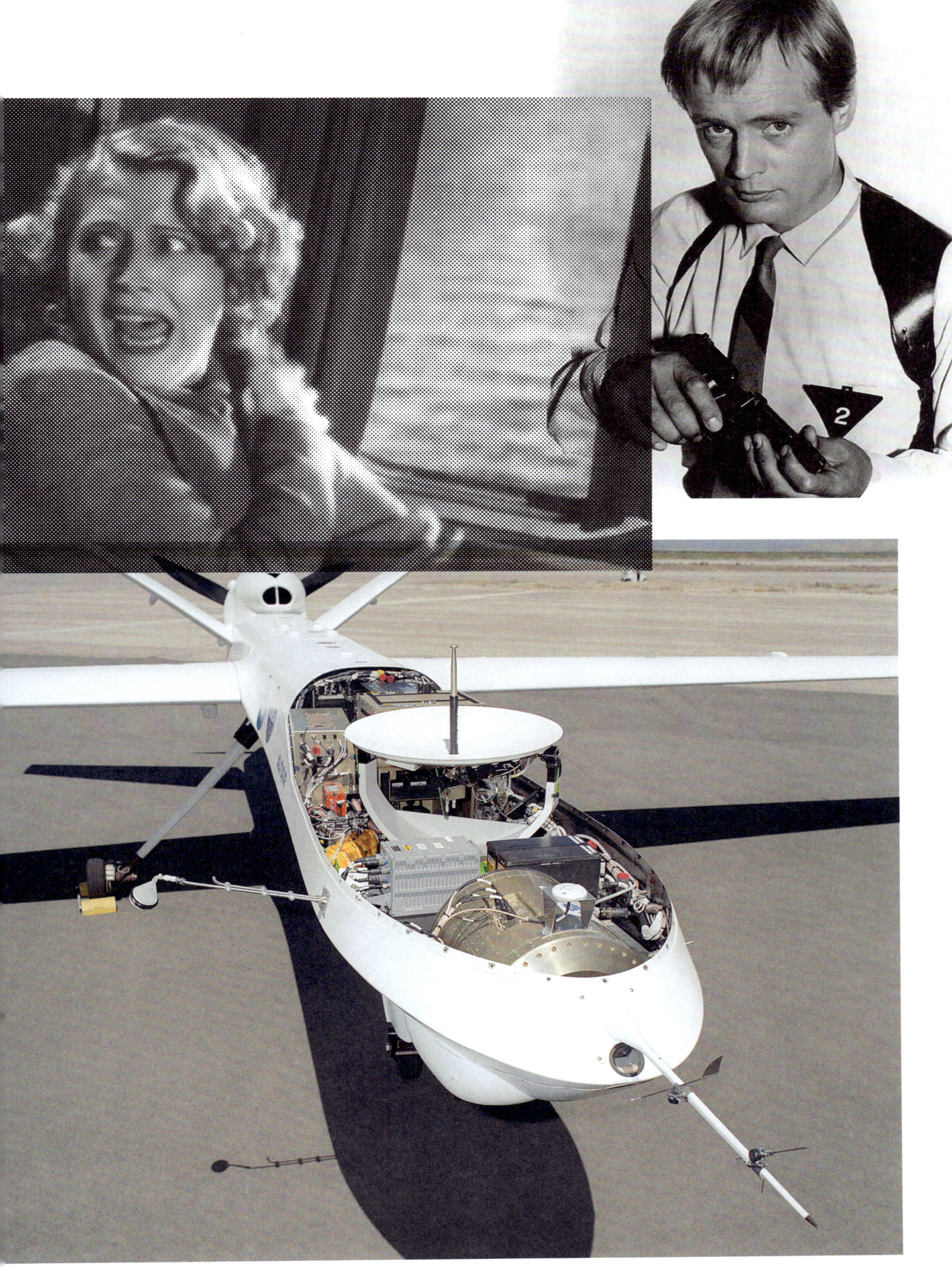

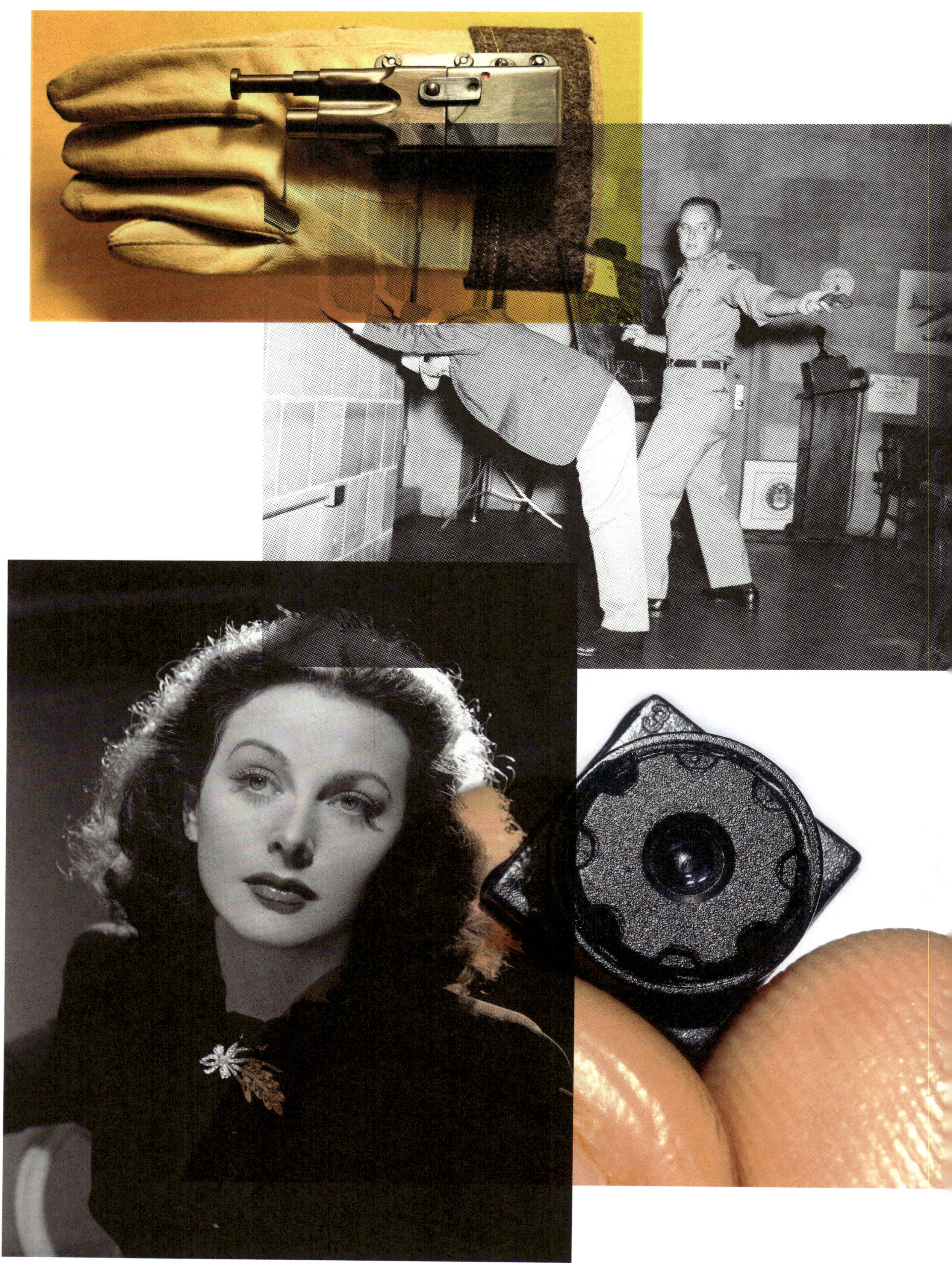

We Never Sleep

Edited by / Herausgegeben von
Cristina Ricupero, Alexandra Midal,
Katharina Dohm (Schirn)

Schirn Kunsthalle Frankfurt
Snoeck

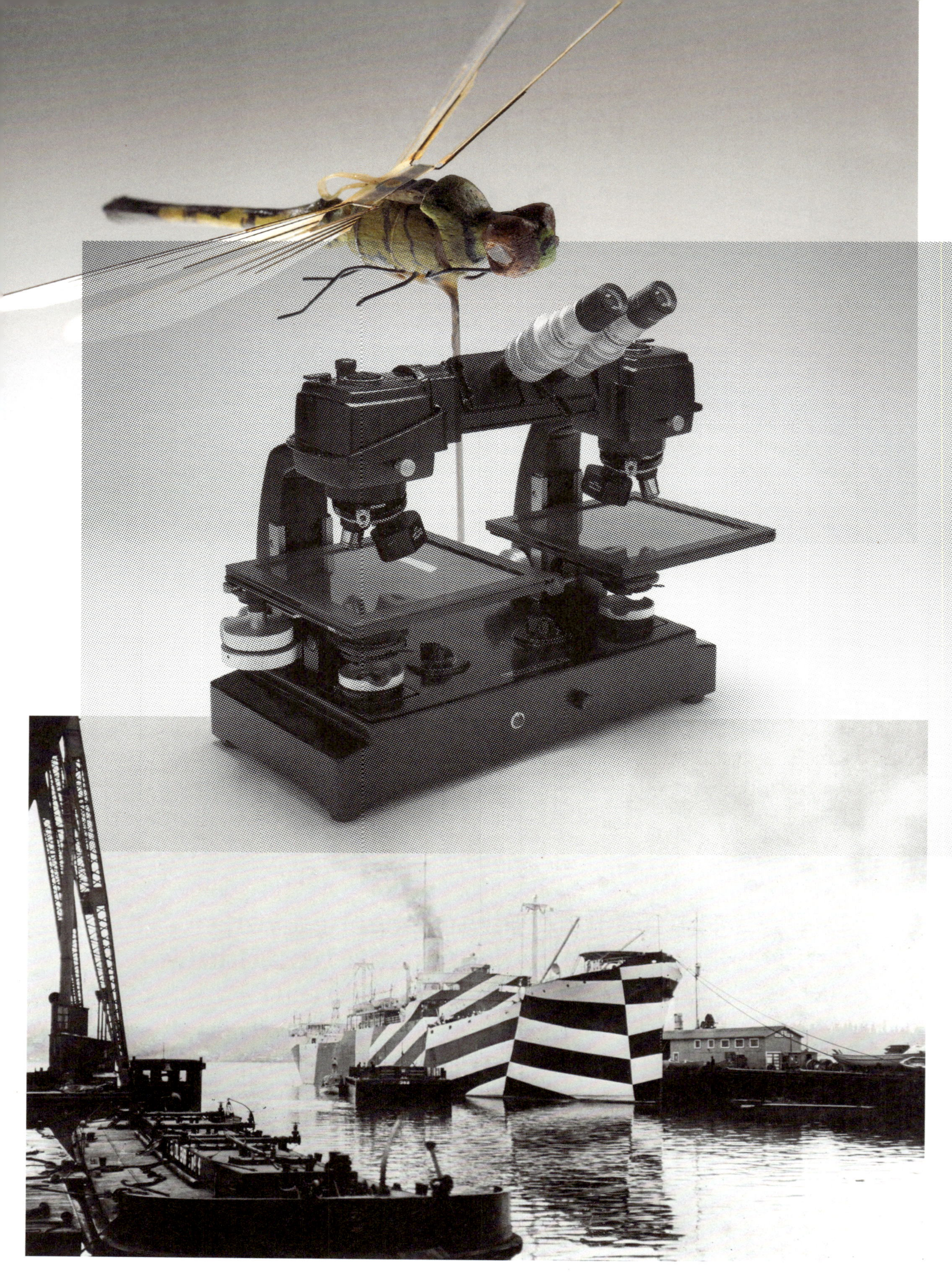

Contents / Inhalt

Foreword / Vorwort
11 / 15

We Never Sleep
Or How to Curate an Art Exhibition
on Espionage / We Never Sleep
oder: Wie man eine Kunstausstellung
über Spionage kuratiert
Cristina Ricupero
19 / 29

The Secret Life of Art During and
After the Cold War / Das verborgene
Leben der Kunst während und nach
dem Kalten Krieg
Jörg Heiser
41 / 51

The Motion Picture as an Art of
Espionage / Film als Spionagekunst
Jelena Martinovic
61 / 65

All the Mystery, and Fear, and Terror
that Love Can Hold
Noam Toran
71

The Agent in Plain Sight /
Das exponierte Agententum
Wladimir Velminski
101 / 113

Mask: The Political Space behind
the War on Terror / Maske: Der
politische Raum hinter dem Krieg
gegen den Terror
Marina Otero Verzier
125 / 129

Facsimiles / Faksimiles

Propaganda (Art) Struggle
Jonas Staal
137

Captives of the Cloud: Part I
Metahaven
151

The artist who spied on MI6
Joanna Moorhead
167

Der Spion, der sich als Künstler tarnte
Ulrike Knöfel
173

Author Biographies /
Autorenbiografien
176

List of Works /
Werkliste
178

Image and Text Credits /
Bild- und Textnachweise
182

Colophon /
Impressum
183

Supported by /
Gefördert durch

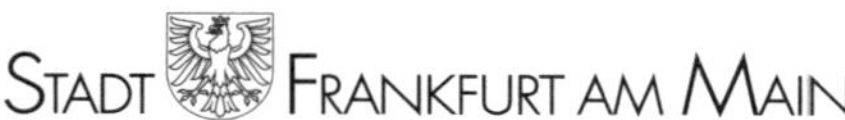 STADT FRANKFURT AM MAIN

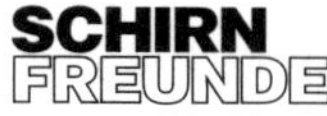 SCHIRN FREUNDE

With the support of /
Mit Unterstützung von

Members of the Executive Board and the Board of Trustees
of the Friends of the Schirn Kunsthalle e. V. / Mitglieder des
Vorstands und des Kuratoriums der Schirn Freunde e. V.

Foreword

"WE NEVER SLEEP."—This is the slogan of Pinkerton's National Detective Agency, the oldest such agency in the United States, founded in 1850. Among its greatest successes is the foiled assassination attempt on President Abraham Lincoln in 1861. The tagline, which frames an open eye in the agency's logo, soon became common knowledge. This had already become apparent in 1917 in Hollywood's silent movie theaters when the *Lonesome Luke* series ended with the episode "We Never Sleep". An amateurish detective pursues the wrong man, superbly impersonated by the famous comedian Harold Lloyd. Meanwhile, the First World War raged in Europe. Detectives, agents, and spies—regardless of their respective clients, their activities are characterized by espionage and the procurement of secret information, which could possibly prevent a war or at least bring it to an early end. In the exhibition *We Never Sleep*, contemporary artists in their works address aspects of espionage such as surveillance, paranoia, threat, and camouflage, cryptography, manipulation, cold-bloodedness, and treason. A variety of artistic strategies and bizarre objects in the exhibition brings into focus both the "heyday" of espionage activity during the Cold War and the current debate on media exposure and monitoring.

The exhibition was conceived long before the start of the coronavirus crisis, yet it became quite apparent even during the pandemic that secret services were doing exactly what they have always been doing. They procure information that is hard to obtain for the rest of us. They can neither cure nor stop a virus, and at best they can provide information, uncover fake news, or contradict conspiracy theories: Did the virus originate in a laboratory in Wuhan? Is Bill Gates really behind it, or are elitist secret societies trying to create an authoritarian world order? How great is the desire for security in relation to the loss of (personal) freedom? The exhibition *We Never Sleep* does not provide final answers, but it raises questions that seem more virulent today than ever before. The catalogue provides a further, supplementary "tool" for the study of the subject matter from a variety of historical and contemporary perspectives. *We Never Sleep* continues the Schirn's tradition of raising socially relevant issues with major themed exhibitions that tie in with current discourse—such as *Infinite Jest* (2014), *Peace* (2017), or *Power to the People* (2018). In 2014, the exhibition *Secret Societies*, curated by Cristina Ricupero together with Alexis Vaillant, already examined secret societies and their impact. This is now complemented by the theme of espionage with *We Never Sleep*.

I wish to first of all thank the many artists who have contributed to this comprehensive project with both existing and new works: Lawrence Abu Hamdan, Maja Bajevic, Jean-Luc Blanc, Nina Childress, Guy de Cointet, Thomas

Demand, Simon Denny, Mauricio Dias & Walter Riedweg, Stan Douglas, Charles and Ray Eames, Forensic Architecture, Dora García, Mathis Gasser, Rodney Graham, Eva Grubinger, Humans since 1982, Alfredo Jaar, Kiluanji Kia Henda, Gabriel Lester, Lim Minouk, Dora Longo Bahia, Jill Magid, Fabian Marti, Josephine Meckseper, Mieko Meguro, Metahaven, Aleksandra Mir, Henrike Naumann, Trevor Paglen, Park Chan-Kyong and Park Chan-Wook, Cornelia Schleime, Jim Shaw, Taryn Simon, Jonas Staal, Noam Toran, Suzanne Treister, Nomeda & Gediminas Urbonas, Jane and Louise Wilson, Liam Young, and Tamir Zadok. I very much appreciate their collaboration with the curators, Cristina Ricupero and Alexandra Midal. I would like to express my sincere thanks to Cristina Ricupero and Alexandra Midal, who initiated and conceived this exhibition project following in-depth research and extensive preparations. Cristina Ricupero, together with Katharina Dohm, was also responsible for the development and elaborate realization of the exhibition. I am grateful for their close cooperation and dedication to the exhibition project, as well as for the preparation of this publication, which provides a wealth of insights into the extensive spectrum of espionage-related topics. I also thank Alica Sänger for her assistance in preparing the exhibition and the catalogue.

Numerous international museums, institutions, and private lenders have contributed to this comprehensive exhibition project by generously providing works on loan. I am grateful to Weiss Falk, Basel; Saatchi Gallery, Berkshire; Deutsche Kinemathek, Berlin; Deutsches Spionagemuseum, Berlin; Galerie Buchholz, Berlin; Stasimuseum, Berlin; Deutsche Bank Collection, Düsseldorf; Deutsches Filmmuseum, Frankfurt am Main; Sammlung von Kelterborn / Von Kelterborn Collection, Frankfurt am Main; Sfeir-Semler Gallery, Hamburg / Beirut; Bürgerkomitee Leipzig e. V. für die Auflösung der ehemaligen Staatssicherheit (MfS); Annely Juda Fine Art, London; Timothy Taylor Gallery, London; Eames Office, Los Angeles; Combined Military Services Museum, Maldon, Essex; 303 Gallery, New York; Air de Paris, Paris; Heinz Nixdorf MuseumsForum, Paderborn; Archives nationales, Paris; La Cinémathèque Française, Paris; Musée de l'Armée, Paris; Galerie Bernard Jordan, Paris; Praz-Delavallade, Paris and Los Angeles; Voorlinden Museum & Gardens, Wassenaar; Galerie Peter Kilchmann, Zurich; and all private institutions and lenders.

Furthermore, I am grateful to all authors for their informative contributions to this publication. I would first of all like to thank Cristina Ricupero, Jörg Heiser, Jelena Martinovic, and Noam Toran for their valuable insights, as well as Ulrike Knöfel, Metahaven, Joanna Moorhead, Marina Otero Verzier, Jonas Staal, and Wladimir Velminski, whose previously published texts have been reprinted in this catalogue. In addition, I extend my gratitude to the artists Gabriel Lester, Simon Menner, and Noam Toran for the distinct choice of images they contributed to the design of the catalogue. Thanks also go to Dawn Michelle d'Atri and Hans-Jörg Huhn for their attentive editing of the texts, and to Stefan Barmann and Susie Hondl for their careful translations. Moreover, I am grateful to Serge Rompza for the creative design of the exhibition catalogue and to Snoeck, especially to the publisher Andreas Balze, for their excellent cooperation in the production of this publication. Finally,

I would like to thank VERY for the convincing graphic design of the exhibition, as well as Adrien Rovero, to whom we owe the elaborate exhibition architecture.

I am delighted about the generous support of the Schirn Friends for this project: my thanks are extended to Christian Strenger, chairman of Schirn Friends, and the managing director Tamara von Clary for their extraordinary commitment and support of this exhibition, and especially to all of the loyal 2,260 members of the association, and their continuous support in a variety of ways. This commitment is additionally supported by donations from the members of the board of trustees and the board of directors of the Verein der Freunde der Schirn Kunsthalle e. V., which made the realization of the artwork by Henrike Naumann possible. I also wish to thank the City of Frankfurt and, on behalf of all decision-makers, Mayor Peter Feldmann and the head of the Department of Culture, Ina Hartwig. My warm thanks are also owed to the national foundations that have helped to make possible the participation of individual artists.

I am grateful to the entire Schirn team for their tireless dedication in the realization of the exhibition and the catalogue. First of all, I would like to thank the deputy director and head of exhibitions Esther Schlicht. I likewise thank Karin Grüning, Elke Walter, and Luise Leyer for the complex organization of the transport as well as the setup and removal of the exhibition. I am grateful as well to Christian Teltz and Oliver Taschke for the technical support and to Anna Noll in her role as assistant to the head of exhibitions. Moreover, I thank Andreas Gundermann and the hanging team as well as the restorers Stefanie Gundermann and Susanne Silbernagel.

Furthermore, I extend my gratitude to Luise Bachmann, Heike Stumpf, Isabel Reiche, and Elena Schmidt for the marketing and design of the campaign. Many thanks to Johanna Pulz, Julia Bastian, Elisabeth Pallentin, and Isabelle Hammer for their press and public relations work. I am particularly indebted to Antonia Lagemann and Anuschka Berthelius for the coordination and production of this publication and for their editing of the Schirn Magazine. I further thank Chantal Eschenfelder with Simone Boscheinen, Laura Heeg, Olga Schaetz, and Anna Haag for the accompanying educational program. In addition, I would like to thank Ute Seiffert and Lena Sobczinski for the development and coordination of the events at the Schirn, and Julia Lange and Hannah Ruiz for the development of financial support and for looking after the sponsors and partners. Last but not least, I would like to thank Heike Berndt, Tanja Mayer, and Boris Deckelmann at the Schirn's administrative office, as well as Andrea Canthal for her assistance in a variety of matters. My thanks go to the messenger Stefan Schell, to Rosaria La Tona and the cleaning team, to Bettina Beyermann, Vilizara Antalavicheva, and Josef Härig at the reception, and to all other employees at the Schirn who were involved in the elaborate organization and realization of this project.

Philipp Demandt
Director
Schirn Kunsthalle Frankfurt

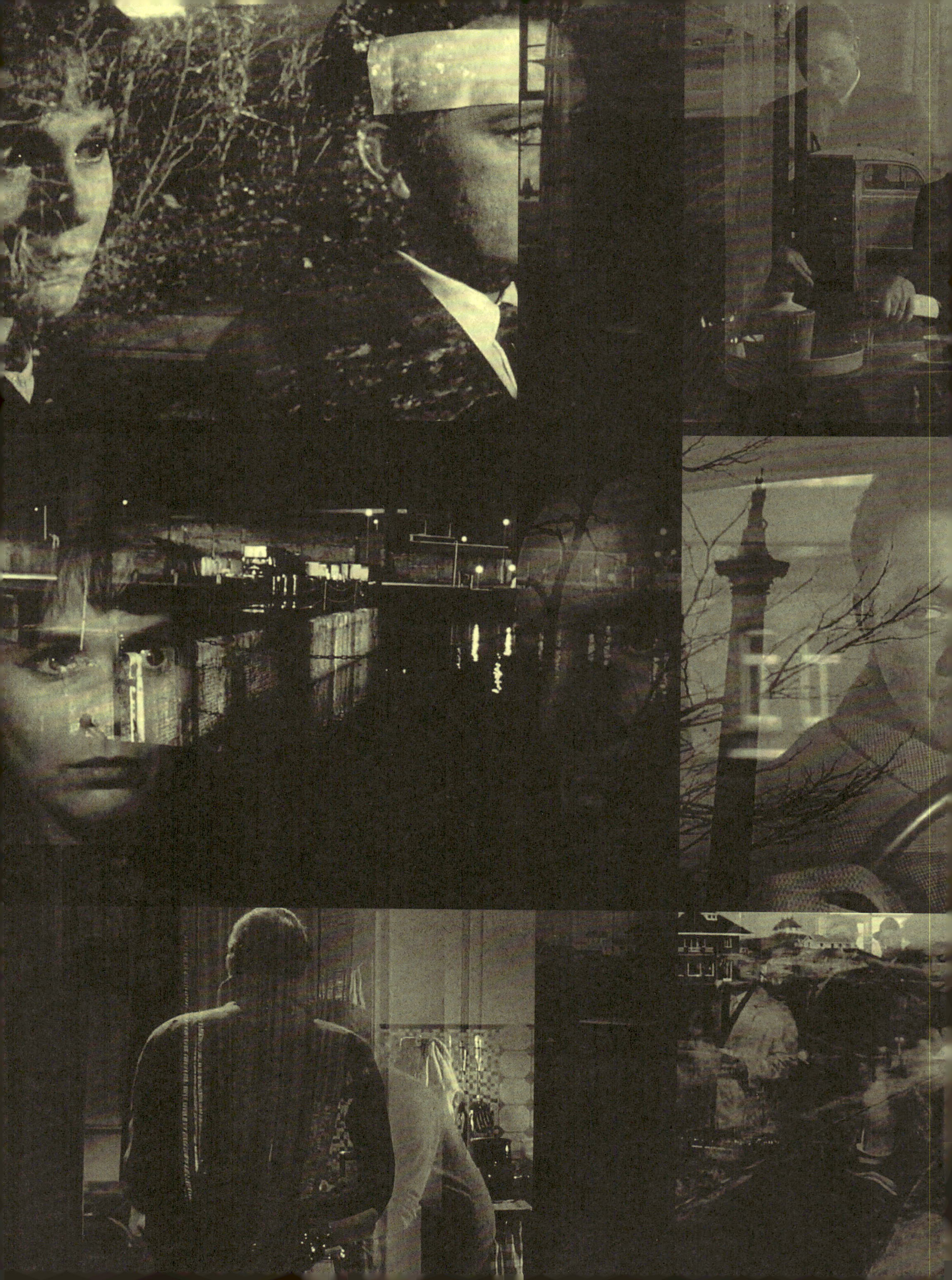

Vorwort

"WE NEVER SLEEP." – So lautet der Slogan der „Pinkerton's National Detective Agency", der ältesten Detektei der Vereinigten Staaten, gegründet 1850. Zu einem ihrer größten Erfolge zählt die Vereitelung des Attentats auf Präsident Abraham Lincoln 1861. Dass dieser Slogan, der im Logo der Detektei ein geöffnetes Auge umrahmt, schnell zum Allgemeingut geworden ist, zeigt sich bereits 1917 in Hollywoods Stummfilmkino, als die „Lonesome Luke"-Serie mit der Folge *We Never Sleep* endet. Ein unbeholfener Detektiv verfolgt den falschen Mann, grandios verkörpert durch den bekannten Komiker Harold Lloyd. Währenddessen tobt in Europa der Erste Weltkrieg. Detektive, Agenten und Spione – unabhängig vom Auftraggeber ist ihre Tätigkeit durch das Ausspähen und Beschaffen geheimer Informationen gekennzeichnet, die womöglich einen Krieg verhindern oder zumindest frühzeitig beenden können. In der Ausstellung *We Never Sleep* widmen sich zeitgenössische Künstlerinnen und Künstler in ihren Werken Aspekten der Spionage wie Überwachung, Paranoia, Bedrohung und Tarnung, Kryptografie, Manipulation, Kaltblütigkeit und Verrat. Mit einer Vielzahl künstlerischer Strategien sowie skurrilen Objekten wird in der Ausstellung der „Höhepunkt" der Spionageaktivitäten während des Kalten Krieges genauso thematisiert wie die aktuelle Verhandlung der medialen Durchleuchtung.

Zwar wurde die Ausstellung lange vor Beginn der Coronakrise konzipiert, doch auch während der Pandemie zeigte sich, dass Geheimdienste genau das machen, was sie immer tun. Sie beschaffen Informationen, an die sonst niemand kommt. Sie können weder heilen noch einen Virus stoppen, aber im besten Fall Informationen liefern, Fake News aufdecken, Verschwörungstheorien widersprechen: Kam der Virus aus einem Labor in Wuhan, steckt Bill Gates dahinter oder versuchen elitäre Geheimgesellschaften eine autoritäre Weltordnung zu erschaffen? Wie groß ist das Bedürfnis nach Sicherheit im Verhältnis zum Verlust der (eigenen) Freiheit? Die Ausstellung *We Never Sleep* liefert keine finalen Antworten, aber sie wirft Fragen auf, die heute virulenter scheinen denn je. Dabei dient der Katalog als weiterführendes, ergänzendes „Werkzeug", um sich mit der Thematik aus vielseitigen, historischen wie zeitgenössischen, Perspektiven auseinanderzusetzen. Mit *We Never Sleep* knüpft die Schirn an ihre Tradition an, mit großen Themenausstellungen gesellschaftlich relevante Fragestellungen aufzuwerfen und damit an aktuelle Debatten anzuknüpfen – wie beispielsweise mit *Unendlicher Spaß* (2014), *Peace* (2017) oder *Power to the People* (2018). Bereits 2011 beschäftigte sich die Ausstellung *Secret Societies*, kuratiert von Cristina Ricupero gemeinsam mit Alexis Vaillant, mit *Geheimgesellschaften* und ihrem Wirken, was mit *We Never Sleep* nun um das Thema der Spionage erweitert wird.

Zuallererst möchte ich allen Künstlerinnen und Künstlern, die zu diesem umfassenden Projekt mit existierenden wie auch neuen Arbeiten beigetragen haben, danken:

Lawrence Abu Hamdan, Maja Bajevic, Jean-Luc Blanc, Nina Childress, Guy de Cointet, Thomas Demand, Simon Denny, Mauricio Dias & Walter Riedweg, Stan Douglas, Charles und Ray Eames, Forensic Architecture, Dora García, Mathis Gasser, Rodney Graham, Eva Grubinger, Humans since 1982, Alfredo Jaar, Kiluanji Kia Henda, Gabriel Lester, Lim Minouk, Dora Longo Bahia, Jill Magid, Fabian Marti, Josephine Meckseper, Mieko Meguro, Metahaven, Aleksandra Mir, Henrike Naumann, Trevor Paglen, Park Chan-Kyong und Park Chan-Wook, Cornelia Schleime, Jim Shaw, Taryn Simon, Jonas Staal, Noam Toran, Suzanne Treister, Nomeda & Gediminas Urbonas, Jane und Louise Wilson, Liam Young, Tamir Zadok. Ihre Zusammenarbeit mit den Kuratorinnen Cristina Ricupero und Alexandra Midal weiß ich überaus zu schätzen. Cristina Ricupero und Alexandra Midal möchte ich meinen herzlichen Dank dafür aussprechen, dass sie dieses Ausstellungsprojekt nach tiefgehender Recherche und umfangreicher Vorbereitung initiiert und konzipiert haben.

Cristina Ricupero haben wir zudem die Entwicklung und aufwendige Realisierung der Ausstellung, gemeinsam mit Katharina Dohm, zu verdanken. Hierfür möchte ich den beiden für ihre vertrauensvolle Zusammenarbeit und Hingabe für das Ausstellungsprojekt sowie für die Erarbeitung der vorliegenden Publikation danken, die vielfache Einblicke in den breiten Themenkosmos rund um das Thema Spionage gibt. Ebenfalls danke ich Alica Sänger für ihre Unterstützung bei der Ausstellungs- und Katalogvorbereitung.

Zahlreiche internationale Museen, Institutionen und Privatleihgeber haben durch die großzügige Bereitstellung der Leihgaben dieses umfassende Ausstellungsprojekt mit ermöglicht. Ihre Unterstützung weiß ich überaus zu schätzen und danke dafür herzlich Weiss Falk, Basel; Saatchi Gallery, Berkshire; Deutsche Kinemathek, Berlin; Deutsches Spionagemuseum, Berlin; Galerie Buchholz, Berlin; Stasimuseum, Berlin; Deutsche Bank Collection, Düsseldorf; Deutsches Filmmuseum, Frankfurt a. M.; Sammlung von Kelterborn / Von Kelterborn Collection, Frankfurt a. M.; Sfeir-Semler Gallery, Hamburg / Beirut; Bürgerkomitee Leipzig e. V. für die Auflösung der ehemaligen Staatssicherheit (MfS); Annely Juda Fine Art, London; Timothy Taylor Gallery, London; Eames Office, Los Angeles; Combined Military Services Museum, Maldon, Essex; 303 Gallery, New York; Air de Paris, Paris; Heinz Nixdorf MuseumsForum, Paderborn; Archives nationales, Paris; La Cinémathèque Française, Paris; Musée de l'Armée, Paris; Galerie Bernard Jordan, Paris; Praz-Delavallade, Paris und Los Angeles; Voorlinden Museum & Gardens, Wassenaar; Galerie Peter Kilchmann, Zürich sowie allen privaten Institutionen und Leihgebern.

Mein Dank richtet sich darüber hinaus an alle Autorinnen und Autoren für ihre aufschlussreichen Textbeiträge in der vorliegenden Publikation. Zuallererst danke ich Cristina Ricupero sowie Jörg Heiser, Jelena Martinovic und Noam Toran für ihre wertvollen Einblicke ebenso wie Ulrike Knöfel, Metahaven, Joanna Moorhead, Marina Otero, Jonas Staal und Wladimir Velminski, deren bereits publizierte Texte in diesem Katalog erneut abgedruckt werden konnten. Außerdem gilt mein Dank den Künstlern Gabriel Lester, Simon Menner und Noam Toran für die prägnanten Bilder, die sie zur Gestaltung des Kataloges beigetragen haben. Dawn Michelle d'Atri und Hans-Jörg Huhn danke ich für das aufmerksame Lektorat der Texte, Stefan Barmann und Susie Hondl für die sensible Übersetzung derselben. Darüber hinaus möchte ich Serge Rompza für die kreative Gestaltung des Ausstellungskataloges danken wie auch Snoeck, insbesondere dem Verleger Andreas Balze, für die gute Zusammenarbeit bei der Produktion der vorliegenden Publikation. Schließlich gilt mein Dank VERY für die stimmige grafische Gestaltung der Ausstellung sowie Adrien Rovero, dem die durchdachte Ausstellungsarchitektur zu verdanken ist.

Ich freue mich sehr, dass die Schirn Freunde dieses Projekt so großzügig unterstützen: So gilt mein Dank für ihr außerordentliches Engagement und die Unterstützung dieser Ausstellung Christian Strenger, dem Vorsitzenden der Schirn Freunde, und der Geschäftsführerin Tamara von Clary wie auch ganz besonders allen treuen 2260 Mitgliedern des Vereins, die uns immerwährend auf unterschiedliche Art und Weise unterstützen. Flankiert wird dieses Engagement zusätzlich von Spenden der Mitglieder des Kuratoriums und des Vorstands des Vereins der Freunde der Schirn Kunsthalle e. V., mit denen die Realisation des Werks von Henrike Naumann mit ermöglicht wurde. Darüber hinaus gilt mein Dank der Stadt Frankfurt sowie, stellvertretend für alle Entscheidungsträger, dem Oberbürgermeister Peter Feldmann und der Kulturdezernentin Ina Hartwig. Danken möchte ich auch den nationalen Stiftungen, die die Partizipation einzelner Künstler mit unterstützt haben.

Für ihren unermüdlichen Einsatz bei der Realisierung der Ausstellung sowie des Kataloges möchte ich dem gesamten Team der Schirn herzlich danken. Mein Dank gilt zuallererst der stellvertretenden Direktorin und Ausstellungsleiterin Esther Schlicht. Ebenso danke ich Karin Grüning, Elke Walter und Luise Leyer für die komplexe Organisation des Transports sowie des Auf- und Abbaus der Ausstellung. Außerdem danken möchte ich Christian Teltz und Oliver Taschke für die technische Betreuung sowie Anna Noll als Assistentin der Ausstellungsleitung. Andreas Gundermann und dem Hängeteam danke ich ebenso wie den Restauratorinnen Stefanie Gundermann und Susanne Silbernagel. Mein Dank gilt darüber hinaus Luise Bachmann, Heike Stumpf, Isabel Reiche und Elena Schmidt für das Marketing und die Gestaltung der Kampagne. Ich danke Johanna Pulz, Julia Bastian, Elisabeth Pallentin und Isabelle Hammer für die Pressearbeit. Antonia Lagemann mit Anuschka Berthelius gilt mein Dank für die Koordination und Produktion der vorliegenden Publikation sowie für die Redaktion des Schirn Magazins. Für das begleitende Vermittlungsprogramm danke ich Chantal Eschenfelder mit Simone Boscheinen, Laura Heeg, Olga Schaetz und Anna Haag. Ich danke Ute Seiffert mit Lena Sobczinski für die Entwicklung und Koordination der Veranstaltungen in der Schirn sowie Julia Lange und Hannah Ruiz für das Sponsoring und die Betreuung der Förderer und Partner. Mein Dank gilt nicht zuletzt Heike Berndt, Tanja Mayer und Boris Deckelmann in der Verwaltung der Schirn sowie Andrea Canthal für ihre Assistenz in zahlreichen Belangen. Ich danke dem Boten Stefan Schell, Rosaria La Tona und dem Team der Gebäudereinigung, Bettina Beyermann, Vilizara Antalavicheva und Josef Härig an der Kasse sowie allen weiteren Kolleginnen und Kollegen an der Schirn, die an der aufwendigen Vorbereitung und Umsetzung dieses Projekts beteiligt waren.

Philipp Demandt
Direktor
Schirn Kunsthalle Frankfurt

We Never Sleep
Or How to Curate an Art Exhibition on Espionage
Cristina Ricupero

"An army without spies is like a man without ears or eyes."
Sun Tzu, *The Art of War*

Who has not dreamed one day of becoming a spy? James Bond, Mata Hari, George Smiley ... Fascination with espionage is a pleasure for all ages and seasons, and practically no one is immune to this cultural temptation.

Artists and spies, why bring them together? What exactly do they have in common? An artist's secret is kept within the space of the studio, while a spy needs to live discreetly, stay undercover, and change identities in order to keep the secret, under threat of losing his or her own life. So, what are the links between art, the artist, and espionage? How to curate an exhibition around espionage, and why? These are some essential questions that Alexandra Midal and I asked ourselves a few years ago when we conceived this exhibition project.

Considered to be one of the oldest activities in the world, espionage has evolved throughout time following the development of new technologies. Fundamentally military, often scientific and industrial, espionage plays a major role in the political sphere of every country, on both national and international levels. If, in the past, national governments spied on individuals, today with WikiLeaks this trend seems to have been reversed, as private individuals are capable of revealing hidden governmental secrets. The desire for transparency seems to have replaced the secret.

What does it mean to live undercover and to have to constantly change one's identity? The world of espionage is closely linked to manipulation, complotting, constant threat, paranoia, and subsequently betrayal (treason). In order to well conduct an inquiry, a spy necessarily needs special tools, gadgets, and machines that enable one to overhear, record, and enlist secret information. And, of course, there are also anonymously coded letters and classified or unclassified secret documents.

Events involving espionage are as old as the invention of war. It is mentioned in the Old Testament of the Christian Bible, the Hebrew Bible, and in the ancient writings of military strategists such as Sun Tzu. But it was only during modern times, in the mid-to-late nineteenth century, that espionage became "professionalized" through the creation of permanent intelligence services. The First World War was crucial for its development with the setup of spy networks and progress in the area of (de) coding and transmissions. Governmental control of censorship, propaganda, and misinformation was put in place. During the Second World War, these aspects were further elaborated, but it wasn't until the Cold War, in a climate of extreme tension between the Western and Soviet blocs, that state secret structures rose to a level that had never been seen before. The secret war became the predominant mode of conflict, assisted by increasingly modernized technologies such as computers and satellites.

For a long time, espionage meant the illegal, unauthorized obtaining of state secrets, often through infiltration from the outside. Historically, the state relied on secrets, a privilege appreciated by those in power. Nowadays the modern state is supposedly based on openness and transparency, even pretending that it hides no secrets. In this new context, whistleblowers expose the state's hidden interior from the inside, disclosing to the public the state's secret mechanisms and operations. In the digital communications era, the mass disclosure of information through leaks and whistleblower initiatives has become quite frequent, almost predictable. But doesn't absolute transparency and an excessive mass of information provide the best possibility for camouflage? Secrets become so obvious today that, paradoxically, we are no longer aware of them.

Parallel to this harsh reality and short history of espionage, popular culture created a glamorous image of it. The spy novel, which appeared as a specific genre of fiction in the nineteenth century, highly contributed to this. It is interesting to note that many authors of spy fiction have themselves been intelligence officers working for British agencies such as MI5 or MI6, or American agencies such as the CIA. John le Carré, Graham Greene, and Ian Fleming, the latter having invented the legendary James Bond, are just a few among many. Numerous spy novels were then adapted to film as the entertainment industry and cinema welcomed espionage with open arms. *Dr. No* (1962) starring Sean Connery as agent 007 and *The Spy Who Came in from the Cold* (1965), inspired by John le Carré's novel, featuring Richard Burton, are good examples. From Fritz Lang's very early *Spione* (1928) to Alfred Hitchcock, who was undeniably a master in the genre with films such as *The 39 Steps* (1935), *Torn Curtain* (1966), *Notorious* (1946), and *North by Northwest* (1959), to Francis Ford Coppola's cult movie *The Conversation* (1974), to more recent examples such as *Tinker Tailor Soldier Spy* (2011) by Tomas Alfredson, film history has definitely done a great deal to popularize espionage. Not to forget the various indelible cult TV series from the 1960s and 1970s, such as *The Avengers*, *The Saint*, and *Mission Impossible*, or the more recent *Homeland*. Everybody knows of Mata Hari, the exotic dancer who also worked as a double agent, using her powers of seduction to extract secrets from her many lovers, but few know that the famous jazz singer and dancer Josephine Baker was recruited, during the Second World War, by French military intelligence as an "honorable correspondent" to later be honored by General Charles de Gaulle. Nor do many know that, during this same period, the glamorous Hollywood star Hedy Lamarr, together with her friend, the avant-garde composer and inventor George Antheil, developed a radio guidance system for Allied torpedoes that could not be tracked or jammed. All of this helps us to understand how fiction has been greatly inspired by the reality of espionage and, above all, how this dark universe has always intrigued and fascinated the general public.

Inversely, sometimes fiction perfectly mimics reality. Some politically oriented secret organizations closely mirror, in a sort of perverse way, the vices, faults, and shortcomings of the political superstructures they vow to destroy. In the early twentieth century, when international anarchist movements were as widespread and feared as Isis is today, G. K. Chesterton wrote *The Man Who Was Thursday*, an ironic commentary on the dangers of allowing paranoia and politically manipulated fear to become the decisive factor in domestic politics.

We all have heard stories about some artists being spies or, at least, being accused of spying, such as Kazimir Malevich, who was imprisoned and interrogated for passing information to Germany under Hitler's regime, or about artists who have used their works to dissimulate and hide secret messages in order to communicate information. And, of course, portraits of famous spies have been painted. It is also interesting to look at what happens behind the "scene," to dig into stories that have been dissimilated. For many years, in the art world, it was either a rumor or a joke, but now it has been confirmed that the CIA used American modern art, including works by artists such as Jackson Pollock, Willem de Kooning, and Mark Rothko, to secretly promote itself; and it also used modern art as a weapon during the Cold War. As mentioned above, many famous authors, actors, and celebrities have led double lives, secretively working for intelligence agencies. One could also say that the modus operandi of certain artists, who often have to interpret codes or deal with archiving and telecommunications, could be similar to that of a spy.

The dark side of human nature has always fascinated and inspired many artists. The world of espionage is filled with enigmas, secret codes to be deciphered, double agents, camouflage, cold blood, complotting, suspicion, surveillance, paranoia, and ultimately betrayal. Spy stories usually have complicated schemes, and one sometimes feels a bit lost within its labyrinthine plot, having difficulty making sense of what is true or false. But the feeling of permanently experiencing danger and fear also creates great excitement. As Guy Burgess, a real-life spy, used say: to let the cat out of the bag, espionage is an aphrodisiac.

The world of espionage thus seems to be a gold mine that artists can dig into. It is clear that the post-apocalyptic mood associated with the most recent terrorist attacks and leaks initiated by hackers during presidential elections have created the perfect ground for a renewed interest in espionage. Themes of threat, paranoia, surveillance, and violence can be reminders of the state of the world and at the same time also materialize in new forms of nihilism, melancholy, and explorations of extremes. Artists are ready to embrace these topics in order to reinvent visual culture—topics that have been dealt with in the recent past by artists like Julia Scher or Bruce Nauman, to name just a few. More recently, a certain number of artists—such as Lawrence Abu Hamdan, Simon Denny, Forensic Architecture, Jill Magid, Metahaven, Trevor Paglen, Jonas Staal, and Suzanne Treister, among others who are presented in the exhibition—have taken a special interest in coded signs, secret documents, and sociopolitical conspiracies, so basically what could be called the mechanisms of contemporary secrecy.

Espionage is not only an individual vocation for deceit, for leading a double life, for treason, for pretending to be loyal. The essence of being a spy involves the search for information to which one is not entitled, along with the use of illicit means to get that information and to pass it on to the enemy. Spies lead dangerous lives and, if caught, are sometimes tortured, executed, or, if lucky, exchanged for other spies. A romantic aura surrounds spies' achievements. Espionage novels—from James Bond's frivolous genre to John le Carré's dark dramas, not to forget Graham Greene's morally ambiguous dilemmas—have always fascinated readers. Fascination in such cases is born of feeling and experiencing the danger, fear, and adventure of an old-age profession at the service of one state against another country. Nowadays, however, the worldwide spread of cybercrime has given rise to quite a different and much less heroic type of spy: the hacker who violates privacy to make a financial profit or to engage in blackmail.

Cybernetics has opened the road to novel and undreamed of possibilities in terms of getting and spreading information. On the one hand, it gave some courageous individuals the opportunity to "blow the whistle" on an unprecedented scale, to denounce their own government's machinations and conspiracies against other countries or against foreign politicians. In some cases, hackers with a conscience have been new heroes, like Edward Snowden, in fighting the Big Brother, that is, the government spying on its own citizens.

The extraordinary development of all these varied modalities of getting and spreading sensitive information brings us to a subject that is at the root of a good deal of this new phenomenon: the profound, intense urge felt by ordinary people to spread information about themselves, their families, and their hobbies on Facebook or elsewhere worldwide, and even, in extreme cases, about what otherwise would have been their best-hidden ugly secrets. What is behind such an urge that sometimes takes the form of self-exposure, self-flagellation, or bullying? Is it simply the natural, understandable human impulse for recognition, for communication, for overcoming the solitude of modern times? Is it another expression of Guy Debord's *La société du spectacle*? These are only some of the questions that present-day society challenges contemporary artists to explore.

We Never Sleep deals with the general theme of espionage through the prism of contemporary art and design, from the twentieth century through its "golden age" during the Cold War to its current context of media super-exposure. The exhibition brings together challenging works encompassing a multitude of artistic strategies. New and already existing projects, as well as a collection of unexpected objects (posters, book covers, secret coded documents, and all sorts of gadgets from reality and fiction like the red telephone or the lie-detecting machine), will be immersed in unorthodox ways within a specific environment.

Rather than "revealing" or "explaining," the main idea is to create surprises and raise questions. The exhibition does not aim to illustrate or to offer mere commentary on the main topic. Instead, the participating artists deal in different ways with the overall theme. Some works directly address this theme, whereas others function in a more mental, historical, or conceptual way, through subthemes such as the secret agent and its myths in Hollywood glamour; women and espionage; Cold War and its return; camouflage and its visual history; cryptography and code breakers; surveillance and threat; the double agent and schizophrenia; manipulation and mind control; propaganda-related information and disinformation; and overhearing: sound and espionage as well as

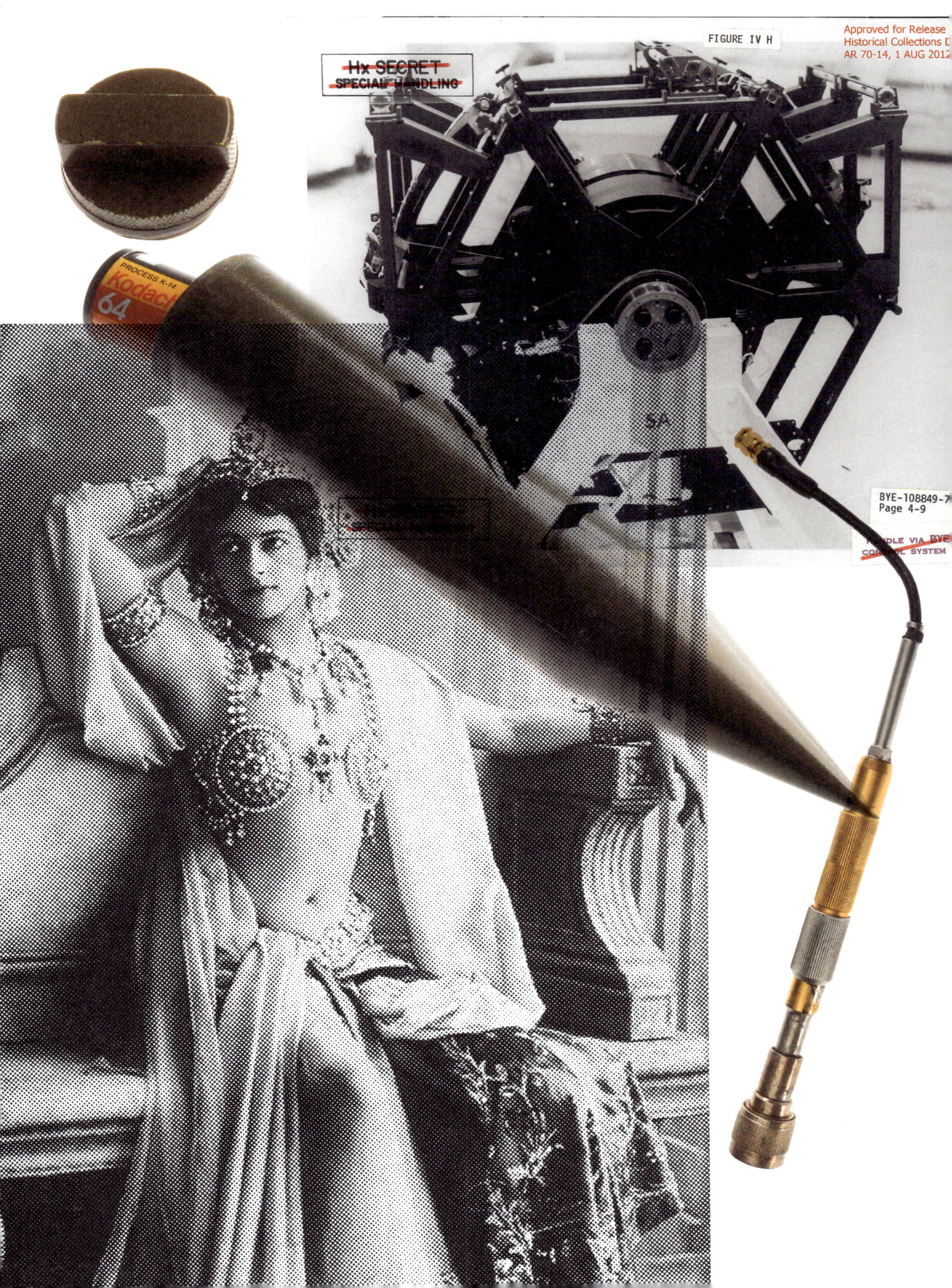
FIGURE IV H
Approved for Release
Historical Collections D
AR 70-14, 1 AUG 2012
Hx SECRET
SPECIAL HANDLING
PROCESS K-14
Kodac
64
SA
BYE-108849-7
Page 4-9
HANDLE VIA BYE
CONTROL SYSTEM

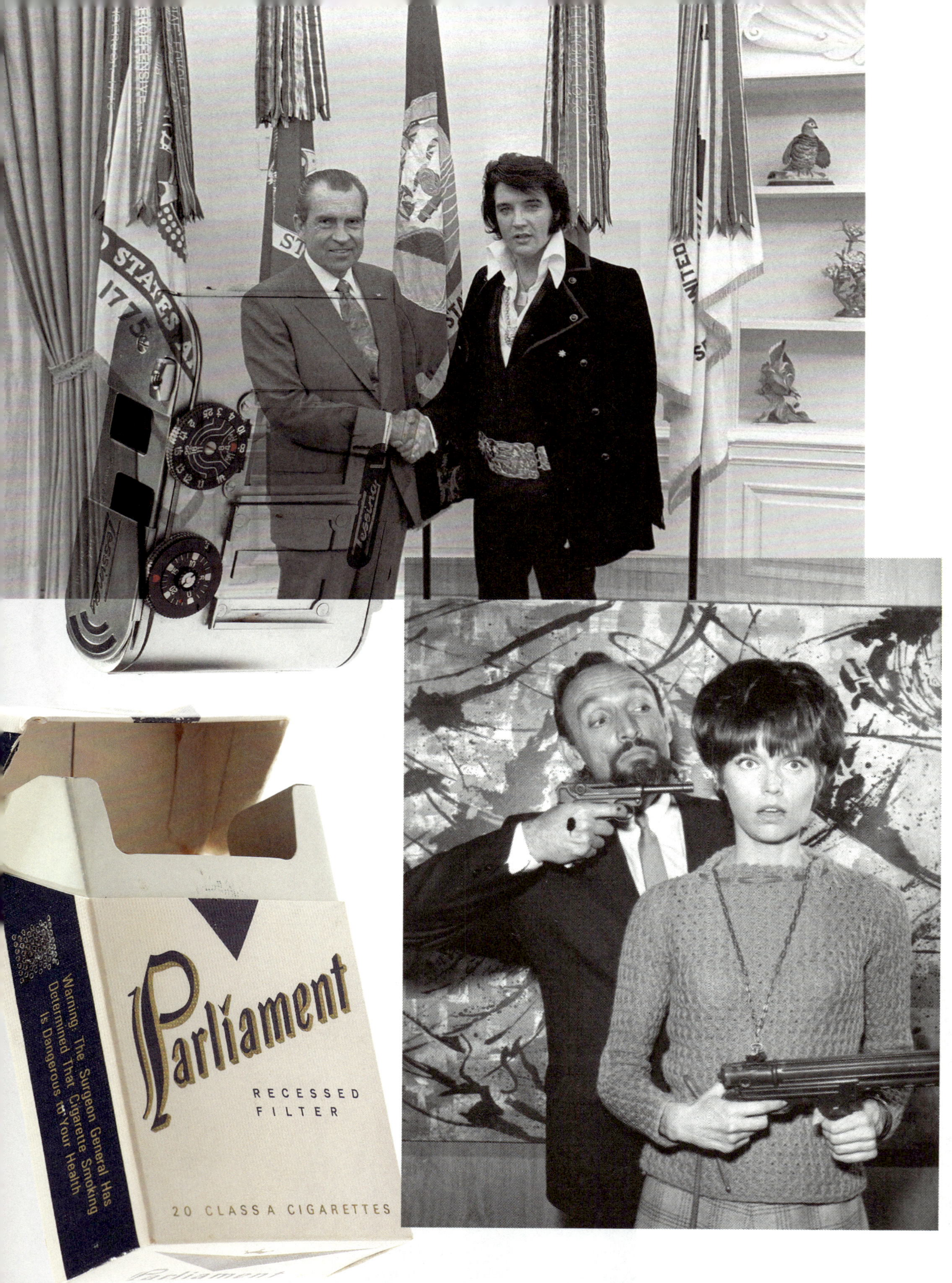
Parliament
RECESSED
FILTER
Warning: The Surgeon General Has
Determined That Cigarette Smoking
Is Dangerous to Your Health
20 CLASS A CIGARETTES

conspiracy and paranoia. But there will be no rooms dedicated to specific themes, as the overall perception is meant to be more fluid and organic.

The main idea is to create a special environment that will guide the viewer through routes containing different chapters of our main narrative. The designer Adrien Rovero has responded to the long, narrow space of the Schirn Kunsthalle Frankfurt by proposing a very extensive corridor, which evokes images that one might see in spy films, progressively giving the visitor access to different spaces containing unexpected material. The entrance, composed of a dazzle immersive camouflage pattern that hides its motifs, immediately sets the tone as we directly enter the unstable, confusing world of espionage. The exhibition is highly staged and it functions as an overall environment. Its space is divided into loose zones that cover topics related to espionage, always interconnected. Just like in a spy novel that slowly unfolds, the gradually revealing spaces transform viewers into amateur spies, highlighting their own ambiguous-voyeuristic sides. Following the labyrinthine logic of a spy story, the architecture conceals and reveals at the same time, always shifting between reality and fiction. Finally, like in the murky world of espionage, the truth should remain a mystery.

For this publication, we chose to bring together a heterogeneous collection of voices, reflecting a diversity of interests, experiences, and points of view. It does not aim to be an exhaustive catalogue of current debates around espionage, but rather a selection of essays and opinions particularly relevant to and innovative for our context. Instead of a conventional catalogue, it should be relatively independent from the exhibition as a resource in itself rather than simply documentation or commentary. Some essays are more analytical, while others are theoretical in character, some are new commissions, others already existing texts, a few of them are printed as facsimiles, and two are intriguing articles from *The Guardian* and from the magazine *Der Spiegel*, both dealing with the dichotomy of artist as spy / spy as artist.

In his new contribution "The Secret Life of Art During and After the Cold War," Jörg Heiser, who is a writer, professor, and curator based in Berlin, examines the paradigm shifts that have occurred in our current multipolar global scenario, in regard to the way the art and the spy worlds interact. In the Cold War era, an English art historian (Anthony Blunt) could be the personal artistic adviser to a head of state (the Queen), while acting, at the same time, for decades as a spy at the service of the Soviet Union. In the art world today, there are occasions and parties where it is possible for a corporate multi-billion-aire (Jeff Bezos) to rub shoulders with royalty (Mohammed bin Salman of Saudi Arabia), possibly resulting in phone spyware being used for blackmailing (eventually leading to Bezos's public divorce) and for hunting down a dissident (the brutal assassination of Jamal Khashoggi, who was a columnist for the Bezos-owned *Washington Post*). The Cold War power games, Heiser argues, seem to be returning in uncanny, shape-shifting disguises, with art being caught in the middle.

Jelena Martinovic, a London-based scholar, writer, and educator, offers a new text called "The Motion Picture as an Art of Espionage," where she assimilates the art of espionage of mid-twentieth century political thrillers to Cold War brainwashing techniques. It focuses on a case study of behavior therapy in which audiovisual technology and script writing are used to turn the patient into a double agent through the manipulation of subliminal images, motion pictures, and codified messages.

A very personal text–image essay is the contribution by Noam Toran, one of the artists participating in the exhibition. In this original essay, he combines autobiographical, fictional, and historical materials to portray his family's troubled encounters with the militarization of American culture and its corresponding paranoia in the late 1970s. In addition, he also contributes *Camp 33*, a collection of stills drawn from government-sponsored educational films produced in the United States from 1946 to 1961. Screened in schoolhouses, churches, and community halls, and produced by organizations such as the Office of Civil Defense and the National Education Programming Department, the films provide methods for safeguarding the population from potential threats to "the American way of life," such as socialism, communism, homosexuality, immigration, and desegregation.

Another participating artist, Gabriel Lester, proposes a selection of cross-dissolves that he calls *Double-Crossed* as they appear in films before the 1970s. The dissolve was one of the first visual transition techniques transposed from theater to cinema. Mimicking the theatrical transition from darkness to light, the dissolve is a gradual increase of appearance of a cinematic image. When images dissolve or melt into each other, that is, when they cross-dissolve, they create a technique used between scenes indicating a leap in time or location. For this publication, Lester has selected cross-dissolves from two classic cult espionage films: *The Spy Who Came in from the Cold* (1965), featuring Richard

Burton, and *Dishonored* (1931), with Marlene Dietrich playing Mata Hari.

A series of particularly interesting and significant essays were selected for republication. "Mask: The Political Space behind the War on Terror" by Marina Otero Verzier, a Rotterdam-based architect and scholar, first published in the online journal *Quaderns*, narrates the author's daily life and experience with the public space in New York under Operation Nexus. A New York Police Department operation adopted after 9/11, Operation Nexus established a nationwide network formed by everyday local businesses with the intention of providing information to prevent a new terrorist attack. Through her interactions with the owner of her local laundromat, Otero Verzier unpacks how contemporary "security architecture" is designed as much for our protection as for the destruction of what makes possible our life in common, including our freedom and our political capacity.

"The Agent in Plain Sight" by Wladimir Velminski, an author and scholar based in Berlin, was first published in the book *Diagnose: Krim*, written after the annexation of Crimea. Using examples from art and politics, such as the artist Viktor Pivovarov's aesthetic works and Vladimir Putin's political strategies, the author examines the exposed structures of secrets in his text. Pivovarov, a co-founder of Moscow Conceptualism, discloses the aesthetic practices of agents to initiate the viewer into the game of secrets, to infect him, to lure him to his side, and thus to form an aesthetic collective body. In applying these revelations to Crimea's annexation, it becomes particularly clear how the practices of the former secret agents have changed and how those of art have been appropriated.

Also participating in the exhibition, Metahaven and Jonas Staal provide essays previously published in *e-flux journal*, which now appear as facsimiles. In "Captives of the Cloud: Part I," first published in September 2012, Metahaven look into our systematic online surveillance. In this article, they state that in a society permanently connected through pervasive broadband networks, the shared Internet is, bit by bit and piece by piece, overshadowed by the "cloud." As voluntary prisoners of the cloud, we are being watched over by governments we did not elect. They also quote Wael Ghonim, Google's Egyptian executive: "If you want to liberate a society just give them the internet. But how does one liberate a society that already has the internet?"

In "Propaganda (Art) Struggle," first published in October 2018, Jonas Staal states that our reality is defined, in part, by a propaganda struggle, understood not as a singular term, but as a result of various competing works of propaganda. Various performances of power aim to construct reality according to their interests, resulting in overlapping claims that shape the arena of the contemporary. What visual forms are assumed by this manifold propaganda and by the realities it wants to create? What kind of artistic morphologies and cultural narratives does the propaganda struggle bring about? These are some important questions raised in the text.

Both this publication and the exhibition have been a collective endeavor. They are based on the research that I conducted together with Alexandra Midal, a writer, professor, and curator based in Paris, over the last few years. The exhibition and the publication would not have been possible without her original outlook and contribution. Katharina Dohm, curator at the Schirn, has totally embraced the project, and her tireless commitment and input have been central to its realization. Adrien Rovero's audacious approach to the scenography has been equally fundamental. I have also involved a certain number of the participating artists in the project's overall construction; their innovative ideas have been very inspiring. An attitude of openness and flexibility has thus been central to the project's approach. Rather than making purely subjective and unilateral choices, our proposal was to opt for partnership, both at the intellectual level and in terms of creating a platform.

In many unexpected ways, the coronavirus pandemic has provided a fertile environment for the present exhibition. This unprecedented crisis has made the world's structural inequalities and injustices especially visible. Various governments have introduced contact-tracing apps and centralized data gathering, causing many to wonder whether these methods are actually seemingly abusive and anti-democratic surveillance measures under the pretext of fighting the pandemic. Fear haunts the world and conspiracy theories blossom. Paranoia, fake news, and misinformation proliferate through social media. Spies, hackers, and net activists are exceptionally active at the moment. Feeling threatened and unsure of what is happening, the public is easy prey to manipulation and abuse. In times of acute crisis triggered by uncertainty and growing anxiety, such as the pandemic, artists may be among the best equipped to decode the unknown and demystify conspiracy theories in order to propose innovative, compelling new paths to our future.

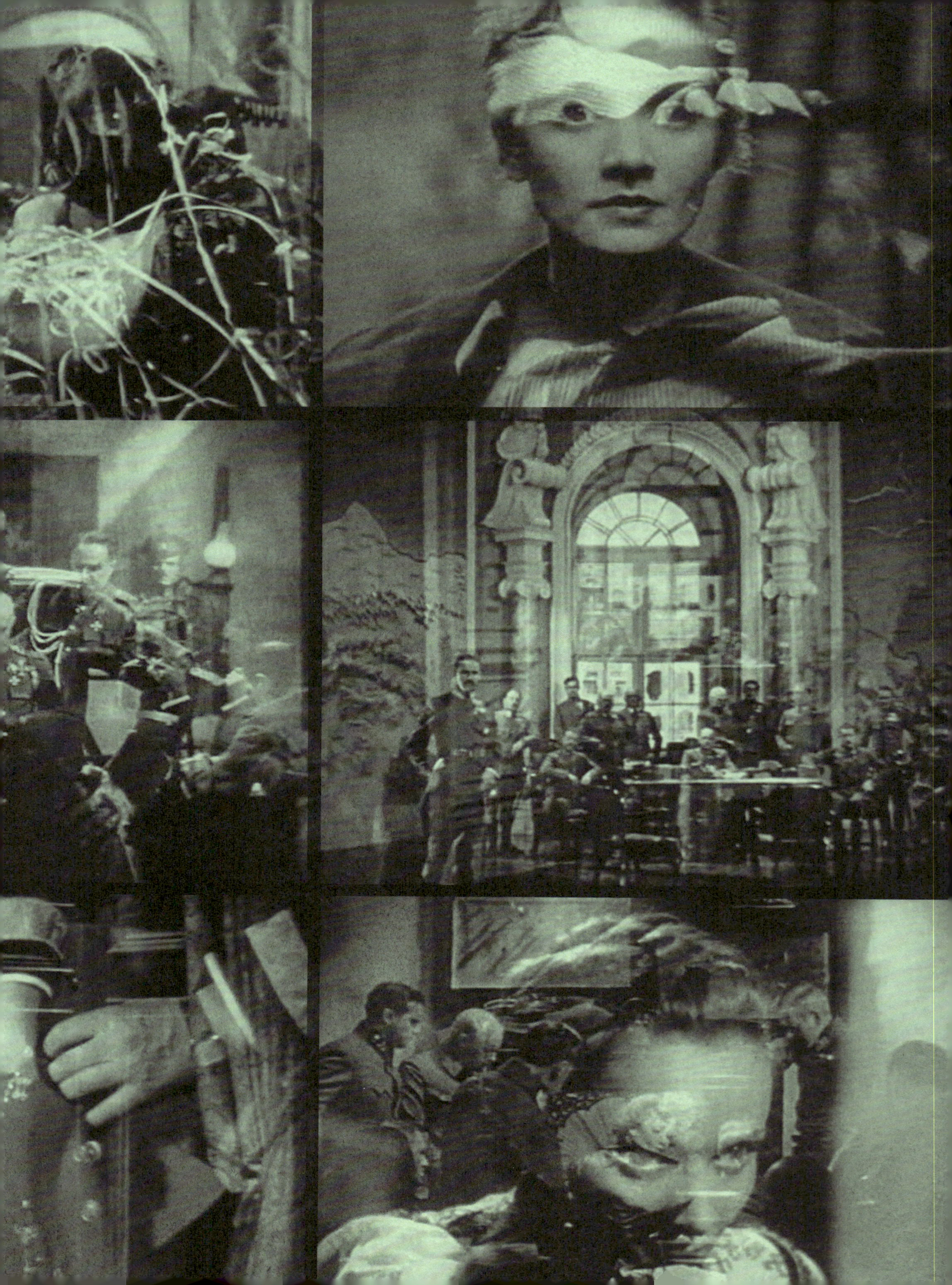

We Never Sleep
oder: Wie man eine Kunstausstellung über Spionage kuratiert
Cristina Ricupero

„Eine Armee ohne Spione ist wie ein Mensch ohne Augen oder Ohren."

Sunzi, *Die Kunst des Krieges*

Wer hat nicht irgendwann einmal davon geträumt, Spion zu werden? James Bond, Mata Hari, George Smiley ... Die Faszination für Spionage kennt weder Alter noch Saison, und so gut wie niemand ist vor ihrem kulturellen Reiz gefeit.

Warum Kunst und Spionage zusammenbringen? Was genau haben sie gemein? Künstlerinnen und Künstler wahren ihre Geheimnisse im Atelier, Spioninnen und Spione dagegen bleiben im Dienst der Geheimhaltung undercover, ändern ihre Identität und verbringen ihr ganzes Leben unauffällig – weil sie es sonst zu verlieren drohen. Was also ist der Zusammenhang zwischen Kunst, Künstlern und Spionage? Wie und wieso eine Ausstellung zur Spionage kuratieren? Das waren im Kern die Fragen, die Alexandra Midal und ich uns vor ein paar Jahren stellten, als wir dieses Projekt entwarfen.

Spionage, die als eine der ältesten Tätigkeiten der Welt gilt, hat sich infolge des technischen Fortschritts weiterentwickelt. Meist auf militärischem, oft aber auch auf wissenschaftlichem und industriellem Gebiet eingesetzt, spielt sie in der Politik aller Länder eine wichtige Rolle, nach innen wie nach außen. Spähten früher nationale Regierungen Individuen aus, so hat dieser Trend sich heute, da Privatleute Regierungsgeheimnisse zu enthüllen imstande sind, mit WikiLeaks offenbar umgekehrt. Das Verlangen nach Transparenz, so scheint es, hat das Geheimnis abgelöst.

Was bedeutet ein Leben undercover unter ständigem Wandel der Identität? Die Welt der Spionage ist eng verknüpft mit Manipulation, Verschwörung, steter Bedrohung, Paranoia und letzten Endes Verrat. Für eine erfolgreiche Ermittlung braucht ein Spion spezielle Werkzeuge, Geräte und Maschinen, mit denen er geheime Informationen abhören, aufzeichnen und weitergeben kann. Und natürlich gibt es auch verschlüsselte anonyme Briefe und offiziell und inoffiziell als geheim eingestufte Dokumente.

Spähaktionen gibt es seit Erfindung des Krieges. Im Alten Testament der christlichen Bibel, dem Tanach, finden sie ebenso Erwähnung wie in antiken Schriften von Militärstrategen wie Sunzi. Doch erst in der Moderne des mittleren bis auslaufenden 19. Jahrhunderts wurde Spionage im Zuge der Einrichtung ständiger Nachrichtendienste zum „Beruf". Einen wichtigen Entwicklungsschritt bedeutete der Erste Weltkrieg mit seinem Aufbau von Spionagenetzwerken sowie der Verbesserung der Ver- bzw. Entschlüsselungs- und Übertragungstechnik.

Damals wurde die administrative Kontrolle über Zensur, Propaganda und Desinformation installiert und später, im Zweiten Weltkrieg, weiter ausgebaut. Doch erst im Kalten Krieg, im Klima äußerster Anspannung zwischen West und Ost, erreichten staatliche Geheimstrukturen ungeahnte Ausmaße. Der von immer moderneren Technologien wie Computern und Satelliten unterstützte Geheimkrieg avancierte zum vorherrschenden Konfliktmodus.

Lange Zeit hieß Spionage unautorisierter, illegaler Zugriff auf Staatsgeheimnisse, oft durch Infiltrierung von außen. Früher basierte ein Staat auf Geheimnissen, deren Kenntnis das Privileg der Machthaber war. Der moderne Staat von heute fußt vermeintlich auf Offenheit und Transparenz, ja gibt vor, er habe nichts zu verbergen. In diesem aktuellen Kontext kehren „Whistleblower" das versteckte Innere des Staats nach außen, indem sie seine geheimen Mechanismen und Operationen der Öffentlichkeit offenlegen. Derlei massenhafte Informationsenthüllung ist im Zeitalter digitaler Kommunikation recht häufig und nahezu vorhersagbar. Doch bieten absolute Transparenz und eine überbordende Informationsmenge nicht gerade die besten Tarnungsmöglichkeiten? Geheimnisse treten heute so offensichtlich auf, dass wir uns ihrer paradoxerweise gar nicht mehr bewusst sind.

Parallel zur harten Wirklichkeit der Spionage schuf die Populärkultur ein glamouröses Bild von ihr. Der Spionageroman, der als eigene Erzählgattung im 19. Jahrhundert aufkam, hat dazu kräftig beigetragen. Interessanterweise waren manche seiner Autoren früher selbst als Nachrichtenoffiziere tätig gewesen, für britische Dienste wie M15 oder M16 oder amerikanische wie die CIA. John le Carré, Graham Greene und Ian Fleming, der den legendären James Bond erfand, sind nur wenige unter vielen. Zahlreiche Agentenromane fanden auch das rege Interesse der Unterhaltungsindustrie und Kinobranche und wurden verfilmt. *007 jagt Dr. No* (1962) mit Sean Connery in der Titelrolle und *Der Spion, der aus der Kälte kam* (1965) nach John Le Carrés Roman mit Richard Burton als Hauptdarsteller sind dafür gute Beispiele. Von Fritz Langs sehr frühem *Spione* (1928) über Alfred Hitchcock – mit Filmen wie *Die 39 Stufen* (1935), *Der zerrissene Vorhang* (1966), *Berüchtigt* (1946) und *Der unsichtbare Dritte* (1959) unbestrittener Meister des Fachs – bis zu Francis Ford Coppolas Kultfilm *Der Dialog* (1974) und jüngeren Beispielen wie *Dame, König, As, Spion* (2011) von Tomas Alfredson hat die Filmgeschichte viel dazu beigetragen, das Thema Spionage populär zu machen. Nicht zu vergessen unvergängliche TV-Kultserien aus den 1960er und 1970er Jahren wie *Mit Schirm, Charme und Melone*, *Simon Templar* und *Kobra, übernehmen Sie* oder, aus jüngerer Zeit, *Homeland*. Mata Hari, die exotische Tänzerin, die auch als Doppelagentin arbeitete und mithilfe ihrer Verführungskünste etlichen Liebhabern Geheimnisse entlockte, kennen alle, aber nur wenige wissen, dass die berühmte Jazzsängerin und Tänzerin Josephine Baker im Zweiten Weltkrieg vom französischen militärischen Abwehrdienst als „Ehrenkorrespondentin" angeworben und später von General Charles de Gaulle dafür geehrt wurde. Auch ist nur wenigen bekannt, dass die Hollywood-Diva Hedy Lamarr gemeinsam mit ihrem Freund, dem Avantgarde-Komponisten und Erfinder Georges Antheil, ein Funkleitsystem für alliierte Torpedos entwickelte, das nicht nachverfolgt oder gestört werden konnte. All das zeigt, wie stark die Fiktion sich von der Spionagerealität anregen ließ und, vor allem, wie fasziniert und gebannt das breite Publikum auf diese dunkle Welt immer schon zu starren gewillt war.

Umgekehrt scheint die Realität zuweilen auch der Fiktion entsprungen. Manche politisch ausgerichteten Geheimorganisationen spiegeln auf geradezu perverse Weise die Untugenden, Fehler und Mängel der politischen Überbauten, die sie zu zerstören geloben. Im frühen 20. Jahrhundert, als internationale anarchistische Bewegungen so verbreitet und gefürchtet waren wie heute der IS, schrieb G. K. Chesterton *Der Mann, der Donnerstag war* – ein ironischer Kommentar über die Gefahren, die lauern, wenn Paranoia und politisch manipulierte Angst zu Triebfedern der Innenpolitik werden.

Wir alle haben Geschichten über Künstlerinnen und Künstler gehört, die Spioninnen und Spione oder wenigstens der Spionage angeklagt waren, etwa Kasimir Malewitsch, der wegen angeblicher Weitergabe von Informationen an Nazideutschland festgenommen und verhört wurde, oder über Künstler, die durch versteckte Botschaften in ihren Werken Informationen übermittelten. Natürlich gibt es zudem gemalte Porträts berühmter Spioninnen und Spione. Interessant ist auch ein Blick hinter die Kulissen, der so manchen Schleier lüftet. So ist, was in der Kunstwelt jahrelang als Gerücht oder Scherz umging, mittlerweile bestätigt: Die CIA hat moderne amerikanische Kunst, darunter Werke von Jackson Pollock, Willem de Kooning und Mark Rothko, heimlich zum eigenen Vorteil genutzt und auch als Waffe im Kalten Krieg eingesetzt. Etliche berühmte Autoren, Schauspieler und Prominente haben, wie gesagt, ein Doppelleben geführt und

insgeheim für Nachrichtendienste gearbeitet. Auch könnte man sagen, dass die Arbeitsweise mancher Künstler, die oft Codes interpretieren oder mit Archivierung und Telekommunikation umgehen müssen, der von Spionen ähnelt.

Seit jeher hat die dunkle Seite der menschlichen Natur viele Künstlerinnen und Künstler fasziniert und inspiriert. Die Welt der Spionage ist voll von Rätseln, zu entschlüsselnden Geheimcodes, Doppelagenten, Tarnungen, kaltblütigem Verhalten, Komplotten, Argwohn, Überwachung, Paranoia und letztlich Verrat. Spionagegeschichten haben für gewöhnlich komplizierte Handlungsfäden, und manchmal fühlt man sich etwas verloren in diesem Labyrinth, in dem sich wahr und falsch kaum unterscheiden lassen. Aber ständig lauernde Gefahr und Furcht sorgen auch für hohe Spannung. Wie Guy Burgess, ein Spion aus dem wirklichen Leben, zu sagen pflegte: „Um die Katze aus dem Sack zu lassen: Spionage ist ein Aphrodisiakum."

Die Welt der Spionage scheint also eine Goldmine für Künstler zu sein. Klar ist, dass eine postapokalyptische Stimmung, gepaart mit jüngsten Terrorattentaten und Hacker-Leaks bei Präsidentschaftswahlen, den perfekten Boden für ein erneuertes Interesse an Spionage gesorgt hat. Topoi wie Gefahr, Paranoia, Überwachung und Gewalt erinnern uns an den Zustand der Welt und können zugleich in neuartigen Formen des Nihilismus, der Melancholie und der Auslotung der Extreme Gestalt annehmen. Künstlerinnen und Künstler – in jüngerer Vergangenheit etwa Julia Scher oder Bruce Nauman, um nur die beiden zu nennen – nutzen solche Themen, um die visuelle Kultur einer Runderneuerung zu unterziehen. Noch jüngeren Datum ist das spezielle Interesse, das eine ganze Reihe von Künstlern – Lawrence Abu Hamdan, Simon Denny, Forensic Architecture, Jill Magid, Metahaven, Trevor Paglen, Jonas Staal und Suzanne Treister neben anderen, in der Ausstellung gezeigten – an codierten Zeichen, geheimen Dokumenten und soziopolitischen Verschwörungen, generell gesagt also an den Mechanismen heutiger Geheimhaltung, bekunden.

Spionage ist nicht nur individuelle Berufung zu Betrug, doppelter Lebensführung, Verrat und vorgeschützter Loyalität. Zum Wesen von Spioninnen und Spionen gehört es, nach Informationen zu suchen, auf die sie kein Anrecht haben, und hierfür, wie auch zwecks Weiterleitung an den Feind, zu rechtswidrigen Methoden zu greifen. Sie leben ein gefährliches Leben und werden, wenn man sie schnappt, für gewöhnlich gefoltert, hingerichtet oder, wenn sie Glück haben, gegen andere Spione ausgetauscht. Eine romantische Aura umgibt ihre Erfolge. Daher sind Spionageromane – vom frivolen James-Bond-Genre bis zu John Le Carrés düsteren Dramen, nicht zu vergessen Graham Greenes moralisch zwiespältige Zwangsszenarien – für ihre Leserschaft stets ein Faszinosum, das dem Nacherlebnis der Gefahren, Ängste und Abenteuer eines altehrwürdigen Berufs im Dienste des einen Staates gegen einen anderen entspringt. Freilich hat die weltweit um sich greifende Cyberkriminalität unterdessen einen ganz anderen und weit weniger heldenhaften Typus von Spion hervorgebracht: den Hacker, der zum Zweck des finanziellen Gewinns oder der Erpressung die Privatsphäre verletzt.

Die Digitalisierung öffnete den Weg zu ungeahnten neuen Möglichkeiten, Informationen einzuholen und zu verbreiten. Immerhin bekamen mutige Einzelne dadurch Gelegenheit, in beispielloser Größenordnung zu (ver) „pfeifen" und die Machenschaften und Verschwörungen der eigenen Regierung gegen andere Staaten oder ausländische Politiker anzuprangern. Mitunter sind Hacker mit Gewissen wie Edward Snowdon zu neuen Helden im Kampf gegen den Big Brother geworden – gegen eine Regierung, die ihre eigenen Bürger ausspäht.

Die ungemeine Entwicklung all der technischen Möglichkeiten, sensible Informationen zu erlangen und zu streuen, führt zu einem Thema, das für dieses neue Phänomen in vielerlei Hinsicht den Nährboden bildet: das starke Bedürfnis vieler Normalbürgerinnen und -bürger, Informationen über sich selbst, ihre Familien und ihre Steckenpferde – im Extremfall sogar zu ihren Geheimnissen, die sie besser niemals und niemandem preisgeben sollten – weltweit auf Facebook oder anderswo auszubreiten. Was steckt hinter diesem Drang, der mitunter die Form von Selbstentblößung, Selbstgeißelung oder auch Schikanierung annimmt? Schlicht das natürliche – verständliche menschliche – Bedürfnis nach Anerkennung, Kommunikation und Überwindung der Einsamkeit in modernen Zeiten? Ist es ein anderer Ausdruck von Guy Debords *Gesellschaft des Spektakels*? Dies sind nur einige der Fragen, zu deren Sondierung die heutige Gesellschaft Künstlerinnen und Künstler herausfordert.

We Never Sleep beleuchtet das allgemeine Thema Spionage durch das Prisma zeitgenössischer Kunst und Gestaltung von der ersten Hälfte des 20. Jahrhunderts über den „Höhepunkt" im Kalten Krieg bis zum aktuellen Kontext medialer Überexponierung. Die Ausstellung versammelt herausfordernde Werke und umfasst vielfältige künstlerische Strategien. Neue und schon vorhandene Projekte werden ebenso wie eine Sammlung

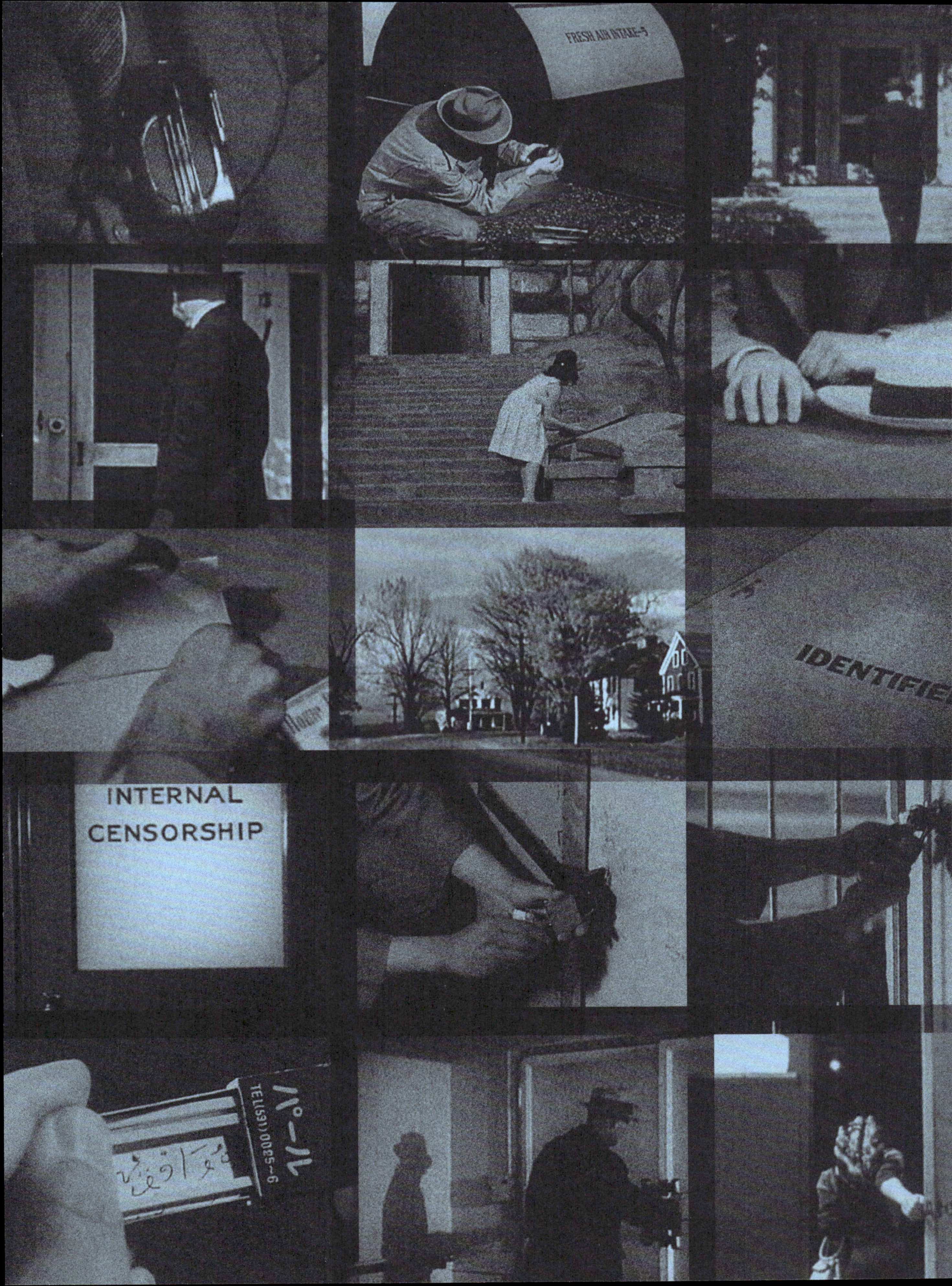
FRESH AIR INTAKE—5
IDENTIFIE
INTERNAL
CENSORSHIP
TELLS31)0005-6

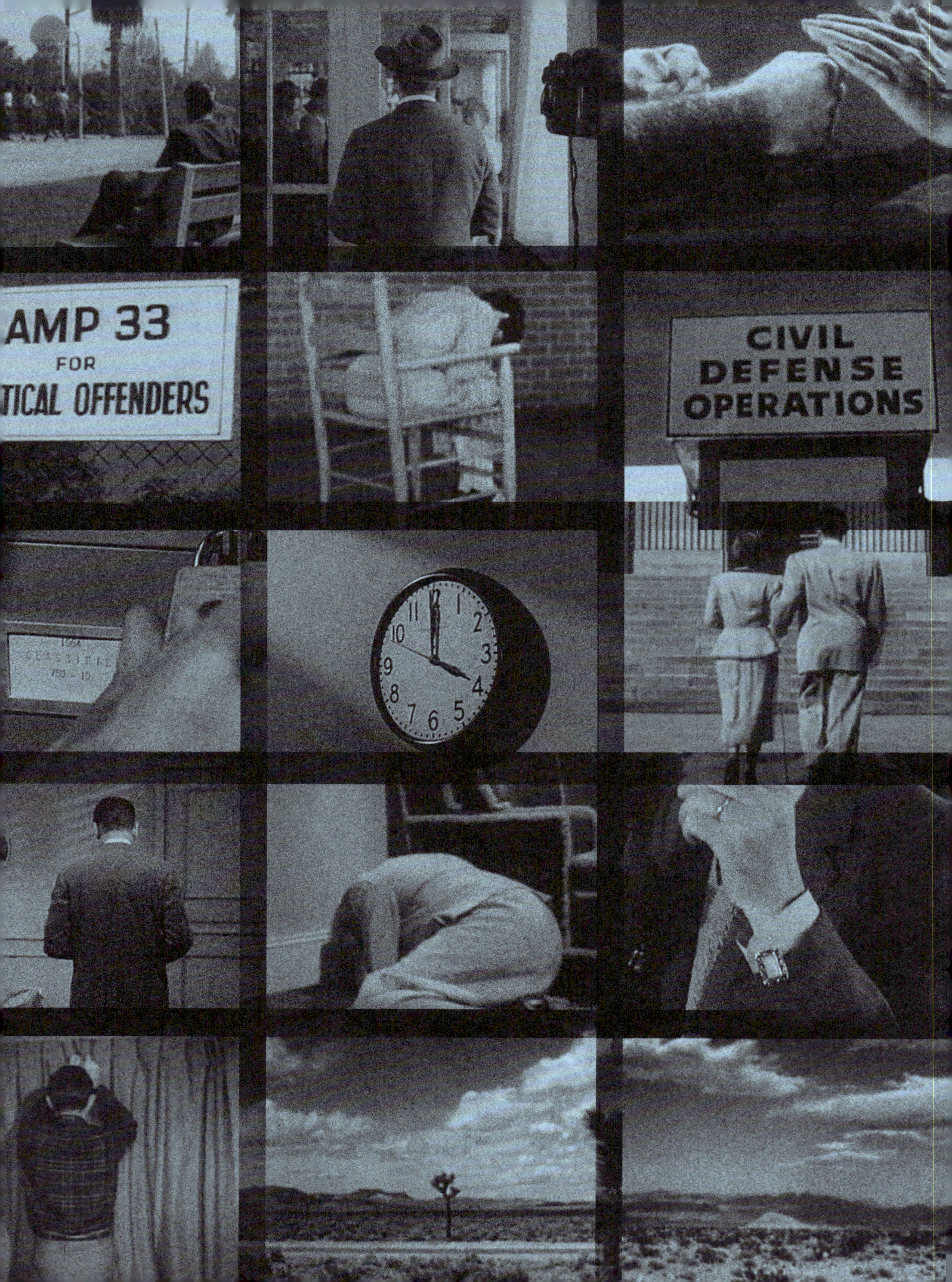
AMP 33
FOR
TICAL OFFENDERS
CIVIL
DEFENSE
OPERATIONS

überraschender Objekte (Plakate, Bucheinbände, codierte Geheimdokumente und allerlei Apparaturen aus Realität und Fiktion wie das rote Telefon oder der Lügendetektor) auf unorthodoxe Weisen einem charakteristischen Environment implementiert.

Statt zu „entlarven" oder zu „erklären", geht es vor allem darum, Überraschungen und Fragen zu provozieren. Die Ausstellung zielt nicht darauf, das Hauptthema zu illustrieren oder zu kommentieren. Vielmehr verfahren die teilnehmenden Künstlerinnen und Künstler damit auf ihre je ganz eigene Art und Weise. Manche Werke sprechen das Thema direkt an, während sich andere eher verstandesmäßig, historisch oder konzeptuell über Subthemen nähern wie: der Geheimagent und seine Mythen im Hollywood-Glamour; Frauen und Spionage; Kalter Krieg und seine Wiederkehr; Tarnung und Bildgeschichte; Kryptografie und Codebrecher; Überwachung und Bedrohung; Doppelagent und Schizophrenie; Manipulation und Bewusstseinskontrolle; propagandistische Information und Desinformation; Lauschangriff: Sound und Spionage ebenso wie Verschwörung und Paranoia. Doch sind im Sinne einer eher fließend-organischen Gesamtwahrnehmung den einzelnen Themen keine bestimmten Räume zugeordnet.

Vornan stand der Gedanke, ein besonderes Environment zu schaffen und die Besucher auf Routen zu geleiten, auf denen die verschiedenen Kapitel unseres Haupterzählstrangs verhandelt werden. Dem langen schmalen Raum der Schirn Kunsthalle Frankfurt gemäß hat Adrien Rovero einen ausgedehnten Korridor designt, der Bilder, die aus Spionagefilmen stammen könnten, wachruft und die Besucherinnen und Besucher nacheinander an unterschiedliche Plätze leitet,

wo überraschende Objekte auf sie warten. Ein schillernd-immersives, seine Motive kaschierendes Tarnmuster zeigt gleich eingangs die unbeständige, verwirrende Welt der Spionage an, in die wir eintreten. Die völlig durchinszenierte Ausstellung ist als Gesamtenvironment ausgelegt. Der Raum teilt sich in lose Bereiche, die, stets miteinander verbunden, spionagebezogene Themen behandeln. Wie in einem sich allmählich entfaltenden Spionageroman verwandeln die Schritt für Schritt sich öffnenden Räume die Besucher in Amateurspione und lassen dabei auch deren zweideutige voyeuristische Seite hervortreten. Die Architektur, der labyrinthischen Logik einer Spionagegeschichte folgend, verbirgt und entbirgt zugleich, changiert ständig zwischen Realität und Fiktion. Am Ende soll, wie in der nebulösen Welt der Spionage, die Wahrheit ein Mysterium bleiben.

Für die vorliegende Publikation haben wir einen vielstimmigen Chor versammelt, der eine Vielfalt von Interessen, Erfahrungen und Ansichten widerspiegelt. Sie stellt keinen erschöpfenden Katalog aktueller Spionagedebatten dar, sondern eine Auswahl für unseren Kontext besonders relevanter und innovativer Essays; ist weniger konventionell dokumentierendes oder kommentierendes Begleitwerk als vielmehr eine von der Ausstellung relativ unabhängige Ressource an sich. Einige Texte sind eher analytisch, andere eher theoretisch, einige entstanden im Auftrag, andere existierten bereits zuvor und werden zum Teil als Faksimiles präsentiert. Zwei spannende Artikel aus *The Guardian* und dem *Spiegel* handeln von der Dichotomie Künstler als Spion – Spion als Künstler.

In seinem eigens verfassten Beitrag „Das verborgene Leben der Kunst während und nach dem Kalten Krieg" untersucht der in Berlin ansässige Autor, Hochschullehrer und Kurator Jörg Heiser die in unserem gegenwärtigen multipolaren globalen Szenario eingetretenen Paradigmenverschiebungen im Hinblick auf das Zusammenspiel der Welten von Kunst und Spionage. In Zeiten des Kalten Kriegs konnte ein englischer Kunsthistoriker (Anthony Blunt) persönlicher Berater des Staatsoberhaupts (der Queen) und gleichzeitig jahrzehntelang Spion im Dienst der Sowjetunion sein. Heute scheinen Kunstprofis eher Gelegenheiten zu schaffen oder Partys zu besuchen, bei denen ein milliardenschwerer Unternehmer (Jeff Bezos) den Schulterschluss mit dem Königtum (Mohammed bin Salman von Saudi-Arabien) sucht, was möglicherweise in eine durch Telefonspyware ermöglichte Erpressung mündet (die letztlich zu Bezos' öffentlicher Scheidung führt) oder dafür sorgt, einen Dissidenten zur Strecke zu bringen (die brutale Ermordung von Jamal Khashoggi, der Kolumnist in der Bezos gehörenden *Washington Post* war). Die Machtspiele des Kalten Kriegs, so Heisers Fazit, scheinen in wechselnden Gestalten und unheimlichen Verkleidungen wiederzukehren, mit der Kunst zwischen allen Fronten.

Die in London lebende Wissenschaftlerin, Schriftstellerin und Hochschullehrerin Jelena Martinovic bringt in ihrem neuen Text „Film als Spionagekunst" das Agentenwesen in politischen Thrillern aus der Mitte des 20. Jahrhunderts in Zusammenhang mit Gehirnwäschetechniken im Kalten Krieg. Schwerpunkt ist eine Fallstudie zur Verhaltenstherapie, in der audiovisuelle Technik und Skripts eingesetzt werden, um eine Patientin mithilfe von subliminalen Bildern, Filmen und ver-

schlüsselten Mitteilungen zu einer Doppelagentin zu machen.

Ein sehr persönlicher Bild-Text-Essay kommt von einem an der Ausstellung teilnehmenden Künstler, Noam Toran. In seinem originellen Beitrag kombiniert er autobiografische, fiktionale und historische Materialien zu einer Schilderung der verstörenden Erfahrungen seiner Familie mit der Militarisierung der US-amerikanischen Kultur in den späten 1970er Jahren und der damit einhergegangenen Paranoia. Außerdem steuert er *Camp 33* bei, eine Reihe von Standbildern aus Schulungsfilmen, die in den USA von 1946 bis 1961 mit Regierungsmitteln hergestellt wurden. Die von Organisationen wie dem Office of Civil Defense und dem National Education Programming Department produzierten und in Schulen, Kirchen und Gemeindesälen gezeigten Filme propagieren Methoden, mit denen sich die Bevölkerung vor potenziellen Gefahren für den „American way of life", wie Sozialismus, Kommunismus, Homosexualität, Einwanderung und Aufhebung der Rassentrennung schützen ließe.

Ein weiterer teilnehmender Künstler, Gabriel Lester, legt unter dem Titel *Double-Crossed* eine Reihe von Überblendungen aus vor 1970 gedrehten Filmen vor. Eine der ersten von der Bühne auf das Kino übertragenen Lichttechniken war die Aufblende. Sie ahmt den Übergang vom Dunkel zum Licht im Theater nach und lässt das Filmbild zusehends klarer werden. Wenn Bilder aufscheinen oder miteinander verschmelzen – sich überblenden –, markiert dies einen Zeit- oder Ortsprung zwischen Szenen. Lester hat für diese Publikation Überblendungen aus zwei Kultklassikern des Spionagefilms ausgewählt, aus *Der Spion, der aus der Kälte kam* (1956) mit Richard Burton in der Hauptrolle und aus *Entehrt* (1931) mit Marlene Dietrich als Mata Hari.

Einige besonders aufschlussreiche Essays wurden zur Wiederveröffentlichung ausgesucht. „Maske: Der politische Raum hinter dem Krieg gegen den Terror" von der in Rotterdam ansässigen Architektin und Wissenschaftlerin Marina Otero Verzier, erstmals erschienen im Online-Journal *Quaderns*, schildert die Alltagserlebnisse der Autorin im öffentlichen Raum New Yorks unter dem Einfluss der Operation Nexus. Diese nach 9/11 eingeleitete Operation der New Yorker Polizeibehörde baute aus gewöhnlichen Geschäften vor Ort ein landesweites Netzwerk auf, das Informationen liefern und damit einen erneuten Terrorangriff verhindern sollte. Am Umgang mit dem Inhaber ihrer nachbarschaftlichen Wäscherei verdeutlicht Otero, dass zeitgenössische „Sicherheitsarchitektur" ebenso zu unserem Schutz dient wie zur Zerstörung dessen beiträgt, was unser Leben in Gemeinschaft ermöglicht, einschließlich unserer Freiheit und politischen Handlungsfähigkeit.

„Das exponierte Agententum" von Wladimir Velminski, Autor und Wissenschaftler in Berlin, erschien erstmals in dem nach der russischen Annexion der Krim verfassten Band *Diagnose: Krim*. Anhand von Beispielen aus Kunst und Politik wie den ästhetischen Arbeiten des Künstlers Viktor Pivovarov oder Wladimir Putins politischen Strategien geht der Autor in seinem Text den herausgestellten Strukturen des Geheimen nach. Pivovarov, Mitgründer des Moskauer Konzeptualismus, bringt die ästhetischen Praktiken des Agententums zum Vorschein, um die Betrachter ins Spiel des Verborgenen hineinzuziehen, sie anzustecken, auf seine Seite zu locken und damit einen ästhetischen Kollektivkörper zu bilden. Bezieht man

derartige Einsichten auf die Annexion der Krim, tritt besonders klar hervor, wie die Praktiken früherer Geheimagenten sich verändert haben und welche aus der Kunst übernommen worden sind.

Von Metahaven und Jonas Staal, ebenfalls an der Ausstellung beteiligt, erscheinen als Faksimiles zuvor im *e-flux journal* veröffentlichte Essays. In „Captives of the Cloud: Part I", erstveröffentlicht im September 2012, inspizieren Metahaven die Systematik unserer Online-Überwachung. Sie stellen fest, dass in einer ständig über flächendeckende Breitbandnetzwerke verbundenen Gesellschaft das gemeinsam benutzte Internet bis ins kleinste Detail von der „Cloud" überschattet wird. Als freiwillige Gefangene der Cloud haben uns Regierungen im Auge, die wir nicht gewählt haben. Zitiert wird auch der ägyptische Google-Manager Wael Ghonim: „Wenn du eine Gesellschaft befreien willst, gib ihr einfach das Internet. Aber wie befreit man eine Gesellschaft, die das Internet schon hat?"

In „Propaganda (Art) Struggle", ursprünglich veröffentlicht im Oktober 2018, gibt Jonas Staal zu bedenken, dass unsere Wirklichkeit zum Teil determiniert ist durch einen Propagandakampf – dieser aber nicht im Sinn einer Einzelkampagne, sondern als resultierender Gesamtvorgang mehrerer konkurrierender Propagandaschlachten. Verschiedene Mächte seien darauf aus, die Wirklichkeit nach ihren Interessen zu gestalten, was dazu führe, dass die zeitgenössische Arena durch einander überlappende Ansprüche geprägt werde. Welche visuellen Formen werden von dieser mannigfaltigen Propaganda und den Realitäten, die sie erzeugen will, vorausgesetzt bzw. angestrebt? Welcherart künstlerische Morphologien und kulturellen Narrative bringt der Propagandakampf

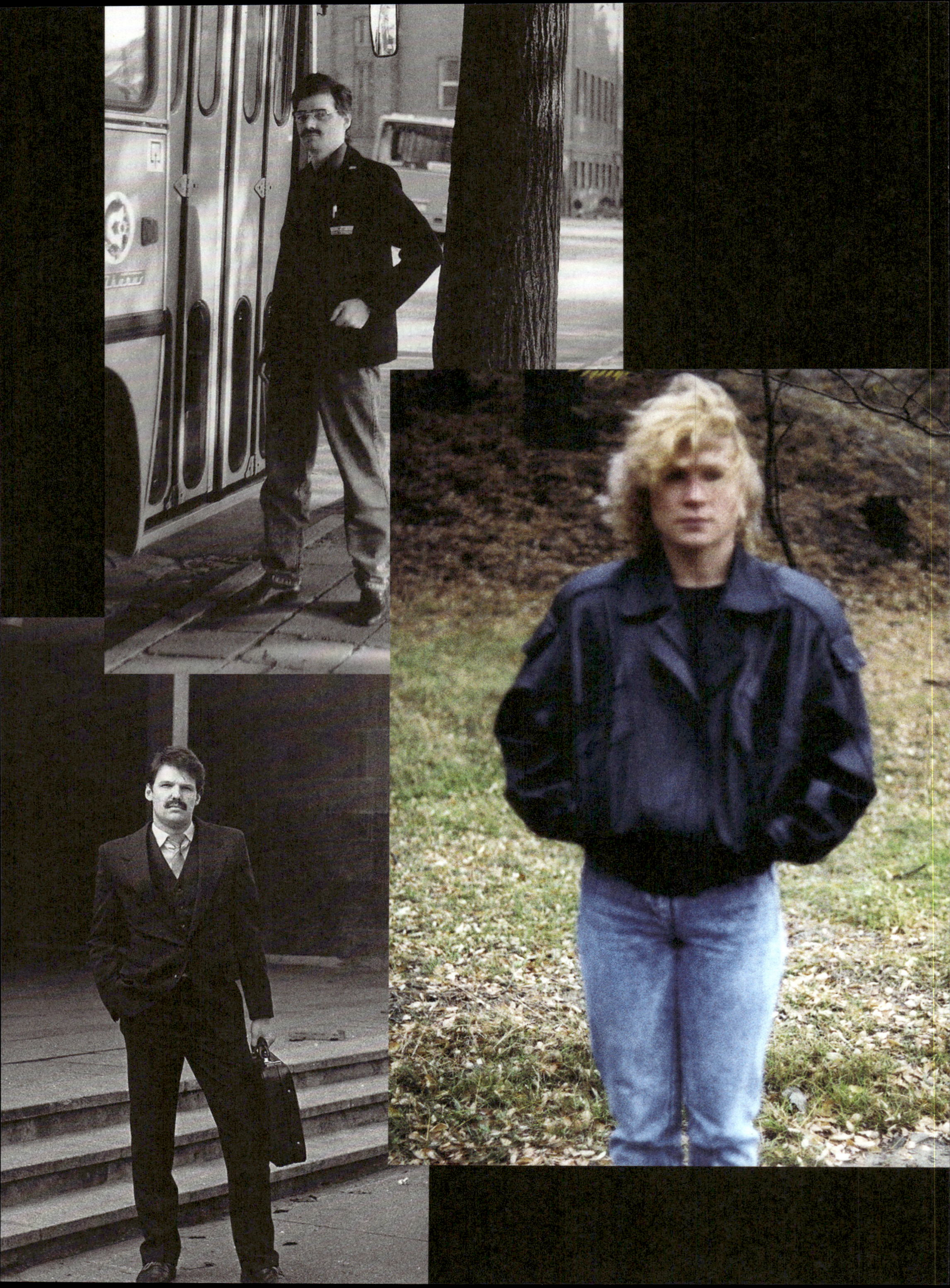

mit sich? Dies sind einige der wichtigen Fragen, die der Text aufwirft.

Publikation wie Ausstellung sind ein gemeinschaftliches Unterfangen. Sie fußen auf Recherchen, die ich mit der in Paris lebenden Autorin, Hochschullehrerin und Kuratorin Alexandra Midal in den vergangenen Jahren betrieben habe. Ohne ihren Weitblick und Beitrag wären beide nicht zustande gekommen. Katharina Dohm, Kuratorin an der Schirn, hat sich des Projekts zur Gänze verschrieben, ihr unermüdliches Engagement und Mitwirken war für seine Verwirklichung unerlässlich. Adrien Roveros kühner szenografischer Wurf war gleichermaßen fundamental. Auch waren einige Künstlerinnen und Künstler in die Gesamtkonstruktion des Projekts mit eingebunden, deren innovative Ideen sehr inspirierend wirkten. Für die Realisierung des Projekts wesentlich war eine offene und flexible Haltung aller Beteiligten. Statt subjektive und einseitige Beschlüsse zu fassen, pflegten wir gedanklichen und praktischen Austausch in Partnerschaft.

Auf viele unvermutete Weisen liefert die Corona-Pandemie die perfekte Umgebung für die vorliegende Ausstellung. Die beispiellose Krise hat die strukturellen Ungleichheiten und Ungerechtigkeiten auf der Welt besonders sichtbar gemacht. Antidemokratische Tendenzen wurden verstärkt, als manche Regierungen unter dem Vorwand der Pandemiebekämpfung im Wege kontaktverfolgender Apps und zentraler Datenerfassung neue Überwachungsmaßnahmen erließen. Angst geht um in der Welt, und Verschwörungstheorien blühen. In den sozialen Medien sprießen Paranoia, Fake News und Desinformation. Spione, Hacker und Netzaktivisten sind im Augenblick ganz besonders rege. Eine sich bedroht fühlende und um die Zukunft besorgte Öffentlichkeit gibt für Manipulation und Missbrauch eine leichte Beute ab. In Zeiten einer von Ungewissheit und wachsender Furcht angestachelten Krise, wie sie die Pandemie darstellt, sind Künstlerinnen und Künstler vielleicht mit am besten gerüstet, das Unbekannte zu entschlüsseln und Verschwörungstheorien zu entmystifizieren, um innovative, überzeugende Linien in die Zukunft zu ziehen.

The Secret Life of Art During and After the Cold War
Jörg Heiser

For years, the wallpaper of the laptop on which I am writing this text has shown a painting by the Venetian painter Lorenzo Lotto (fig. 1). I love this painting. The original from around 1530 is on display at the Kunsthistorisches Museum in Vienna. In landscape format—highly unusual for portrait painting at the time—it depicts a middle-aged man with curly brown hair and a reddish full beard from three sides simultaneously, as though he were looking into a makeup mirror. In his hand rests a jewelry box: he is a goldsmith. One reason for this rather unusual form of depiction may have been that Lotto's painting was part of a then virulent debate about which of the two disciplines of painting and sculpture was the more excellent art form (whereby the argument in favor of the latter was that it offered more than just one perspective, which Lotto in turn refuted, employing the wit of literalness).

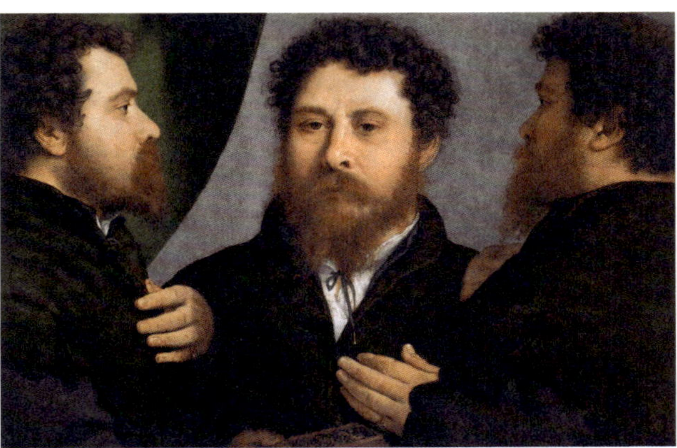

Fig. / Abb. 1: Lorenzo Lotto, *Portrait of a Goldsmith in Three Positions / Ein Goldschmied in drei Ansichten*, ca. 1530
Kunsthistorisches Museum Wien

Another reason may have been that it alluded to the sitter's hometown, Treviso, which literally means "three views."[1] These two readings are not mutually exclusive, but rather are to be seen as moments of a deliberate overdetermination, or rather multiple meaning, demonstrating artistic refinement. Things that at first appear trivial gain in importance, while others that seem to imply something specific suddenly mean the opposite. It may be seen as a pastime of the well educated, as an intellectual game of insinuation among aristocratic and clerical elites. More importantly, however, it is reminiscent of the between-the-lines tactic, which is well known from eras and from places and societies where freedom of expression is not guaranteed—in other words, in global and epochal history almost everywhere and always. And anyone who, in the 1530s within the sphere of Roman influence, even mentioned anything related to the new teachings of a certain Martin Luther had to expect consequences, such as being drowned in the Canal Grande. The eyes and ears of the clergy were everywhere—and the confessionals were the wiretapping systems of their time. Which brings us to a third level of meaning of the image: according to Inquisition records from the 1570s, the goldsmith Bartolomeo Carpan, whom Lotto had portrayed four decades earlier, was the head of the Lutheran congregation, which—despite the relative tolerance of Venice as a commercial hub—had remained clandestine.[2]

In 1964, the art historian Anthony Blunt explained this very painting to a distinguished English audience using a slide projection. He eloquently reported that the painting had long been wrongly attributed to Titian, and he connected the issue of the two or three faces of the person portrayed with the idea of a hidden layer, a double life—or even triple life—beneath a thin veneer of representation: "Truth may lie beneath the surface, buried, forgotten, but time has a way of uncovering it."[3]

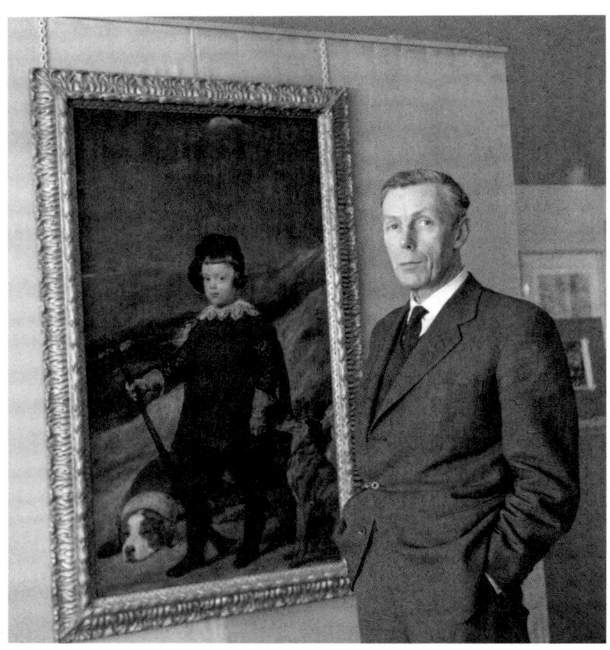

Fig. / Abb. 2: Blunt and / und Velasquez, 1962

The scene described did not actually take place in reality, at least not in the exact same way. Rather, it is the fictionalized, albeit fact-based, portrayal in the first episode of the third season of the Netflix series *The Crown*. Anthony Blunt was indeed the art historian at Buckingham Palace and was in active, direct contact with Queen Elizabeth II (fig. 2). He was in charge of the Royal Collection and was furthermore director of the Courtauld Institute of Art. His students included Brian Sewell, the art critic of the *Evening Standard*, and Nicholas Serota, the founder of Tate Modern. And, above all, Blunt was, as a direct confidant of the British head of state, the fourth of the Cambridge Four, the spy ring that revealed state secrets to the Soviet Union during World War II and into the early 1950s. He would on occasion spend his Christmas holidays together with Sir Dick White, initially head of MI5 and then of MI6. In 1964, the British secret service finally found him out. They granted him immunity, apparently because the embarrassment about him remaining undiscovered for such a long time was too great. It was not until 1979 that Blunt was publicly exposed by Margaret Thatcher in the House of Commons. His handler at the NKVD (later KGB) had already suspected Blunt of being a triple agent (a triple agent is a double agent who pretends loyalty to one side while they are actually loyal to the other).

The point of the Netflix scene is that, right afterward, Blunt was arrested and interrogated—if he had indeed been a triple agent, then the triple portrait by Lotto was a good choice. The relationship between the art world and the world of espionage during the Cold War era is summed up as follows: an honorable, highly educated art connoisseur, who was acting on behalf of the head of state, while eavesdropping on state secrets in the back room over whiskey and cigars, and later exchanging them, over vodka and cigarettes, for other (supposed) state secrets. Because, deep down, he was following an ideological conviction, or enjoyed playing with fire—likely both at once.

The changes in a world where walls have fallen and the attacks of 9/11 took place also become apparent in the relationship between the art world and the world of espionage. The vast majority of heads of state (presumably including the Queen) meanwhile probably take little interest in art historians. Some autocrats, however, certainly rely on contemporary art in their self-representation. Espionage, in the meantime, takes place less ad personam in back rooms than on digital devices. And today we see global players who influence the fate of the world in unprecedented ways—and in doing so, they also bring art as a milieu into play, incidentally, but in a conspicuous way.

A big Hollywood dinner was held on April 4, 2018, hosted by the film producer Brian Grazer and his wife Veronica Smiley Grazer, as well as by Ari Emanuel, the head of the William Morris Endeavor talent agency, its portfolio listing actors such as Robert De Niro, but also sports tournaments, the Miss Universe Pageant, and the company Frieze, including the art fairs and magazine of the same name (for which the author of this text worked as an editor from 1997 to 2017). By this time, Emanuel had already secured financial support for his firm from a special guest of honor at the gala evening: Crown Prince Mohammed bin Salman, also known by the acronym MBS, who was about to enter into a $400 million share deal in Endeavor through the Saudi investment fund he controls.[4] MBS was thus present in person at this glamorous event alongside stars such as basketball legend Kobe Bryant and Disney boss Bob Iger. As a party report in the glossy gossip magazine *Vanity Fair* describes in a smug and bitterly ironic way: "Topics that were deemed off-limits included the 32-year-old's bombing campaign in Yemen, which has killed thousands of civilians; his abduction of Lebanon's prime minister, Saad Hariri, in November [2017]; and the decidedly un-Hollywood-like repression of independent media and journalists, one of whom was recently imprisoned for five years for 'insulting' the royal court."[5]

MBS had demonstrated his interest in investing in the cultural and arts sector in other places as well, albeit rather discreetly. According to credible rumors, he was personally behind the 450 million dollar purchase of the world's most expensive painting, *Salvator Mundi*, attributed to Leonardo da Vinci. The "missing" painting is believed to be on his yacht, *Serene*.[6] In any case, the 400-million-dollar deal that had made the Saudi crown prince de facto an indirect shareholder in the art company Frieze for a short time (which, among other things, triggered speculation that the eponymous fair would soon be held in the Persian Gulf[7]) was ultimately reversed barely a year later. This is because something drastic had happened in the meantime: in October 2018, the dissident and journalist Jamal Khashoggi was brutally murdered in the Saudi consulate in Istanbul by henchmen of the MBS regime. And since Turkey had made intelligence information about this assassination public, the criminal, unbridled despotism could no longer be glossed over as a regrettable transitional phenomenon of the actions of an actually reform-minded heir to the throne. Emanuel therefore reached the only correct conclusion—albeit almost half a year later—and annulled the deal after he had secured alternative investors. In this, he was an exception—other companies allowed similar investment deals to quietly continue.[8] Yet the story did not end there. Khashoggi was a columnist for *The Washington Post*,

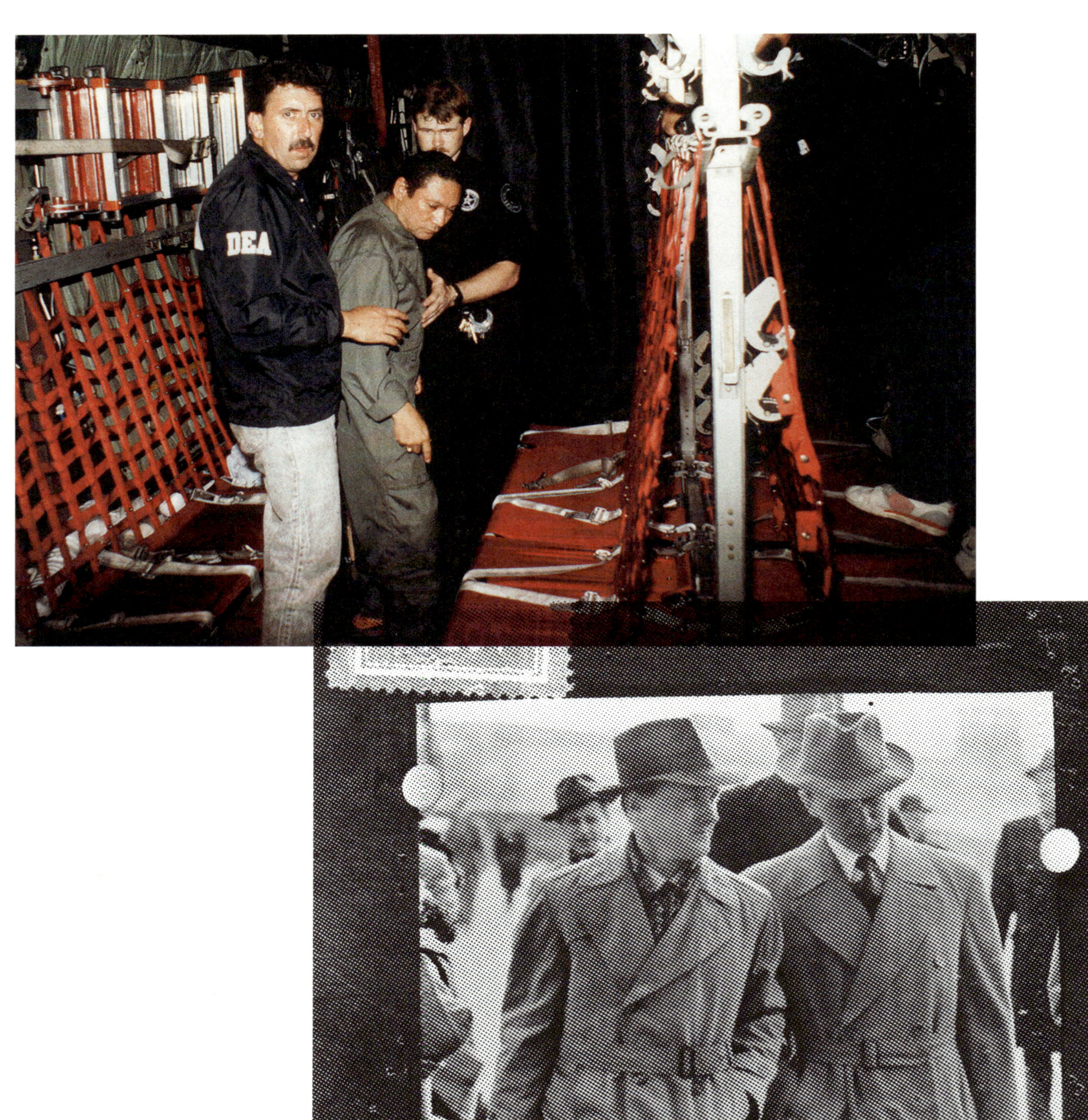

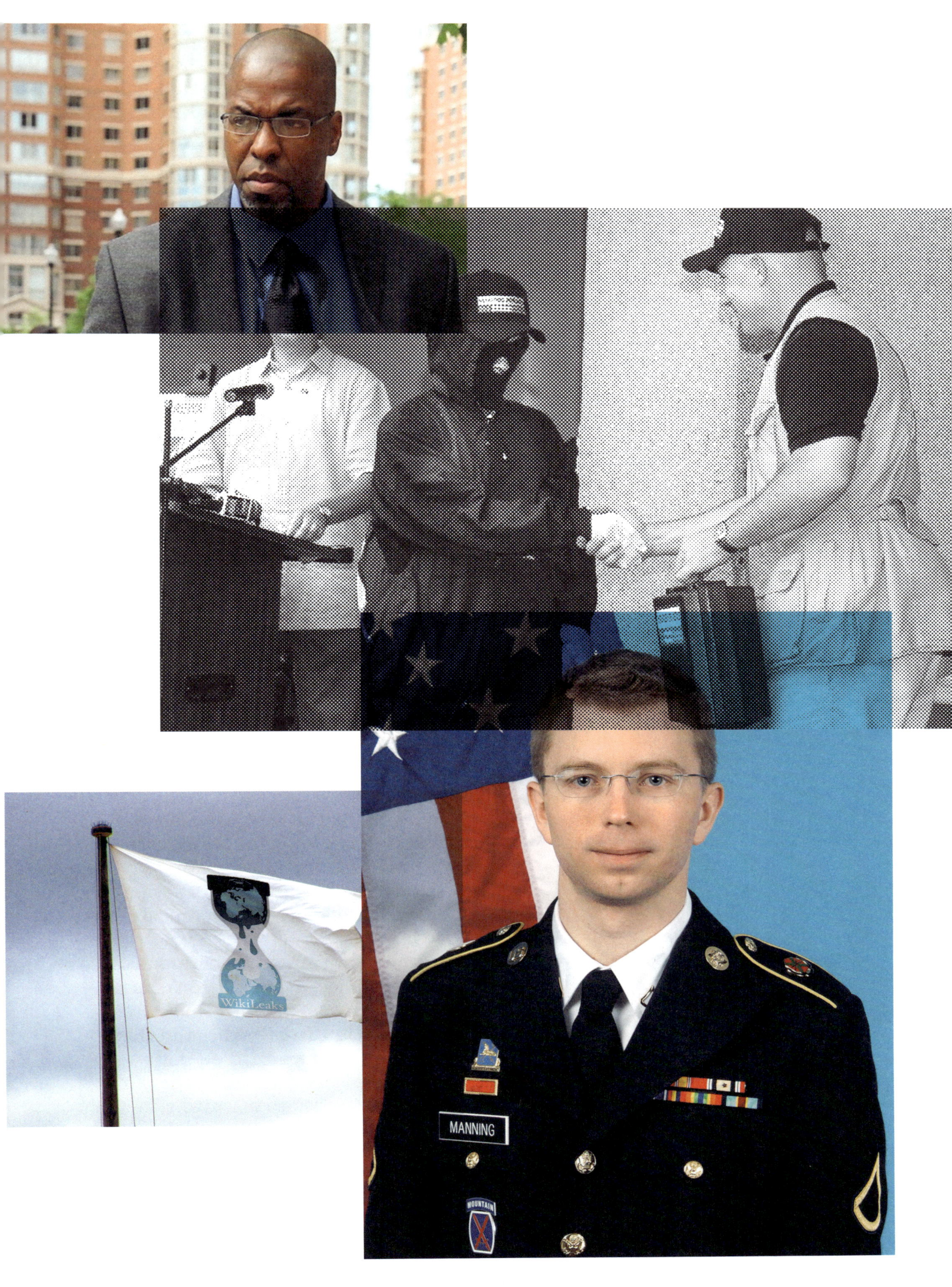

among other publications. And its owner, the richest man in the world, the Amazon boss Jeff Bezos, was also present at that memorable Hollywood dinner in April 2018. Moreover, he exchanged cell phone numbers with MBS that very night. They hooked up via WhatsApp.

What now followed only became fully known in January 2020: Bezos's mobile phone was spied on in early May 2018 by means of a file that landed on his phone through a personal WhatsApp message from MBS (fig. 3).[9] Intimate photos of Bezos, a married man engaging in an affair, were offered to the American tabloid *National Enquirer*. Jeff Bezos beat most of the publications to the punch by openly admitting to his extramarital affair.[10] Yet this was not enough to prevent divorce from his wife MacKenzie Bezos—she received a 38 billion dollar share of his assets. What is clear, however, is that MBS had personally attacked Bezos because of *The Washington Post*'s coverage of its columnist Khashoggi; and also that the intention to strong-arm Bezos had indeed already existed before Khashoggi was murdered for his journalistic work for *The Washington Post*.

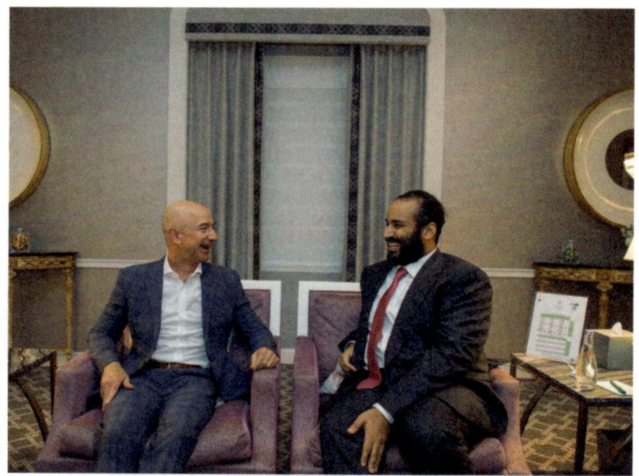

Fig. / Abb. 3: Meeting of Mohammed bin Salman, the Crown Prince of Saudi Arabia, and Jeff Bezos, the founder of Amazon and owner of *The Washington Post* / Treffen des saudischen Kronprinzen Mohammed bin Salman mit Amazon-Gründer und Besitzer der *Washington Post* Jeff Bezos, 2018

The Saudi secret service had apparently also spied on Khashoggi before his murder by means of a spyware that had landed on his mobile phone. This malware called Pegasus is offered to governmental organizations by the Israeli company NSO Group Technologies. The Mexican government is also alleged to have used the program against journalists investigating the unsolved case of a bus hijacking in 2014 during which forty-three students were murdered. This brings the story back to the art world once more. In June 2019, research by the British news magazine *The Guardian* led, within just a few days, to the resignation of Yana Peel, the managing director of the Serpentine Gallery in London.[11]

What had happened? Peel, a former Goldman Sachs banker, had put her money into an investment fund. This fund in turn acquired the aforementioned software company NSO. According to *The Guardian*, Peel was now co-owner of the company that produced Pegasus, the software that government organizations—that is, secret service agencies—were particularly fond of using in their attacks on unpopular opponents of the regime, dissidents, and journalists. And this despite the fact that she had staged herself in the art public as a liberal, ethically conscientious person, serving, for instance, as a jury member for the Freedom of Expression Award, which in 2018 was bestowed on a human rights organization that had been targeted by the secret services in Egypt through cyberattacks.

But why did Peel's resignation come about so fast? It was, among others, the German artist Hito Steyerl and the British designer James Bridle—both had realized projects with the Serpentine Gallery—who decided to intervene.

Immediately after *The Guardian* published the accusations, they drummed up signatures from members of the art world for a letter of protest. The pressure built up quickly. In the times of Donald Trump's presidency, in which the obscenity of a massive preference for the super-rich combined with the most vile right-wing populism has been openly exposed, parts of the art world have become even more critical of the role of the same super-rich within this sphere. Yet there is another factor that plays a part in this: a number of artists, including Steyerl and Bridle, but also others such as Trevor Paglen and the group Forensic Architecture around the architect Eyal Weizman, have themselves actively and investigatively researched intelligence surveillance techniques in the digital age. They know very well what can be accomplished with a software such as Pegasus. Actual agent activity has become a serious subject of artistic work. At documenta 14 (2017), for example, Forensic Architecture showed a work in which they were able to prove, by means of a virtual 3D reconstruction based on ballistic details and spatial visual axes, that Andreas Temme, an agent of the Hessian Verfassungsschutz (Office for the Protection of the Constitution), who was in the adjacent room when Halit Yozgat was murdered by the right-wing extremist terrorist group NSU in an Internet café in Kassel in 2006, must have lied: he testified that he had not heard the shots and had not seen the body behind the counter when leaving the premises—a claim that Forensic Architecture managed to refute convincingly.[12]

Artists, as well as civil society as a whole, are thus today in a position to apply and use the digital possibilities of spying, or rather the forensic reconstruction of events, against those authorities that use these capabilities in secret by their very nature. Yet the fate of whistleblowers like Edward Snowden, Chelsea Manning, and Julian Assange illustrates that this happens at the price of exposing oneself to possible criminalization and prosecution. But we should not delude ourselves that the end of the Cold War in today's multipolar world has ushered in a golden age of journalistic and artistic liberation from entanglement in the (by all means espionage-led) activities of the super-rich and autocrats. On the contrary: for one, art has long been a lubricant—in multiple allegorical respects—for the triangle of money, power, and injustice, since autocrats and the super-rich who do business with artists apply an artistic varnish to themselves that signals cosmopolitanism, in order to relativize and cover up their other activities—keyword: "artwashing." Furthermore, it may also happen that in the middle of this new multipolar, virtually and physically globalized world, practices from the Cold War era are being used again under new auspices. Such as the one—in the Soviet secret service tradition since the good old KGB days—that has been referred to with the eerie term "kompromat." We may never know for sure, but one can certainly speculate how it came about that the Russian dissident and artist Pyotr Pavlensky, from his place of exile in France, chose to resort to such blackmail methods in February 2020 using intimate visual material, which is considered a secret service kompromat par excellence. Pavlensky had offered a masturbation video of Benjamin Griveaux—the candidate of Macron's party La République en Marche for the post of mayor of Paris—to the investigative news platform Mediapart for publication. He had obtained this video through his French girlfriend Alexandra de Taddeo, who in turn had engaged in an affair with Griveaux—she had therefore, knowingly or not, been the "honeytrap" for Griveaux. Mediapart refused to publish this information because it is an unwritten law in France that the private and sex lives of prominent politicians are sacrosanct, as long as their political actions are not significantly affected by this behavior.[13] It was at this point that Pavlensky made the video public on his own website. Griveaux withdrew his candidacy.

Here, a further comparison with Anthony Blunt is worthwhile. There is serious circumstantial evidence, which also found its way into the aforementioned episode of *The Crown*, that Blunt used his knowledge of Prince Philip—the Queen's husband—having an indirect connection to the Profumo affair of 1963 against Philip, in order to prevent his own public exposure. Profumo, the British Secretary of State for War, had met the showgirl Christine Keeler through the osteopath and artist Stephen Ward. Ward, in turn, had made several portrait drawings of Prince Philip and was himself a spy for the Soviets; his handler Eugene Ivanov managed to eavesdrop on various meetings between Profumo and Keeler. Ward had auctioned off the portraits of the prince—and Blunt is said to have bought them to protect the royal house; or indeed to have a weapon in hand should his public exposure ever be imminent.[14]

Regarding Pavlensky, one must assume that he never even remotely belonged to the inner intelligence circle in which Blunt had been active for decades. Nevertheless, it would be naive to believe that the dissident artist would resort, en passant, to the means of

exposing the (sexual) private life of a politician with whom he had no previous dealings. A quick recap: in 2012, Pavlensky had sewn up his mouth in protest against the imprisonment of the members of the band Pussy Riot in a penal camp. In 2013, he nailed his scrotum to Red Square to protest against police violence and general indifference. In November 2015, he set fire to an entrance door of the Russian domestic secret service FSB in Moscow, whereupon he was arrested and transferred to a psychiatric ward (fig. 4). Instead of a prison sentence, he was later fined the equivalent of 13,500 euros. In February 2017, he eventually fled to seek asylum in France.

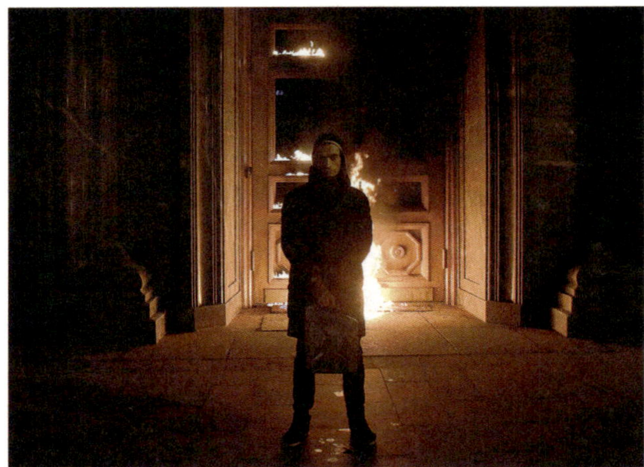

Fig. / Abb. 4: Nigina Beroeva, The artist Pyotr Pavlensky during his action *Threat*, shown against the burning door of the Russian domestic secret service FSB in Moscow / Der Künstler Pjotr Pawlenski bei seiner Aktion *Bedrohung* vor brennender Tür des russischen Geheimdienstes FSB in Moskau, 2015

It is no secret that Russia's President Putin himself was a KGB officer, stationed in Dresden in the GDR from 1985 to 1990. During this time, he also held a Stasi identity card.[15] In this respect, it may come as no surprise that, under his present rule, well-known secret service methods like kompromat, bribery, and media manipulation—supplemented by today's digital means in information warfare—have once again become state doctrine, so to speak. The indications that Russia has tried to influence the US elections (to harm Hillary Clinton and help Trump), the UK Brexit referendum, and the French presidential elections (to support Marine Le Pen and prevent Macron from being elected) through hacker attacks, but also through an indirect manipulation of public opinion in social media (via troll farms, etc.), have intensified in recent years. It is thus not surprising that, immediately after the Griveaux affair became public knowledge, Macron vehemently proclaimed the containment of such Russian attempts to influence elections in Europe.[16] Given the temporal proximity of the events, it is reasonable to wonder whether Pavlensky might have been made an offer by the state before he fled to France, an offer he could not refuse. This is a classic instrument of power: either you do XY, or you will be sent to penal camp (like Pussy Riot), or something even worse will happen to you. Especially since, in this case, the "XY" was completely tailored to Pavlensky's obvious desire for breaking taboos and for public agitation through provocation of powerful politicians—a classic "turning" of a subject by a secret service agency. Admittedly, this is mere speculation. But even if Pavlensky was acting of his own free will and on his own account, it is clear that in today's attention economy he was engaged in something that—although, or precisely because, it is presented as (conceptual, activist) art—follows classic secret service patterns and thus, intentionally or not, plays into their hands.[17]

So what can we learn from all this? First of all, the unsurprising circumstance that the art world can hardly wriggle "innocently" and unaffectedly out of the fact that, particularly in the last two decades, it has become a plaything of oligarchs, autocrats, and the super-rich, including their involvement in intelligence-assisted human rights violations and their undermining of democratic and civil society structures. The glamorous days when Cold War spies made pretty portrait drawings of princes or gave scholarly lectures on Renaissance artists are over. Instead, participants in the art world run the risk of being caught up in artwashing or even, as in Pavlensky's case, in the direct undermining of democratic and civil society standards. All the more important are, therefore, those artists who—like Steyerl, Paglen, and Forensic Architecture—work tirelessly to uncover and artistically comment on such circumstances.

1   See David Alan Brown, Peter Humfrey, and Mauro Lucco, eds., *Lorenzo Lotto: Rediscovered Master of the Renaissance*, exh. cat. The National Gallery of Art, Washington, DC; Accademia Carrara di Belle Arti, Bergamo; and Galeries nationales du Grand Palais, Paris (New Haven, CT, and London, 1997), pp. 176–77.

2   John Jeffries Martin, *Venice's Hidden Enemies: Italian Heretics in a Renaissance Society* (Baltimore and London, 1993), pp. 89, 132, and 158.

3   Cited from *The Crown*, TV series, Netflix, 2019, season 3, episode 1.

4   Nancy Tartaglione, "Saudi Arabia Fund Deal For Endeavor Stake Could Close In Week's Time For $400M," *Deadline*, March 16, 2018, https://deadline.com/2018/03/saudi-arabia-fund-endeavor-stake-talks-400-to-500-million-1202243920/ (alls URLs accessed in April 2020).

5   Isobel Thompson, "Prince Mohammed Does Hollywood," *Vanity Fair*, April 6, 2018, https://www.vanityfair.com/news/2018/04/prince-mohammed-does-hollywood.

6   Kenny Schachter, "Where In the World Is 'Salvator Mundi'? Kenny Schachter Reveals the Location of the Lost $450 Million Leonardo," *artnet news*, June 10, 2019, https://news.artnet.com/opinion/kenny-schachter-on-the-missing-salvator-mundi-1565674.

7   Ibid.

8   Kate Kelly and Ben Hubbard, "Endeavor Returns Money to Saudi Arabia, Protesting Khashoggi Murder," *The New York Times*, March 8, 2019, https://www.nytimes.com/2019/03/08/business/endeavor-saudi-arabia.html.

9   Stephanie Kirchgaessner, "Jeff Bezos Hack: Amazon Boss's Phone 'Hacked by Saudi Crown Prince'," *The Guardian*, January 22, 2020, https://www.theguardian.com/technology/2020/jan/21/amazon-boss-jeff-bezoss-phone-hacked-by-saudi-crown-prince.

10 Jeff Bezos, "No thank you, Mr. Pecker," *Medium*, February 7, 2019, https://medium.com/@jeffreypbezos/no-thank-you-mr-pecker-146e3922310f.

11 "UK News: Yana Peel," *The Guardian*, June 14, 2019, https://www.theguardian.com/law/2019/jun/14/yana-peel-uk-rights-advocate-serpentine-nso-spyware-pegasus; Jon Swaine, Stephanie Kirchgaessner, and Patrick Greenfield, "Serpentine Galleries Chief Resigns," *The Guardian*, June 18, 2019, https://www.theguardian.com/artanddesign/2019/jun/18/serpentine-galleries-chief-resigns.

12 "The Murder of Halit Yozgat," *Forensic Architecture*, n.d., https://forensic-architecture.org/investigation/the-murder-of-halit-yozgat.

13 Cyril Delaune, "Sextape de Benjamin Griveaux: pourquoi Mediapart a refusé de diffuser les vidéos de Piotr Pavlenski," *Voici*, March 8, 2020, https://www.voici.fr/news-people/actu-people/sextape-de-benjamin-griveaux-pourquoi-mediapart-a-refuse-de-diffuser-les-videos-de-piotr-pavlenski-676011.

14 See Chloe Foussianes, "How Prince Philip Was Connected to the Profumo Affair—and How Anthony Blunt May Have Covered For Him," *Town & Country*, November 17, 2019, https://www.townandcountrymag.com/society/tradition/a29322952/profumo-affair-true-story-prince-philip-anthony-blunt-connection/.

15 "Wladimir Putins Stasi-Ausweis in Dresdner Archiv entdeckt," *Der Tagesspiegel*, December 11, 2018, https://www.tagesspiegel.de/politik/aus-kgb-zeit-in-der-ddr-wladimir-putins-stasi-ausweis-in-dresdner-archiv-entdeckt/23745760.html.

16 Laurens Cerulus, "Macron Calls for Attribution, Cybersanctions to Stop Russian Election Meddling," *Politico*, February 15, 2020, https://www.politico.eu/article/macron-calls-for-attribution-cybersanctions-to-stop-russian-election-meddling/.

17 According to a Russian acquintance who has friends in Moscow closely following the political developments, they do not think that it is likely that Pavlensky was recruited, simply because he was too uncontrollable of a person for any such recruitment. However, in my humble opinion, a certain volatility, even crazyness, seems like something that is precisely welcome and employed by state agencies under other circumstances as well, against the background of an age of online trolling and the supporting of irresponsible clowns as heads of state. That said, as is the nature of these things, unless documents are revealed, which may not be the case for decades to come if ever, any such assessment admittedly remains a speculation.

Das verborgene Leben der Kunst während und nach dem Kalten Krieg
Jörg Heiser

Der Bildschirmhintergrund des Laptops, auf dem ich diesen Text schreibe, ist seit Jahren ein Gemälde des venezianischen Malers Lorenzo Lotto (Abb. 1, S. 41). Ich liebe dieses Bild. Das Original von ca. 1530 hängt im Kunsthistorischen Museum in Wien. Im – für damalige Porträtmalerei sehr ungewöhnlichen – Querformat zeigt es einen Mann mittleren Alters mit lockig braunem Haupthaar und rötlichem Vollbart von drei Seiten gleichzeitig, so als schaue er in einen Schminkspiegel. In seiner Hand ein Schmuckkästchen: Er ist Goldschmied. Ein Grund für diese recht ungewöhnliche Form der Darstellung mag gewesen sein, dass Lotto mit dem Bild auf eine damals virulente Debatte darüber einging, welche der beiden Disziplinen Malerei und Bildhauerei die vortrefflichere Kunstform sei (wobei für Letztere vorgebracht wurde, sie böte schließlich mehr als nur eine Perspektive, was Lotto mit dem Witz der Buchstäblichkeit widerlegte). Ein anderer Grund mag gewesen sein, dass sich so eine Anspielung auf den Heimatort des Dargestellten ergab – Treviso, wörtlich „drei Ansichten".[1] Diese beiden Lesarten schließen sich nicht aus, sondern sind eher als Momente einer bewussten, die künstlerische Verfeinerung demonstrierenden Überdeterminierung beziehungsweise Mehrfachbedeutung anzusehen. Dinge, die zunächst nebensächlich erscheinen, bekommen Gewicht, oder Dinge, die etwas Bestimmtes zu bedeuten scheinen, bedeuten plötzlich das Gegenteil davon. Man kann das als Zeitvertreib der Gebildeten verstehen, als intellektuelles Spiel der Andeutung unter aristokratischen und klerikalen Eliten. Wichtiger aber ist: Es erinnert an die Zwischen-den-Zeilen-Taktik, die wohlbekannt ist aus Zeiten und von Orten und Gesellschaften, wo freie Meinungsäußerung nicht garantiert ist – also global- und epochenhistorisch betrachtet fast überall und immer. Und wer in den 1530er Jahren im Einflussbereich von Rom etwas – beispielsweise – über die neuen Lehren eines gewissen Luther verlor, musste mit Konsequenzen rechnen, bis hin dazu, im Canal Grande ersäuft zu werden. Die Augen und Ohren des Klerus waren überall – und die Beichtstühle waren die Abhöranlagen ihrer Zeit. Womit wir bei einer dritten Bedeutungsebene des Bildes wären: Wie aus Inquisitionsakten der 1570er Jahre hervorgeht, war der Goldschmied Bartolomeo Carpan, den Lotto vier Jahrzehnte zuvor porträtiert hatte, Kopf jener lutherischen Gemeinde, welche trotz der relativen Toleranz des Handelsplatzes Venedigs klandestin geblieben war.[2]

Ebenjenes Bild erläutert der Kunsthistoriker Anthony Blunt 1964 vor einem distinguierten englischen Publikum anhand einer Diaprojektion. Eloquent berichtet er, dass das Bild lange fälschlich Tizian zugeschrieben worden sei, und er verknüpft die Frage nach den zwei oder drei Gesichtern des

Dargestellten mit der Vorstellung einer verborgenen Schicht, eines Doppellebens – oder gar Dreifachlebens – unter einer dünnen Oberfläche der Repräsentation: „Die Wahrheit mag unter der Oberfläche liegen, vergraben, vergessen, aber die Zeit weiß Wege, sie wieder zum Vorschein zu bringen."[3]

Die geschilderte Szene fand allerdings in der Realität nicht statt, zumindest nicht genau so – sondern sie ist die fiktionalisierte, allerdings auf Tatsachen beruhende Darstellung in der ersten Folge der dritten Staffel der Netflix-Serie *The Crown*. Anthony Blunt war tatsächlich der Kunsthistoriker des Buckinghampalastes und stand in regem direkten Kontakt mit Königin Elisabeth II (Abb. 2., S. 42). Er betreute die königliche Sammlung und war zudem Direktor des Courtauld Institute of Art; zu seinen Schülern zählten unter anderem Brian Sewell, der Kunstkritiker des *Evening Standard*, und Nicholas Serota, der Gründer der Tate Modern. Und Blunt war vor allem, als unmittelbarer Vertrauter des britischen Staatsoberhaupts, der Vierte der Cambridge Four, des Spionagerings, welcher im Zweiten Weltkrieg und bis in die frühen 1950er Jahre Staatsgeheimnisse an die Sowjetunion verriet. Seine Weihnachtsferien hatte er mitunter gemeinsam mit Sir Dick White, erst Chef des MI5 und dann des MI6, verbracht. Der britische Geheimdienst kam ihm erst 1964 auf die Schliche; und billigte ihm Immunität zu, offenbar weil die Beschämung darüber, dass er so lange unentdeckt geblieben war, zu groß war; erst 1979 wurde er von Margaret Thatcher im Unterhaus öffentlich enttarnt. Bereits sein Kontaktmann beim NKVD (später KGB) hatte Blunt verdächtigt, ein Triple Agent zu sein (ein Triple Agent ist ein Doppelagent, der vorgibt, seine Loyalität liege auf der einen Seite, während sie tatsächlich auf der anderen liegt).

Die Pointe der Netflix-Szene ist, dass Blunt just nach ihr festgenommen und verhört wird – falls Blunt tatsächlich ein Triple Agent war, so ist das Dreifachporträt Lottos gut gewählt. Das Verhältnis zwischen Kunstwelt und Spionagewelt in der Ära des Kalten Krieges ist so auf den Punkt gebracht: Ein ehrenwerter, hochgebildeter Kunstkenner, der im Auftrag des Staatsoberhaupts handelt, während er im Hinterzimmer bei Whiskey und Zigarren Staatsgeheimnisse belauscht und später, bei Wodka und Zigaretten, gegen andere (vermeintliche) Staatsgeheimnisse eintauscht. Weil er tief im Inneren einer ideologischen Überzeugung folgt; oder auch, weil er Spaß am Spiel mit dem Feuer hat – wahrscheinlich beides zugleich.

Die Veränderungen in einer Welt, in der die Mauer gefallen sind und die Angriffe des 11. September stattgefunden haben, zeigen sich nun auch am Verhältnis von Kunstwelt und Spionagewelt. Für Kunsthistoriker interessieren sich wohl die allermeisten Staatsoberhäupter (mutmaßlich inklusive der Queen) inzwischen eher wenig. Manch Autokrat setzt jedoch in seiner Selbstrepräsentation durchaus auch auf zeitgenössische Kunst. Spionage findet derweil weniger ad personam im Hinterzimmer statt als auf dem digitalen Endgerät. Und wir sehen heute globale Player, die in nie gesehener Weise Einfluss auf die Weltgeschicke nehmen – und dabei nebenbei, aber in auffälliger Weise, auch die Kunst als Milieu mit ins Spiel bringen.

Am 4. April 2018 findet ein großes Hollywood-Dinner statt, dessen Gastgeber der Filmproduzent Brian Grazer und seine Frau Veronica Smiley Grazer sind, sowie Ari Emanuel, Chef der Talent

Agency William Morris Endeavor, zu deren Portfolio Schauspieler wie Robert De Niro gehören, aber auch Sportturniere, die Miss-Universe-Wahlen sowie die Firma *Frieze* mitsamt den gleichnamigen Kunstmessen und dem Kunstmagazin (für welches wiederum der Autor dieses Textes als Redakteur von 1997 bis 2017 gearbeitet hat). Emanuel hatte seiner Firma zu diesem Zeitpunkt bereits die finanzielle Unterstützung durch einen besonderen Ehrengast dieses Galaabends gesichert: Kronprinz Mohammed bin Salman, auch bekannt unter dem Kürzel MBS, welcher einen 400-Millionen-Dollar-Anteil-Deal an Endeavor durch den saudischen Investment-Fonds einge-hen wollte, den er kontrolliert.[4] MBS war also neben Stars wie Basketball-legende Kobe Bryant oder Disney-Chef Bob Iger bei diesem Glamourevent per-sönlich zugegen. Und wie es ein Party-bericht des Edel-Regenbogenblatts *Vanity Fair* süffisant und bitter ironisch formuliert, galten in seiner Gegenwart „bestimmte Themen als unschicklich, inklusive des Kriegsbombardements des Yemen durch den Zweiunddreißig-jährigen, dem Tausende Zivilisten zum Opfer gefallen sind; seine Entführung des libanesischen Premierminister Saad Harari im November [2017]; und die dezidiert nicht hollywoodhafte Unter-drückung unabhängiger Medien und Journalisten, von denen zuletzt einer für fünf Jahre hinter Gitter ging aufgrund der ‚Beleidigung‘ des Königshauses."[5]

MBS hatte auch an anderen Stellen, wenn auch eher diskret, sein Interesse an Investitionen in den Kultur- und Kunst-sektor gezeigt. So soll er ernsthaften Gerüchten zufolge persönlich hinter dem 450-Millionen-Dollar-Kauf des teu-ersten Gemäldes der Welt, des Leonardo da Vinci zugeschriebenen *Salvator Mundi*, stecken. Das „verschwundene"

Gemälde soll sich auf seiner Yacht *Serene* befinden.[6] Der 400-Millionen-Deal jedenfalls, der den saudischen Kron-prinz de facto kurzzeitig zum indirekten Anteilseigner am Kunstunternehmen *Frieze* gemacht hatte (was unter anderem Spekulationen auslöste, die gleichnamige Messe würde nun bald auch am arabi-schen Golf stattfinden[7]), wurde allerdings am Ende, knapp ein Jahr später, rück-gängig gemacht. Denn inzwischen war etwas Einschneidendes passiert: Im sau-dischen Konsulat in Istanbul war im Oktober 2018 der Dissident und Journa-list Jamal Khashoggi von Schergen des MBS-Regimes bestialisch ermordet worden. Und da die Türkei geheim-dienstliche Erkenntnisse über dieses Attentat öffentlich gemacht hatte, war das Verbrecherische, zügellos Despoti-sche endgültig nicht mehr als bedauerli-ches Übergangsphänomen des Vorge-hens eines eigentlich reformerisch denkenden Thronfolgers zu beschönigen. Emanuel zog also – wenn auch erst fast ein halbes Jahr später – den einzig richtigen Schluss und annullierte den Deal, nachdem er alternative Investoren gefunden hatte. Dabei war er durchaus eine Ausnahme, denn andere Unterneh-men ließen ähnliche Investmentdeals stillschweigend weiterlaufen.[8] Doch war die Geschichte damit noch nicht zu Ende. Denn Khashoggi war unter ande-rem Kolumnist der *Washington Post*. Und deren Eigentümer, der reichste Mann der Welt, Amazon-Chef Jeff Bezos, war ebenfalls bei jenem denkwürdigen Hollywood-Dinner im April 2018 zugegen. Noch mehr, er tauschte just an diesem Abend Handynummern aus mit MBS. Man verknüpfte sich auf WhatsApp.

Was nun folgte, ist erst im Januar 2020 in vollem Ausmaß bekannt gewor-den: Bezos' Handy wurde Anfang Mai 2018 ausspioniert mittels einer Datei, die durch eine persönliche WhatsApp-Nachricht von MBS auf Bezos' Telefon landete (Abb. 3, S. 46).[9] Intime Fotos einer Affäre des Verheirateten wurden dem amerikanischen Boulevardblatt *National Enquirer* angeboten. Bezos kam einem Gutteil der Veröffentlichungen durch ein freimütiges Bekenntnis zu seiner außerehelichen Affäre zuvor.[10] Die Scheidung von seiner Frau MacKenzie Bezos konnte er so nicht verhindern – sie erhielt einen 38-Milliarden-Dollar-Anteil an seinem Vermögen. Klar ist, dass MBS Bezos persönlich angriff aufgrund der Berichterstattung der ihm gehörenden *Washington Post* über ihren Kolumnisten Khashoggi; und dass die Absicht, Bezos unter Druck zu setzen, bereits vor der Ermordung Khashoggis aufgrund dessen journalistischer Tätigkeit für die *Washington Post* bestanden hatte.

Der saudische Geheimdienst hatte übrigens offenbar Khashoggi vor dessen Ermordung ebenfalls mittels einer Spyware ausgespäht, die auf seinem Handy gelandet war. Dieses Schadprogramm namens Pegasus wird von der israelischen Firma NSO Group Technologies Regierungsorganisationen angeboten. So soll auch die mexikanische Regierung das Programm eingesetzt haben gegen jene Journalisten, die den unaufgeklärten Fall einer Busentführung von 2014 untersuchten, bei der 43 Studenten ermordet worden waren. Womit sich die Geschichte ein weiteres Mal in die Kunstwelt hineindreht. Denn im Juni 2019 führte eine Recherche des britischen Nachrichtenblatts *The Guardian* innerhalb weniger Tage zum Rücktritt der Geschäftsführerin der Londoner Serpentine Gallery, Yana Peel.[11]

Was war geschehen? Die ehemalige Goldman-Sachs-Bankerin Peel hatte ihr Geld in einen Investmentfonds gesteckt. Dieser erwarb wiederum die erwähnte Softwarefirma NSO. Laut *Guardian* war Peel nun also Miteigentümerin jener Firma, welche Pegasus herstellte, also jene Software, mit der Regierungsorganisationen – sprich Geheimdienste – besonders gerne unliebsamen Regimegegnern, Dissidenten und Journalisten zusetzte. Und das, obwohl sie sich in der Kunstöffentlichkeit als liberale, ethisch bewusste Person inszeniert hatte, unter anderem als Jurymitglied des Freedom of Expression Award, welcher 2018 mitunter an eine Menschenrechtsorganisation verliehen wurde, die in Ägypten von Geheimdiensten just mittels Cyberattacken aufs Korn genommen wurde.

Warum aber ging Peels Rücktritt so schnell vonstatten? Es waren u. a. die deutsche Künstlerin Hito Steyerl und der britische Designer James Bridle, welche beide mit der Serpentine Gallery Projekte realisiert hatten und nun intervenierten. Unmittelbar nach Bekanntwerden der Vorwürfe durch den *Guardian* trommelten sie Unterschriften aus der Kunstwelt für ein Protestschreiben zusammen. Der Druck baute sich schnell auf. Teile der Kunstwelt sind in Zeiten der Präsidentschaft eines Donald Trumps, in der die Obszönität einer massiven Bevorzugung der Superreichen in Kombination mit niederträchtigstem Rechtspopulismus offen zutage tritt, noch kritischer gegenüber der Rolle ebensolcher Superreicher in der Kunstwelt geworden. Ein weiterer Faktor spielt hier aber ebenso hinein: Einige Künstlerinnen und Künstler, darunter Steyerl und Bridle, aber auch andere wie Trevor Paglen oder die Gruppe Forensic Architecture um den Architekten Eyal Weizman, haben selbst aktiv und investigativ zu geheimdienstlichen Überwachungstechniken im digitalen Zeitalter recherchiert. Sie kennen sich sehr gut aus mit dem, was man

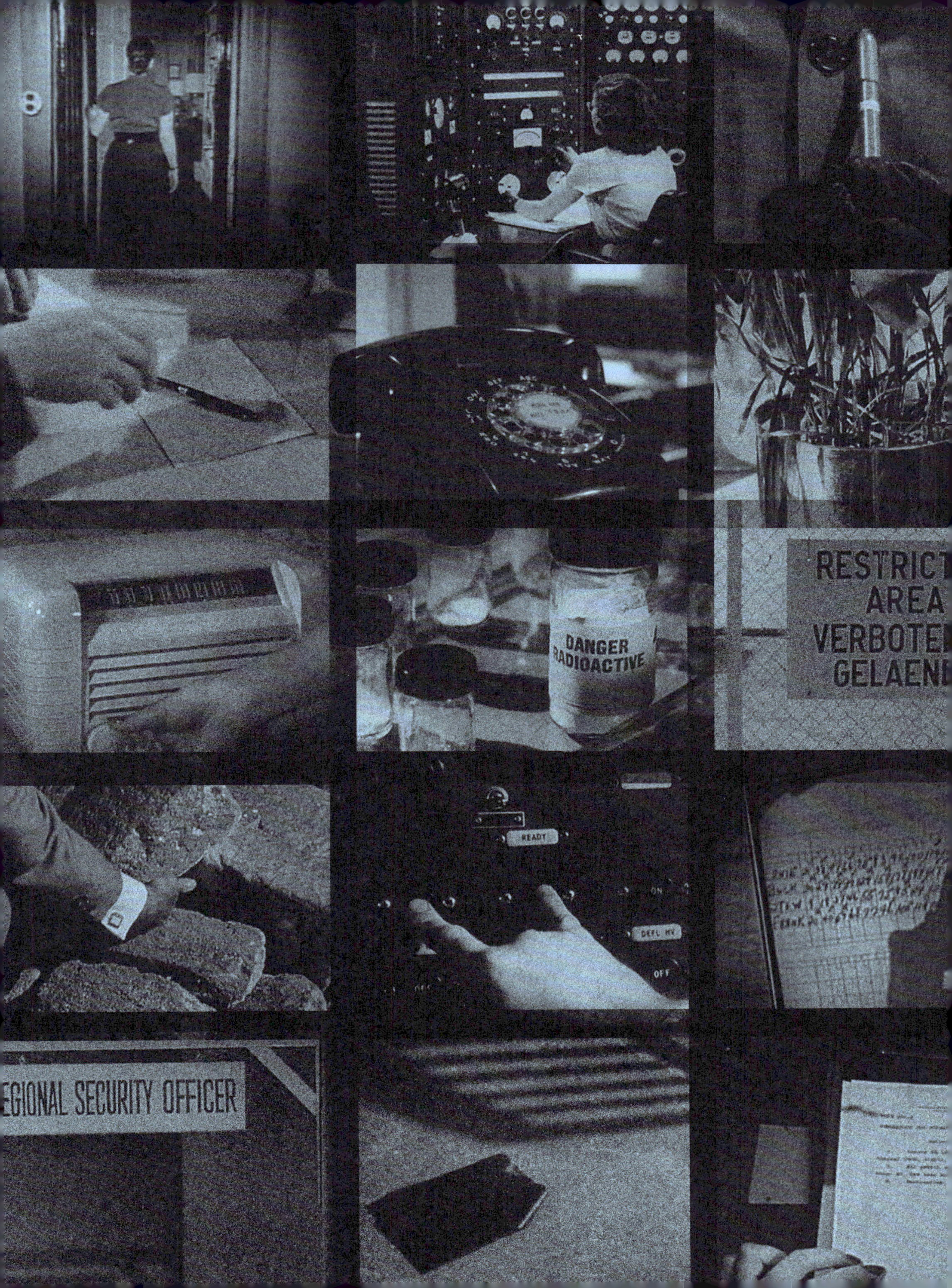

DANGER
RADIOACTIVE
RESTRICT
AREA
VERBOTE
GELAEND
READY
ON
DEFL HV
OFF
EGIONAL SECURITY OFFICER

beispielsweise mit einer Software wie Pegasus anrichten kann. Reale Agententätigkeit ist zum ernsthaften Gegenstand künstlerischer Arbeiten geworden. So haben Forensic Architecture beispielsweise bei der *documenta 14* (2017) eine Arbeit gezeigt, bei der sie anhand einer virtuellen 3-D-Rekonstruktion auf der Grundlage ballistischer Details und räumlicher Sichtachsen nachweisen konnten, dass Andreas Temme, Agent des hessischen Verfassungsschutzes, welcher bei der Ermordung von Halit Yozgat durch die rechtsradikale Terroristengruppe NSU in einem Kasseler Internet-Café 2006 im Nebenraum war, gelogen haben musste: Er hatte ausgesagt, er habe die Schüsse nicht gehört und auch beim Verlassen der Räumlichkeiten die Leiche hinter der Ladentheke nicht gesehen - eine Behauptung, die Forensic Architecture eindrücklich widerlegten.[12]

Künstlerinnen und Künstler, aber auch die Zivilgesellschaft insgesamt sind also heute dazu in der Lage, die digitalen Möglichkeiten zur Ausspähung bzw. forensischen Rekonstruktion von Ereignissen selber gegen jene Instanzen zu wenden und einzusetzen, die diese Möglichkeiten von Haus aus im Geheimen benutzen. Allerdings geschieht dies - siehe das Schicksal von Whistleblowern wie Edward Snowden, Chelsea Manning oder Julian Assange - um den Preis, sich möglicher Kriminalisierung und Verfolgung auszusetzen. Doch sollte man sich keine Illusionen machen, dass mit dem Ende des Kalten Kriegs in unserer heutigen multipolaren Welt eine goldene Zeit der journalistischen und künstlerischen Befreiung von Verstrickungen in die (nicht zuletzt auch mit Spionagemitteln betriebenen) Machenschaften von Superreichen und Autokraten angebrochen sei. Im Gegenteil: Zum einen ist

Kunst längst Schmiermittel - in mehrfach allegorischer Hinsicht - für das Dreieck von Geld, Macht und Unrecht, denn Autokraten und jene Superreichen, die mit ihnen Geschäfte machen, tragen sich ein Weltoffenheit signalisierendes künstlerisches Firnis auf, um ihre sonstigen Machenschaften zu relativieren und zu übertünchen - Stichwort „Artwashing"; zum anderen kann es aber auch passieren, dass mitten in dieser neuen multipolaren, virtuell wie physisch globalisierten Welt Vorgehensweisen aus Zeiten des Kalten Kriegs unter neuen Vorzeichen wieder Verwendung finden. Etwa diejenige, die in der sowjetischen Geheimdienst-Tradition seit guten alten KGB-Zeiten mit dem schönschaurigen Begriff „Kompromat" belegt ist. Wir werden es vielleicht nie genauer erfahren, aber spekulieren darf man sicher schon, wie es kommt, dass der russische Dissident und Künstler Pjotr Pawlensky im französischen Exil im Februar 2020 ausgerechnet auf solche Erpressungsmethoden mittels intimen Bildmaterials verfallen ist, welche als geheimdienstliches Kompromat par excellence gelten können. Pawlensky hatte ein Masturbationsvideo von Benjamin Griveaux - dem Kandidaten der Macron-Partei La République en Marche für den Posten des Pariser Bürgermeisters - der investigativen Nachrichtenplattform Mediapart zwecks Veröffentlichung angeboten. Er war an dieses Video über seine französische Freundin Alexandra de Taddeo gelangt, die wiederum eine Affäre mit Griveaux gehabt hatte - sie war also, ob wissentlich oder nicht, die „honeytrap" für Griveaux gewesen. Mediapart lehnte die Veröffentlichung ab, da es in Frankreich als ungeschriebenes Gesetz gilt, dass das Privat- und Sexleben prominenter Politiker sakrosankt ist, soweit ihr politisches Handeln dadurch nicht nennenswert beeinflusst wird.[13] Daraufhin machte Pawlensky das Video auf einer eigenen Website publik. Griveaux trat von seiner Kandidatur zurück.

Hier lohnt noch einmal der Vergleich mit Anthony Blunt. Es gibt ernsthafte Indizien, die auch Eingang in die erwähnte Folge von *The Crown* gefunden haben, dass Blunt sein Wissen, dass Prince Philip – der Ehemann der Königin – eine indirekte Verbindung zur Profumo-Affäre von 1963 hatte, gegen diesen einsetzte, um seine eigene öffentliche Enttarnung zu verhindern. Kriegsminister Profumo hatte das Showgirl Christine Keeler durch den Osteopathen und Künstler Stephen Ward kennengelernt. Der wiederum hatte mehrere Porträtzeichnungen von Prince Philip angefertigt und war selbst ein Spion für die Sowjets; seinem Kontaktmann Eugene Ivanov wiederum gelang es, diverse Treffen des Kriegsministers mit Keeler abzuhören. Ward hatte die Porträts des Prinzen versteigert – und Blunt soll sie gekauft haben, um das Königshaus zu schützen; oder eben auch, um eine Waffe in der Hand zu haben, sollte seine öffentliche Enttarnung drohen.[14]

Bei Pawlensky muss man davon ausgehen, dass er nie auch nur im Entferntesten jenen inneren Geheimdienstzirkeln angehörte, in denen Blunt über Jahrzehnte tätig war. Dennoch wäre es naiv zu glauben, dass der dissidente Künstler en passant zum Mittel der Exponierung des (sexuellen) Privatlebens eines Politiker greift, mit dem er zuvor nichts zu schaffen hatte. Kurzer Rückblick: 2012 hatte Pawlensky sich den Mund zugenäht aus Protest gegen die Inhaftierung von Mitgliedern der Band Pussy Riot in ein Straflager. 2013 nagelte er sein Skrotum am Roten Platz fest, um gegen Polizeigewalt und allgemeine Gleichgültigkeit zu protestieren. Im November 2015 setzte er dann eine Eingangstür des russischen Inlandsgeheimdienstes FSB in Moskau in Brand und wurde daraufhin verhaftet und in die Psychatrie eingewiesen (Abb. 4, S. 48). Anstatt einer Haftstrafe erhielt er jedoch später eine Geldbuße von umgerechnet 13.500 Euro. Im Februar 2017 erfolgte dann seine Flucht ins französische Asyl.

Bekanntlich war Russlands Präsident Putin selbst KGB-Offizier, stationiert von 1985 bis 1990 in Dresden in der DDR. In dieser Zeit hatte er auch einen Ausweis der Stasi besessen.[15] Insofern mag es wenig überraschen, dass unter seiner Herrschaft die altbekannten Geheimdienstmethoden wie Kompromat, Bestechung und Medienmanipulation – ergänzt durch die heutigen digitalen Mittel im Informationskrieg – gewissermaßen wieder Staatsdoktrin geworden sind. Die Hinweise, dass Russland versucht hat, mittels Hackerangriffen, aber auch indirekten Manipulationen der öffentlichen Meinung in den Sozialen Medien (durch Trollfarmen etc.) Einfluss auf die Wahlen in den USA zu nehmen (um Hillary Clinton zu schaden und Trump zu helfen), auf das Brexitreferendum im Vereinigten Königreich oder etwa die französischen Präsidentschaftswahlen (zur Unterstützung von Marine Le Pen und Verhinderung von Macron) häuften sich in den letzten Jahren. Insofern überrascht es nicht, dass Macron unmittelbar nach Bekanntwerden der Griveaux-Affäre vehement die Eindämmung derartiger russischer Versuche der Einflussnahme auf Wahlen in Europa proklamierte.[16] Angesichts der zeitlichen Nähe der Geschehnisse darf man wohl fragen, ob Pawlensky womöglich vor seiner Flucht nach Frankreich von staatlicher Seite ein Angebot unterbreitet worden war, das er nicht ablehnen konnte. Es ist ein klassisches Mittel der Macht: Entweder du machst XY, oder du wanderst ins Straflager (siehe Pussy Riot), oder Schlimmeres stößt dir zu. Zumal in diesem Fall das „XY" ganz auf die offensichtliche Sehnsucht Pawlenskys nach Tabubruch und öffentlicher Erregung durch Provokation mächtiger Politiker zugeschnitten war – ein klassisches „Umdrehen" eines Probanden durch einen Geheimdienst. Zugegeben, eine Spekulation. Aber selbst wenn Pavlensky aus freien Stücken und auf eigene Rechnung gehandelt haben sollte, so wird doch deutlich, dass er in der heutigen Aufmerksamkeitsökonomie etwas betrieben hat, das, obwohl oder gerade weil es sich als (konzeptuelle, aktivistische) Kunst geriert, klassischen geheimdienstlichen Mustern folgt und so, gewollt oder nicht, in deren Hände spielt.[17]

Was sind die Lehren aus all dem? Erst einmal die wenig überraschende, dass die Kunstwelt sich kaum „unschuldig" und unbeeinträchtigt aus der Tatsache herauswinden kann, dass sie vor allem in den letzten zwei Jahrzehnten zum Spielball von Oligarchen, Autokraten und Superreichen geworden ist; inklusive derer Verstrickungen in geheimdienstlich ermöglichte Menschenrechtsverletzungen und Unterhöhlungen demokratischer und zivilgesellschaftlicher Strukturen. Die glamourösen Zeiten, in denen Kalter-Krieg-Spione hübsche Porträtzeichnungen von Prinzen anfertigten oder gelehrte Vorträge über Renaissancekünstler hielten, sind vorbei. Stattdessen laufen die Teilnehmer der Kunstwelt Gefahr, sich in Artwashing einspannen zu lassen oder gar, wie in Pawlenskys Fall, in die direkte Unterhöhlung demokratischer und zivilgesellschaftlicher Standards. Umso wichtiger sind jene Künstlerinnen und Künstler, die wie Steyerl, Paglen oder Forensic Architecture unermüdlich daran arbeiten, ebensolche Umstände aufzudecken und künstlerisch zu kommentieren.

1   Vgl. David Alan Brown, Peter Humfrey, Mauro Lucco (Hg.), *Lorenzo Lotto. Rediscovered Master of the Renaissance*, Ausst.-Kat. The National Gallery of Art, Washington, DC; Accademia Carrara di Belle Arti, Bergamo; Galeries nationales du Grand Palais, Paris, New Haven/London 1997, S. 176f.

2   John Jeffries Martin, *Venice's Hidden Enemies. Italian Heretics in a Renaissance Society*, Baltimore/London 1993, S. 89, 132, 158.

3   Zit. nach *The Crown*, Fernsehserie, Netflix 2019, 1. Folge, Dritte Staffel.

4   Nancy Tartaglione, „Saudi Arabia Fund Deal For Endeavor Stake Could Close In Week's Time For $400M“, in: *Deadline*, 16. März 2018, https://deadline.com/2018/03/saudi-arabia-fund-endeavor-stake-talks-400-to-500-million-1202243920/ (alle Zugriffe auf URLs erfolgten im April 2020).

5   Isobel Thompson, „Prince Mohammed Does Hollywood“, in: *Vanity Fair*, 6. April 2018, https://www.vanityfair.com/news/2018/04/prince-mohammed-does-hollywood.

6   Kenny Schachter, „Where In the World Is ‚Salvator Mundi'? Kenny Schachter Reveals the Location of the Lost $450 Million Leonardo“, in: *artnet news*, 10. Juni 2019, https://news.artnet.com/opinion/kenny-schachter-on-the-missing-salvator-mundi-1565674.

7   Ebd.

8   Kate Kelly and Ben Hubbard, „Endeavor Returns Money to Saudi Arabia, Protesting Khashoggi Murder“, in: *The New York Times*, 8. März 2019, https://www.nytimes.com/2019/03/08/business/endeavor-saudi-arabia.html.

9   Stephanie Kirchgaessner, „Jeff Bezos Hack: Amazon Boss's Phone ‚Hacked by Saudi Crown Prince'“, in: *The Guardian*, 22. Januar 2020, https://www.theguardian.com/technology/2020/jan/21/amazon-boss-jeff-bezoss-phone-hacked-by-saudi-crown-prince.

10   Jeff Bezos, „No thank you, Mr. Pecker“, in: *Medium*, 7. Februar 2019, https://medium.com/@jeffreypbezos/no-thank-you-mr-pecker-146e3922310f.

11   „UK News: Yana Peel“, in: *The Guardian*, 14. Juni 2019, https://www.theguardian.com/law/2019/jun/14/yana-peel-uk-rights-advocate-serpentine-nso-spyware-pegasus; Jon Swaine, Stephanie Kirchgaessner, Patrick Greenfield, „Serpentine Galleries Chief Resigns“, in: *The Guardian*, 18. Juni 2019, https://www.theguardian.com/artanddesign/2019/jun/18/serpentine-galleries-chief-resigns.

12   „The Murder of Halit Yozgat“, in: *Forensic Architecture*, o. D., https://forensic-architecture.org/investigation/the-murder-of-halit-yozgat.

13   Cyril Delaune, „Sextape de Benjamin Griveaux: pourquoi Mediapart a refusé de diffuser les vidéos de Piotr Pavlenski“, in: *Voici*, 8. März 2020, https://www.voici.fr/news-people/actu-people/sextape-de-benjamin-griveaux-pourquoi-mediapart-a-refuse-de-diffuser-les-videos-de-piotr-pavlenski-676011.

14   Vgl. Chloe Foussianes, „How Prince Philip Was Connected to the Profumo Affair—and How Anthony Blunt May Have Covered For Him“, in: *Town & Country*, 17. November 2019, https://www.townandcountrymag.com/society/tradition/a29322952/profumo-affair-true-story-prince-philip-anthony-blunt-connection/.

15   „Wladimir Putins Stasi-Ausweis in Dresdner Archiv entdeckt“, in: *Der Tagesspiegel*, 11. Dezember 2018, https://www.tagesspiegel.de/politik/aus-kgb-zeit-in-der-ddr-wladimir-putins-stasi-ausweis-in-dresdner-archiv-entdeckt/23745760.html.

16   Laurens Cerulus, „Macron Calls for Attribution, Cybersanctions to Stop Russian Election Meddling“, in: *Politico*, 15. Februar 2020, https://www.politico.eu/article/macron-calls-for-attribution-cybersanctions-to-stop-russian-election-meddling/.

17   Laut eines russischen Bekannten, dessen Moskauer Freunde die politischen Entwicklungen aufmerksam verfolgen, denken Letztere nicht, dass es wahrscheinlich sei, dass Pavlensky rekrutiert worden sei, schlichtweg weil er als Person zu unkontrollierbar sei für eine solche Rekrutierung. Meiner bescheidenen Ansicht nach ist es jedoch so, dass eine gewisse Unbeständigkeit, wenn nicht Verrücktheit, etwas sein könnte, das von staatlichen Diensten eben genau in Kauf genommen, wenn nicht gar bewusst eingesetzt wird, auch unter anderen Umständen, wenn man etwa an den Einsatz von Online-Trolling denkt oder die Unterstützung verantwortungsloser Clowns als Staatsoberhäupter. Davon unbenommen ist, dass solange es keine handfesten Beweise in Form von Dokumenten gibt (was auf Jahrzehnte hin oder nie der Fall sein wird), jedwede solche Einschätzung natürlich Spekulation bleibt.

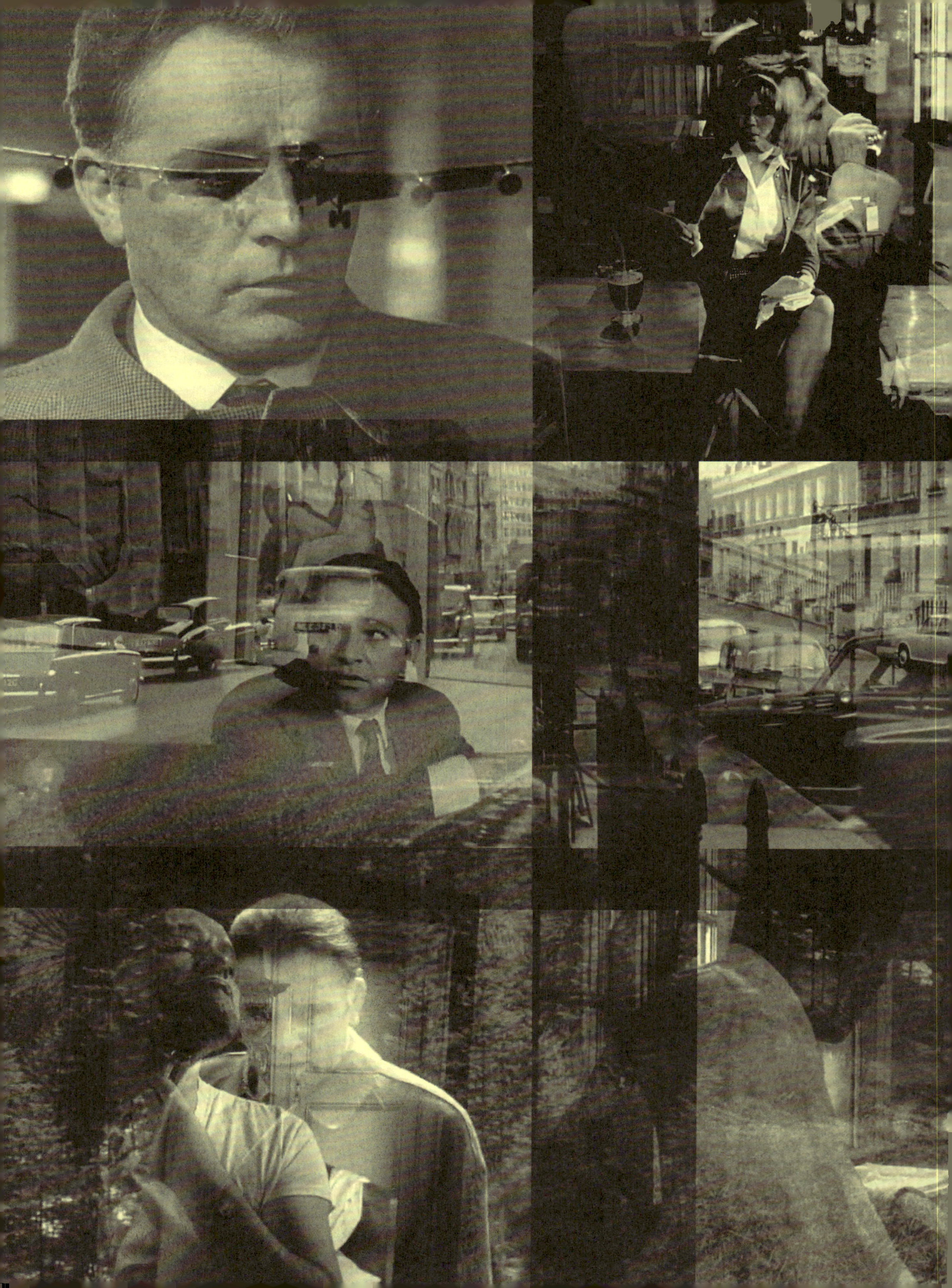

The Motion Picture as an Art of Espionage
Jelena Martinovic

Cinema has showcased multifaceted plots in which people become spies despite themselves or are used against their will as a weapon for counterintelligence. One of the most emblematic cases is the 1962 cinematographic adaptation of Richard Condon's novel *The Manchurian Candidate* (1959) by John Frankenheimer.[1] In the movie, years after returning from the Korean War, Major Bennett Marco is haunted by recurring nightmares in which a fellow officer, Sergeant Raymond Shaw, a highly decorated war hero, is hypnotized and then forced to assassinate two members of his troop. The central scene is the demonstration of a foreign intelligence brainwashing method, visually presented as a hallucinatory information technique infiltrating sleep-deprived bodies. US soldiers appear to be attending a horticultural lecture staged in the Ladies' Garden Club, but they are actually in an auditorium, as the camera pan reveals, where Russian and Chinese intelligence officers are programming Shaw as their sleeping agent. Set in the context of the Cuban Missile Crisis, *The Manchurian Candidate* is a classic Cold War cinematographic plot which combines brainwashing and espionage: a queen of diamonds card activates Shaw, who instinctively executes post-hypnotic suggestions of which he later has no recollection. Toward the end of the movie, the political conspiracy is toppled when it is revealed that the ultimate double-agent is Shaw's mother, who operated the protagonist into killing her main political opponent.[2]

The art of espionage, as illustrated in Cold War political thrillers, found its counterpart in the art of spying and brainwashing in real-life Cold War medical and psychological sciences. Pavlovian conditioning became a key strategy in psychological warfare. The notorious MK-Ultra programs conducted by the CIA had the primary objective to obtain foreign intelligence and to make enemies compliant. However, the experiments were practiced not only in military or scientific laboratories, but also in hospital wards and institutions where real patients' lives and their intimate stories were at stake. One of the key concepts developed in the early 1950s by a psychiatrist, whose research was supported by the CIA, was "psychic driving." Ewen Cameron's technique, which some have rightly credited as a "shock cure," aimed at radically altering the personality of a patient.[3] In one variation, the heavily sedated patient[4] was forced to listen to a prerecorded audio tape, inserted into the patient's pillow. The tape contained intimate information compiled from the talking cure sessions conducted with the patient beforehand. Keywords, or cues, were selected by the psychiatrist, repeated, and arranged into a script that conveyed deliberately intrusive keywords, functioning similarly to post-hypnotic suggestion. The patient, held passive in a semi-comatose state, was thus infiltrated with a secretly devised cryptography for which the patient herself delivered the material, thus becoming a sort of double agent. The audio dictates of this mind-controlling technique had disastrous results: as a consequence of the treatment, patients suffered from anxiety and amnesia.

Another example merits a lengthy description in order to demonstrate how patients were turned into obedient collaborators: a treatment of kleptomania using motion pictures, making deliberate use of subliminal imagery and post-hypnotic suggestion, implanted the art of auto-spying in the patient who became an unwilling, albeit quasi automatic, collaborator of the doctor and his treatment plan.

In December 1967, a forty-eight-year-old housewife was hospitalized at the Morgannwg Hospital in Bridgend, Wales, after a failed suicide attempt, which, according to the medical record, was committed as a consequence of a shoplifting act. The treating doctor, the late Alexander Kellam, presented the production of an elaborate motion picture for the treatment of this patient after the previous failure of conventional aversion therapy.[5] Together with his colleagues from the film unit, Kellam converted a hospital corridor into a temporary cinema and developed a 10-minute, 16mm color film in which a senior psychologist played the main protagonist, the patient.

Shot in a local department store, the opening scene shows the protagonist from the back, wearing an overcoat and headscarf to cover her face, followed by a scene in which she is standing in front of the store, and then a scene inside the commercial establishment where she starts to remove commodities, such as jewelry, stockings, and tins of food. At first sight, the script recalls the structure of a classic film, the silent *The Kleptomaniac* (1905) by Edwin S. Porter, except that in the latter the main act is a bourgeois woman confronted by the police, whereas in the patient movie the censure is orchestrated through montage. In fact, each time the protagonist removes an article, an eight-frame shot (a third of a second each) shows a close-up of a face expressing disapproval at the proof of the crime. (Kellam used nursing cadets and other staff from the hospital to stage these close-ups, but also to play onlookers or to serve as the background crowd in the department store.) In addition, scenes depicting the protagonist entering and exiting the shop alternate with takes from the patient entering and exiting similar doors in the hospital facility. The final scene shows the patient walking through the ward, wearing a similar outfit as the main protagonist so as to further the visual identification.

Treatment was scheduled over the course of five weeks and consisted of a total of forty screenings. An electric shock operator was attached to the patient's left arm, delivering electroshocks each time the "just-recognizable flashes of disapproving faces"[6] appeared on the screen. The rationale behind this setup was to conduct a form of social and physical punishment with the use of quasi-subliminal images and of electroshock signals delivered in vivo, adjusted at a level just beyond the "definitely unpleasant"[7] as indicated by the patient. With the treatment script, Kellam adopted a classical operant conditioning method, using aversive stimuli to "strengthen one very specific response" and to make its repetition more probable in the future.[8] The doctor's main aim was to condition the patient to a state of generalized anxiety and, more particularly, to the specific fear of being watched, building on the patient's fear of social censure. The result of the treatment was dramatic: the patient developed a generalized fear of shops, and of being watched whenever she entered a commercial establishment. This emotion was furthered by the sensation of pain in her left arm, a reminiscence of the shock treatment.

This shoplifting treatment, one might argue, made use of the art of spying by extracting secrets, by adopting alter egos and stage props in order to infiltrate the patient's mind, and ultimately also by enhancing identification with the enemy, the kleptomaniac. In this theater of compliance, the patient becomes a sort of paranoiac double agent: a secret employee of the medical sciences, working on eradicating her own desires while helping to cure a problem which has become one of mental health, rather than of criminal law.

As this example highlights, the use of the motion picture accounts for the behaviorist's phantasm to depattern desire by implementing technology. Kellam made deliberate use of collage and subliminal images to further social censure and compliance. For this reason, one could compare the medical-therapeutic script with the cinematographic script: images are arranged and put into narrativity to enhance identification with the main protagonist.

Throughout history, strong associations have been made between technology and cure, and more particularly between cinema and mental illness / mental health. Since the early twentieth century, psychological concepts of cure merged with cinema theory and hypnosis: two eminent examples are *Le mystère des roches de Kador* (1912) and *Dr. Mabuse, der Spieler* (1922).[9] One could argue that in the context of "permanent war," when fiction merged with science and politics,[10] aversion therapy was both real and fictional. The ultimate phantasm, shared in this coercive collaboration by both patient and doctor, was that humans can function—to refer to Anthony Burgess—as an "orange clockwork": an organism and mechanical device.[11] In the cinematographic adaptation by Stanley Kubrick, *A Clockwork Orange* (1972) is set around a central scene in which Alex, the delinquent protagonist who engages in violent gang actions, is coerced into treatment through aversion therapy. Alex's eyes are kept open with a mechanical device and his body is pumped with drugs, while he is forced to watch a montage of film extracts showing "real" violence (the horrors of mass murders and the Holocaust) and listen to his favorite composer Beethoven. The Ludovico technique, as it is called in the film, relies on brainwashing treatment which combines highly intimate information (Alex's favorite music) with highly aversive feelings (watching mass murders that Alex considers to be the ultimate enemy form of violence as compared to his own form of gang violence, which he believes to have committed in an act of free will).

Interestingly, Burgess intended to take the brainwashing device even further than the Ludovico technique of the cinematographic version. Burgess imagined the plot and structure of his novel, first published in 1962, as a veritable art of spying. He aimed at infiltrating the readers' minds. As Burgess commented in an interview,[12] his objective was to invent a new language, Nadsat, so that readers would be coerced into learning a new language. He deliberately left out a glossary to explain the meaning of the words, a mixture of cockney and Russian, so as to force his readers to assimilate on their own the encrypted words spread throughout the plot. That Burgess wrote the novel while himself on travels in Russia, and that he had a long-standing interest in Russian and Pavlovian science, further attests to his deliberate use of a mind-manipulating technique as an artistic form. Maybe the linguistic art of spying is ultimately a stronger device than cinema, as it perverts the mental space through even more convoluted paths and journeys, thus turning the reader to an unwilling collaborator.

1   A film adaptation of the 1962 novel *The Mandchurian Candidate* was released in 2004, starring Denzel Washington, with a plot set in the aftermath of the Gulf War.

2   Thus, the plot is tied to the prominent conspiracy theory at the time, about the over-domineering mother, a phenomenon that was known as "momism" and gained momentum after Philip Wylie published *Generation of Vipers* in 1942. Laura Mulvey has highlighted this parallel in her paper "From Momism to the Feminine Mystique" given at the conference Brainwash: History, Cinema and the Psy-Professions held at Birkbeck College, University of London, in July 2015.

3   D. Ewen Cameron, "Psychic Driving," *American Journal of Psychiatry* 112, no. 7 (January 1956), pp. 502–9. On the controversies surrounding Cameron's work, see Rebecca Lemov, "Brainwashing's Avatar: The Curious Career of Dr. Ewen Cameron," *Grey Room* 45 (2011), pp. 60–87.

4   All patients in this study were female.

5   Alexander Kellam, "Shoplifting Treatment by Aversion to a Film," *Behavioral Research and Therapy* 7 (1969), pp. 125–27.

6   Ibid., p. 126.

7   Ibid.

8   Kellam refers to Pavlovian conditioning in his study, however his method also heavily borrows ideas from Skinner. In particular, see B. F. Skinner, *Science and Human Behavior* (New York, 1953), pp. 170 and 171–93 (the chapters "Aversion, Avoidance, Anxiety" and "Punishment").

9   Raymond Bellour, *Le corps du cinéma: hypnoses, émotions, animalités* (Paris, 2009). See also Mireille Berton, "Cinéma et sciences du psychisme autour en 1900: la névrose, la paramnésie, la transe," *Gesnerus* 66 (2009), pp. 103–20.

10 This was the case with "brainwashing," a concept initially invented in journalism and then adopted in scientific and military operations. On the merging of fiction, science, and politics during the Cold War, see Timothy Melley, *The Covert Sphere: Secrecy, Fiction, and the National Security State* (Ithaca, NY, 2012).

11 Anthony Burgess, *A Clockwork Orange*, ed. Mark Rawlinson (London, 2011).

12 Anthony Burgess, *You've Had Your Time: Being the Second Part of the Confessions of Anthony Burgess* (New York, 1991).

Film als Spionagekunst
Jelena Martinovic

Immer wieder wartet das Kino mit schillernden Geschichten auf, in denen jemand unwillentlich zum Spion oder unfreiwillig als Waffe für Gegenspionage eingesetzt wird. Eines der prägnantesten Werke dieser Art ist John Frankenheimers 1962 erschienene Verfilmung von Richard Condons Roman *The Manchurian Candidate* (1959).[1] Jahre nach seiner Rückkehr aus dem Koreakrieg wird Major Bennett Marco von wiederkehrenden Albträumen heimgesucht, in denen sein mittlerweile als Kriegsheld hochdekorierter Kampfgefährte Sergeant Raymond Shaw hypnotisiert und anschließend gezwungen wird, zwei Kameraden aus seinem Trupp zu ermorden. Bildkräftig zeigt die geträumte Schlüsselsequenz die Gehirnwäschemethode eines ausländischen Geheimdienstes, unter Schlafentzug halluzinierende Soldaten informatorisch zu infiltrieren. Diese wähnen sich bei einem gartenkundlichen Vortrag im Ladies' Garden Club, befinden sich aber, wie ein Kameraschwenk enthüllt, in einem Auditorium, wo russische und chinesische Geheimdienstoffiziere Shaw als ihren Schläfer programmieren. Im Kontext der kubanischen Raketenkrise angesiedelt, ist *The Manchurian Candidate* eine klassische Kinofabel aus dem Kalten Krieg, die thematisch Gehirnwäsche und Spionage kombiniert: Ausgelöst durch eine Karo-Dame-Karte, setzt Shaw wie triebgesteuert posthypnotische Suggestionen in Taten um,

an die er sich nachher nicht erinnert. Zum Ende des Films hin bricht die politische Verschwörung in sich zusammen, als sich Shaws Mutter als ultimative Doppelagentin entpuppt, die den Protagonisten dazu manipuliert hat, ihren politischen Hauptgegner umzubringen.[2]

Die Kunst der Spionage als Thema in politischen Thrillern zuzeiten des Kalten Kriegs hat ihre Entsprechung in der Kunst des Ausspähens und der Gehirnwäsche in den ganz realen medizinischen und psychologischen Wissenschaften dieser Jahre. Klassische Konditionierung nach Pawlow wurde zu einer Schlüsselstrategie in der psychologischen Kriegsführung. Die berüchtigten MKUltra-Programme der CIA hatten vorrangig zum Ziel, Erkenntnisse über das Ausland zu gewinnen und Feinde gefügig zu machen. Die Experimente wurden jedoch nicht nur in militärischen oder wissenschaftlichen Labors durchgeführt, sondern auch in Krankenstationen und anderen Einrichtungen, in denen es um die realen Leben der Patientinnen und Patienten und deren jeweilige persönlichen Geschichten geht. Zu den Schlüsselkonzepten, die in den frühen 1950er Jahren ein von der CIA in seinen Forschungen unterstützter Psychiater entwickelte, zählt das „psychic driving" (psychische Steuerung). Ewen Camerons Technik, von manchen zu Recht als „Schockbehandlung" bezeichnet, zielte darauf, die Persönlichkeit eines Patienten von Grund auf zu verändern.[3] Die stark sedierte Patientin[4] wurde gezwungen, sich über einen in ihrem Kopfkissen befindlichen Lautsprecher eine Bandaufnahme anzuhören, die intime Auskünfte aus den zuvor mit ihr durchgeführten gesprächstherapeutischen Sitzungen enthielt. Dazu wählte der Psychiater Schlüssel- oder Stichwörter aus, loopte sie und arrangierte sie zu einem Skript, das auch gezielt eingeschleuste weitere Schlüsselwörter umfasste und ähnlich wie eine posthypnotische Suggestion funktionierte. Die in einen halbkomatösen Zustand versetzte Patientin wurde also mit einem im Geheimen kodierten Text infiltriert, für den sie selbst das Material geliefert hatte, und avancierte damit zu einer Art Doppelagentin. Die bei dieser Technik der Bewusstseinskontrolle eingesetzten Audiodiktate zeitigten verheerende Resultate: Infolge der Behandlung litten die Patientinnen an Angstzuständen und Gedächtnisverlust.

Ein weiteres Beispiel verdient ausgiebigere Beschreibung, um zu verdeutlichen, wie Patienten zu fügsamen Mitwirkenden umfunktioniert wurden: Eine Kleptomanie-Behandlung mithilfe von Filmsequenzen, die gezielt subliminale Bilder und posthypnotische Suggestion einsetzte, impfte Patienten die Kunst der Selbstspionage ein, die dann zu unwilligen, wiewohl gewissermaßen automatischen Mitarbeitern des Doktors und seines Behandlungsplans wurden.

Im Dezember 1967 wurde eine 48-jährige Hausfrau nach einem gescheiterten Selbstmordversuch, laut Krankenakte begangen im Gefolge eines Ladendiebstahls, ins Morgannwg Hospital in Bridgend, Wales, eingeliefert. Nachdem eine herkömmliche Aversionstherapie gescheitert war, schlug der inzwischen verstorbene behandelnde Arzt, Alexander Kellam, vor, die Patientin mithilfe eines raffiniert inszenierten Films zu therapieren.[5] Zusammen mit seinen Kollegen aus der Abteilung Film baute er einen Krankenhausflur in ein temporäres Kino um und erarbeitete einen zehnminütigen 16mm-Farbfilm, in dem eine leitende Psychologin die Hauptfigur – die Patientin – spielte.

Der in einem örtlichen Warenhaus gedrehte Film beginnt mit einer Rückenansicht der Protagonistin, die einen Mantel trägt und ihr Gesicht unter einem Kopftuch verbirgt, gefolgt von einer Szene, in der sie vor dem Geschäft steht, und einer weiteren Innenaufnahme, bei der sie Waren wie Schmuck, Strümpfe und Esskonserven zu entwenden beginnt. Auf den ersten Blick erinnert das Drehbuch an den Aufbau des Stummfilmklassikers *The Kleptomaniac* (1905) von Edwin S. Porter, nur dass in diesem die Hauptfigur eine bürgerliche Frau ist, die von der Polizei gestellt wird, während in dem Patientenfilm die soziale Zensur per Montage erfolgt. Jedesmal nämlich, wenn die Hauptfigur einen Artikel an sich nimmt, zeigt eine acht Filmbilder (das heißt eine Drittelsekunde) lange Einstellung die Großaufnahme eines Gesichts, das die offenkundige Straftat mit Missbilligung quittiert. (Kellam setzte sich in der Ausbildung befindliche Krankenpflegerinnen und anderes Personal aus dem Krankenhaus für diese Großaufnahmen ein, zog es aber auch zur Darstellung von Zuschauenden oder als Hintergrundmenge in dem Warenhaus heran.) Außerdem wechseln Szenen, in denen die Hauptfigur das Geschäft betritt und verlässt, mit Aufnahmen, in denen die Patientin durch ähnliche Türen das Klinikgebäude betritt und verlässt. Die Schlussszene zeigt, bei einem Gang über die Station, die Patientin, die zur Erleichterung der visuellen

Identifikation ähnliche Kleidung trägt wie die Hauptfigur.

Die Behandlung war auf fünf Wochen angelegt und bestand aus insgesamt 40 Vorführungen. Am linken Arm der Patientin war eine Vorrichtung befestigt, die jedesmal einen Elektroschock verabreichte, wenn auf der Leinwand „gerade noch wahrnehmbar das missbilligende Gesicht aufblitzte"[6]. Grundgedanke hinter dieser Maßnahme war es, mithilfe von quasi-subliminalen Bildern und in vivo verabreichten Elektroschocksignalen in einer Stärke, die laut der Patientin knapp über dem „eindeutig Unangenehmen"[7] lag, eine Form der sozialen und körperlichen Bestrafung durchzuführen. Mit seinem Behandlungsskript wandte Kellam eine klassische Methode der operanten Konditionierung an, die aversive Reize benutzt, „um eine bestimmte Reaktion zu verstärken" und ihre Wiederholung in der Zukunft wahrscheinlicher werden zu lassen.[8] Hauptziel des Arztes war es, die Patientin auf einen Zustand durchgängiger Ängstlichkeit zu konditionieren, insbesondere auf die Furcht vor Beobachtung, wobei er auf die Angst der Patientin vor sozialer Zensur setzte. Die Behandlung hatte dramatische Auswirkungen: Die Patientin entwickelte eine allgemeine Furcht vor Läden und davor, beobachtet zu werden, wann immer sie ein Geschäft betrat. Noch vermehrt wurde dieses Gefühl durch das gesteigerte Schmerzempfinden in ihrem linken Arm als Nachwirkung der Schockbehandlung.

Diese Ladendiebstahlsbehandlung machte, könnte man folgern, Gebrauch von der Kunst des Spionierens, indem sie Geheimnisse anzapfte, mithilfe von Alter Egos und Requisiten das Bewusstsein der Patientin infiltrierte und schließlich die Identifikation mit dem Feind, der kleptomanischen Person, verstärkte. In dieser ganzen Inszenierung von Konformität wird aus der Patientin eine Art paranoische Doppelagentin: eine heimliche Angestellte der medizinischen Wissenschaft, die daran arbeitet, ihre eigenen Wünsche auszumerzen, und zugleich mithilft, ein Problem zu beheben, das von der Ebene des Strafrechts auf die der geistigen Gesundheit verlegt wurde.

Wie dieses Beispiel veranschaulicht, offenbart sich in der Nutzung filmischer Mittel die der Fantasie entsprungene Idealvorstellung eines Behavioristen, der durch den Einsatz von Technik die an Wünsche geknüpften Verhaltensmuster auflösen will. Kellam machte gezielten Gebrauch von Montage und subliminalen Bildern, um soziale Zensur und komformes Verhalten zu fördern. Deshalb könnte man das medizinisch-therapeutische Skript mit dem kinematografischen Skript vergleichen: Die Bilder werden so angeordnet und in eine Erzähllogik gestellt, dass sie die Identifikation mit der Hauptfigur verstärken.

Immer wieder wurden in der Vergangenheit ausgeprägte Verbindungen zwischen Technologie und ärztlicher Behandlung und insbesondere zwischen Kino und psychischer Krankheit beziehungsweise -gesundheit gezogen. Seit dem frühen 20. Jahrhundert verschmelzen psychologische Behandlungskonzepte mit Filmtheorie und Hypnose: Zwei herausragende Beispiele hierfür sind *Le mystère des roches de Kador* (1912) und *Dr. Mabuse, der Spieler* (1922).[9] Man könnte sagen, dass unter Bedingungen eines „permanenten Kriegs", in dem Fiktion, Wissenschaft und Politik ineinanderflossen[10], die Aversionstherapie auf realer wie auf fiktionaler Ebene zum Tragen kam. Das kühnste, von Patient und Arzt in solchem erzwungenen

Zusammenwirken geteilte Wahngebilde bestand in der Vorstellung, dass Menschen – mit Anthony Burgess zu sprechen – als ein „Orangenuhrwerk" zu funktionieren vermögen: als Organismus und mechanischer Apparat in einem.[11] Stanley Kubricks Verfilmung *A Clockwork Orange* (1972) entfaltet sich rund um eine zentrale Szene, in der der straffällige Protagonist Alex, der eine gewalttätige Bande anführt, einer aversionstherapeutischen Zwangsbehandlung unterzogen wird. Vollgepumpt mit Drogen, werden ihm mit einer mechanischen Vorrichtung seine Augen offengehalten, während er sich eine Montage aus Filmausschnitten, die „reale" Gewalt (die Gräuel von Massenmorden und Holocaust) zeigen, ansehen und Musik von seinem Lieblingskomponisten Beethoven hören muss. Die Ludovico-Technik, wie sie in dem Film heißt, beruht auf einer Methode der Gehirnwäsche, die äußerst intime Information (Alex' Lieblingsmusik) kombiniert mit äußerst aversiven Gefühlen (ausgelöst durch den Anblick von Massenmorden, die Alex, verglichen mit seiner eigenen Form der Bandengewalt, die er in einem Akt des freien Willens verübt zu haben glaubt, als absolut feindliche Gewaltform wahrnimmt).

Interessanterweise hatte Burgess vor, das Verfahren der Gehirnwäsche noch über die in der Kinoversion zu sehende Ludovico-Technik hinauszuführen. Burgess stellte sich Handlung und Struktur seines 1962 veröffentlichten Romans als veritable Spionagekunst vor. Sein Ziel war es, das Bewusstsein der Leser zu infiltrieren. Wie er in einem Interview[12] erläuterte, hatte er sich vorgenommen, ein neues Idiom – Nadsat – zu erfinden und seine Leser hierdurch zum Lernen einer neuen Sprache zu zwingen. Ein Glossar, das die Bedeutung der Wörter, einer Mischung aus Cockney und Russisch, erklärt hätte, ließ er bewusst weg, damit seine Leser sich die über die gesamte Handlung verstreuten verschlüsselten Wörter selber aneignen mussten. Dass Burgess den Roman schrieb, als er in Russland auf Reisen war, spricht, ebenso wie sein langjähriges Interesse an der russischen und Pawlow'schen Wissenschaft, zusätzlich für seinen gezielten Gebrauch bewusstseinsmanipulierender Techniken als künstlerischer Form. Möglicherweise ist die sprachliche Spionagekunst letztlich ein wirksameres Instrument als das Kino, unterwandert sie doch über noch zahlreichere verschlungene Wege und Bewegungen den mentalen Raum und macht dabei die Leserinnen und Leser zu unwillentlichen Mitwirkenden.

1   Deutscher Titel: *Botschafter der Angst*. Eine erneute
     Adaption des Romanstoffs kam 2004 mit Denzel
     Washington in der Hauptrolle heraus, wobei die Handlung
     in die Zeit nach dem Golfkrieg verlegt worden ist.

2   Die Handlung knüpft also an die seinerzeit führende
     Verschwörungstheorie von der überdominanten Mutter
     („Momismus") an, die Verbreitung fand, nachdem 1942
     Generation of Vipers von Philip Wylie erschienen war. Auf
     diese Parallele wurde von Laura Mulvey in ihrem Vortrag
     „From Momism to the Feminine Mystique" hingewiesen,
     den sie auf der am Birkbeck College der University
     of London im Juli 2015 stattgefundenen Konferenz
     „Brainwash: History, Cinema and the Psy Professions"
     gehalten hat.

3   D. Ewen Cameron, „Psychic Driving", *American Journal
     of Psychiatry* 112, Nr. 7 (Januar 1956), S. 502–9. Zu den
     Kontroversen, die über die Arbeit Camerons geführt
     worden sind, vgl. Rebecca Lemov, „Brainwashing's
     Avatar: The Curious Career of Dr. Ewen Cameron", *Grey
     Room* 45 (2011), S. 60–87.

4   Alle in dieser Studie aufgeführten Patienten sind
     weiblich.

5   Alexander Kellam, „Shoplifting Treatment by Aversion
     to a Film", *Behavioral Research and Therapy* 7 (1969),
     S. 125–27.

6   Ebd., S. 126.

7   Ebd.

8   Kellam bezieht sich in seiner Studie auf die Pawlow'sche
     Konditionierung, entlehnt aber in seiner Methode auch in
     hohem Maße Ideen von Skinner, siehe insbesondere: B. F.
     Skinner, *Science and Human Behavior*, New York 1953,
     S. 170 und 171–93 (Kapitel „Aversion, Avoidance, Anxiety"
     and „Punishment").

9   Raymond Bellour, *Le corps du cinéma: hypnoses, émotions,
     animalités*, Paris 2009. Siehe hierzu auch: Mireille Berton,
     „Cinéma et sciences du psychisme autour en 1900: la
     névrose, la paramnésie, la transe", *Gesnerus* 66 (2009),
     S. 103–20.

10   Dies galt etwa für die „Gehirnwäsche", ein ursprünglich
     im Journalismus erfundenes Konzept, das dann in
     wissenschaftlichen und militärischen Operationen
     übernommen wurde. Zum Ineinanderfließen von Fiktion,
     Wissenschaft und Politik im Kalten Krieg siehe Timothy
     Melley, *The Covert Sphere: Secrecy, Fiction, and the
     National Security State*, Ithaca, NY, 2012.

11   Anthony Burgess, *A Clockwork Orange*, hg. v. Mark
     Rawlinson, London 2011.

12   Anthony Burgess, *You've Had Your Time: Being the Second
     Part of the Confessions of Anthony Burgess*, New York 1991.

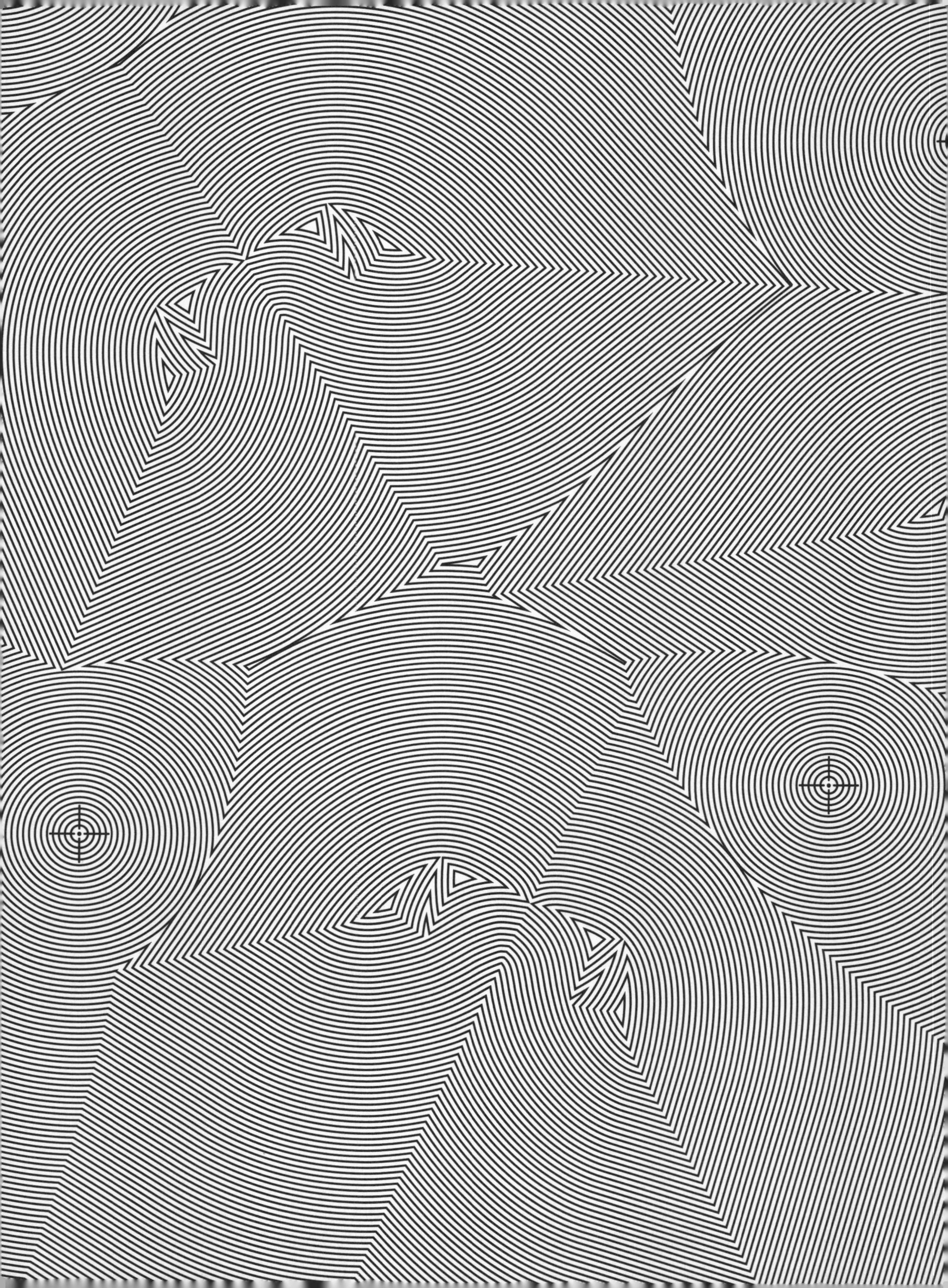

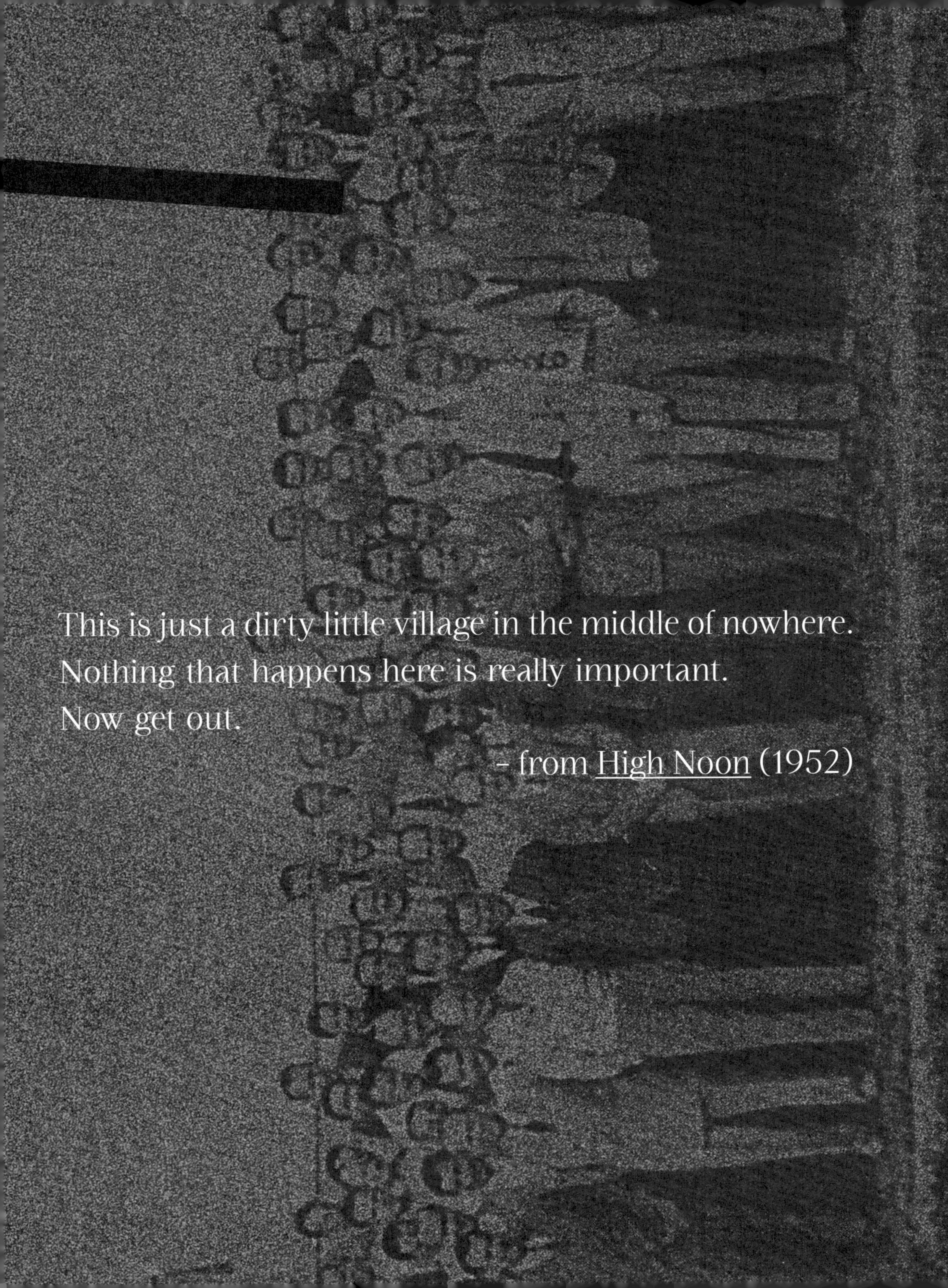

This is just a dirty little village in the middle of nowhere.
Nothing that happens here is really important.
Now get out.
- from High Noon (1952)

All the M[...] and Fear, Terror th[...] Can Hold

Noam Toran

ystery, and at Love

My parents first suspected that their mail was being read when an attempt to re-gum a correspondence from my grandmother in Vilnius seemed to prove too difficult for whoever was doing the covert job. Apparently the glue in Lithuania has a viscosity that even the FBI can't contend with, my father joked. My mother was not amused. In response, she drove to Albuquerque and mailed a letter to herself, which read:

Go fuck y[...]
and stor[...]
fucking [...]
faecist [...]

ourselves

eading my

ail you

ssholes

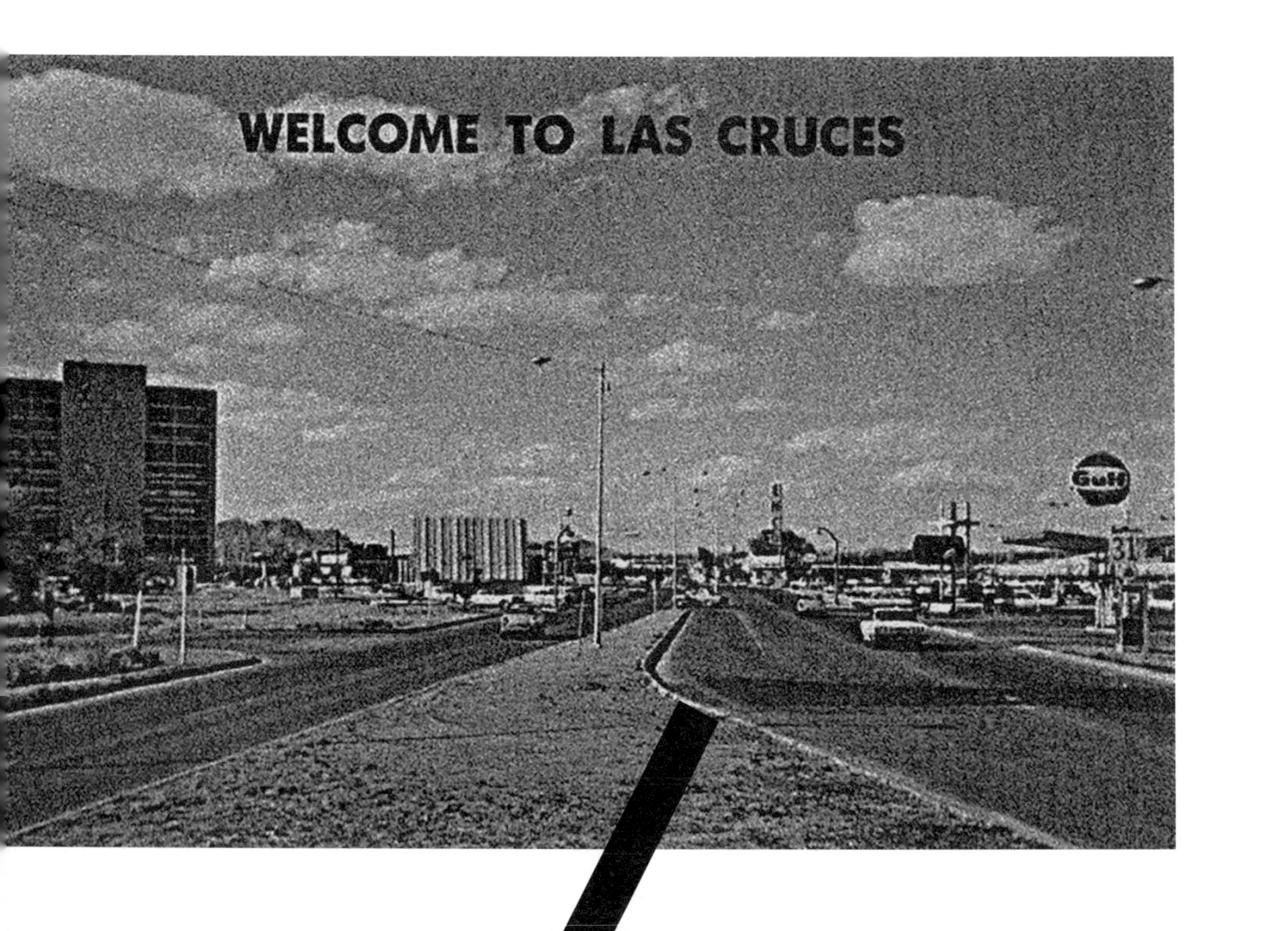
WELCOME TO LAS CRUCES
Gulf

Las Cruces, New Mexico, is not a small town and it's not a big town. It sits at the feet of the toothy, igneous Organ Mountains, in the Rio Grande rift valley, and has the celebrated river running north to south on its western side, irrigating the neighboring farms on its way to serving as a border between the US and Mexico. On windy September days, you can be overwhelmed by the sweet smell of chile as it's being harvested. The desert landscape is arid, rough, and occupied by resilient, callous creatures—humans, animals, and plants alike.

In the 1970s, the town had two main employers, the State University and the White Sands Missile Range (a third player arrived in the 1990s: Walmart). The social and political discord between the two institutions was not palpable when my family first arrived in 1977. The town was by all accounts pretty sleepy, with pockets of southwestern charm, but also painfully disjointed in the typical way that only a really bad 1960s urban renewal project can produce. My parents admitted later that their naivety to the forces that ran the town should have been killed off almost immediately, but they desperately needed to "make it work," and so kept telling themselves that it was all coincidental, or bad luck, until it maybe wasn't. It didn't help that the desert seemed totally ambivalent to honoring the consecrated borders between town and wilderness. Sand and dust storms, tempests of sagebrush pollen, waves of tumbleweed, plagues of wasps and vermin swept through Las Cruces seasonally.

My mother said she should have listened to her instincts when they drove into town for the first time, which was to just keep driving.

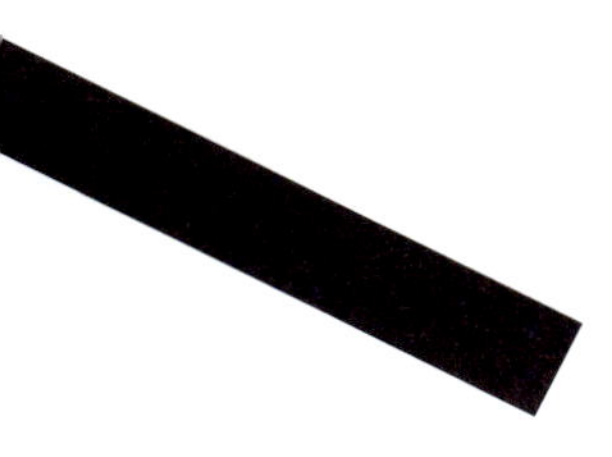

Two janitors are dragging a large black bag across the desert floor. As she approaches, they begin singing a Pedro Infante song; she can't remember which one. Then they point to the array of satellites on the far west side of the compound. They move synchronously upward, pointing toward a single point, maybe a single star. When she looks back, the janitors are gone but the song remains. She remembers it now, it's "No Volveré." The black bag is still there. She pries it open, and sees the decapitated heads of the Rosenbergs, stitched onto the bodies of dogs. A lion's mane of electrodes and wires fan out from their lifeless faces.
A failed experiment.

My parents, Lithuanian and Hungarian Jews with thick hair and accents, and recent appointees to the university faculty as European literature and cinema adjuncts, became instant celebrities within the ragtag circle of academics, poets, and filmmakers that adopted them upon our arrival. They were de facto bohemians: exotic, worldly, possibly communists. None of this was really true. My father adored the attention, cultivated the persona, and quickly procured a permanent position. My mother, far superior as a thinker and teacher but misanthropic, tried to play along, but was unceremoniously let go after her first year.

The region offers very good year-round viewing and pursuit of red-tailed hawk, Gambel's quail, golden eagle, rock squirrel, desert mule deer, black bear, elk, oryx, javelin, cougar and coyote. Also watch for black-throated sparrow, ladder-backed woodpecker, verdin, black-tailed gnatcatcher, lesser nighthawk, Scott's oriole, cactus wren, desert cottontail, and collared and tree lizard in the spring and summer. Please ensure you have a valid hunting license and comply with the state game and fish department requirements associated with that license. Hunting licenses can generally be purchased at any retail outlet that deals in hunting and fishing equipment, such as sporting goods stores.

From a New Mexico Game and Fish pamphlet, 1979

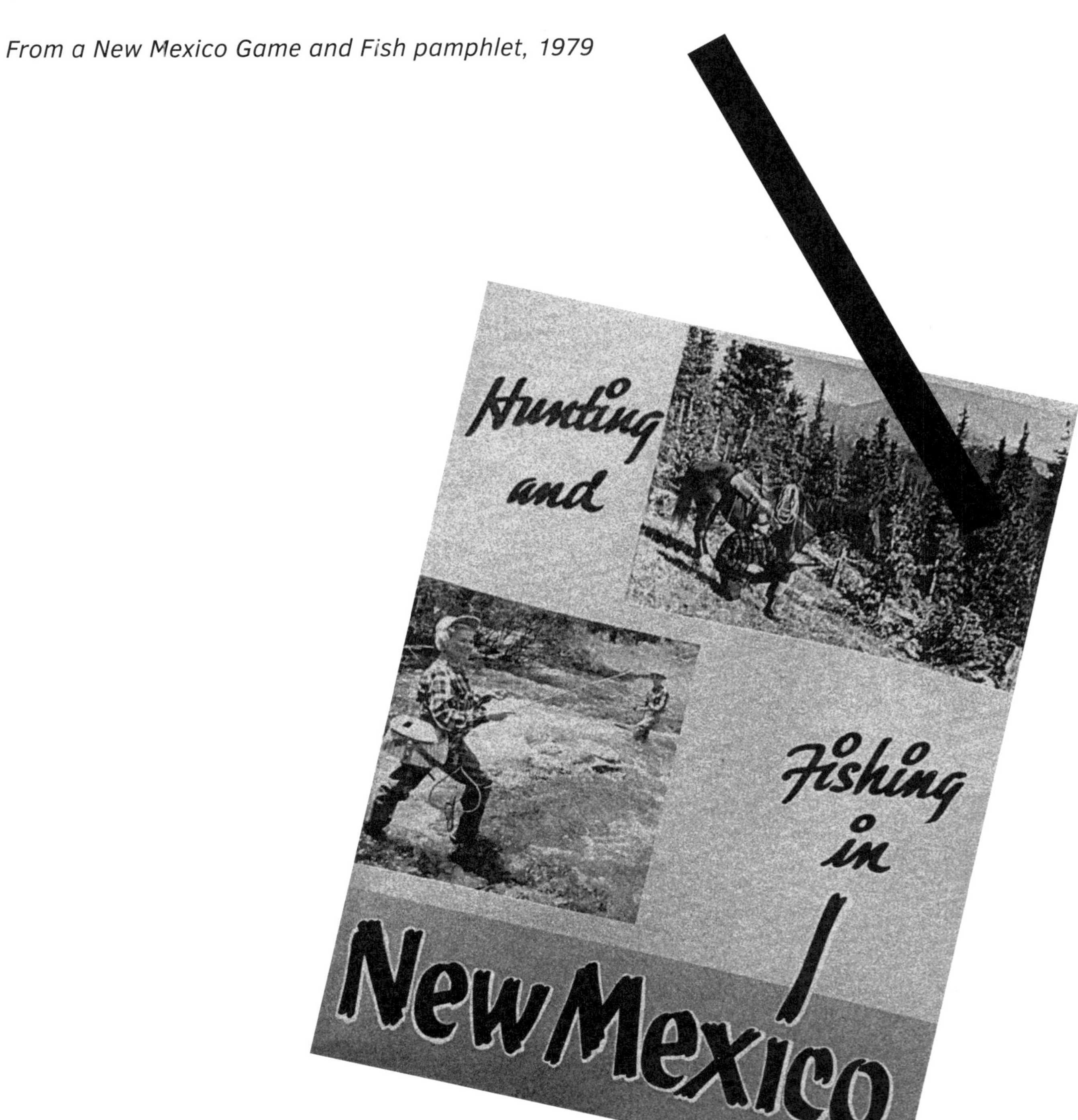

The Department of Defense has conducted a risk assessment that includes prioritizing ranges based on mission criticality, determining their vulnerabilities to foreign encroachment, and assessing the degree to which foreign encroachment could pose a threat to the mission of the ranges. Training ranges are challenged by many forms of so-called encroachment that inhibit training and testing, such as urban growth, competition for radio frequencies and airspace, noise and air pollution, endangered species, anti-military and environmental protests, and other security threats.

At some point I realized that my parents didn't want to return to our apartment. They extended afternoons and evenings out past the point of fun. Double-bill film screenings followed by midnight milkshakes at the Dairy Queen, followed by a long drive, the windows down, the radio on, my father looking intermittently in the rearview mirror. Then at some point I'd be shaken into a half-conscious state, be assisted out of the car and up the fire escape, through my bedroom window and into bed. I'd wake up the next morning with my jeans still on, a ticket stub still in the back pocket.

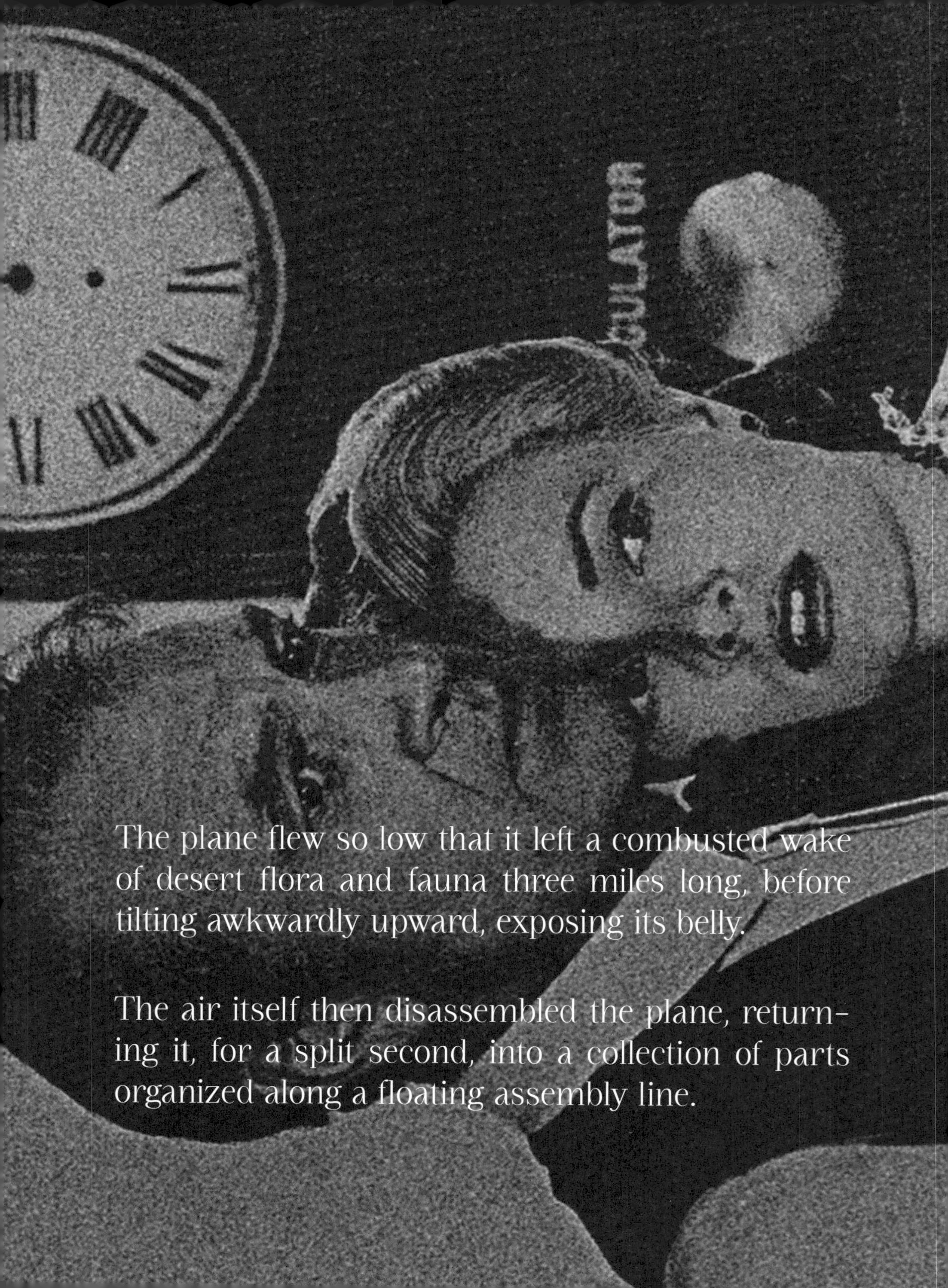

The plane flew so low that it left a combusted wake
of desert flora and fauna three miles long, before
tilting awkwardly upward, exposing its belly.

The air itself then disassembled the plane, returning it, for a split second, into a collection of parts
organized along a floating assembly line.

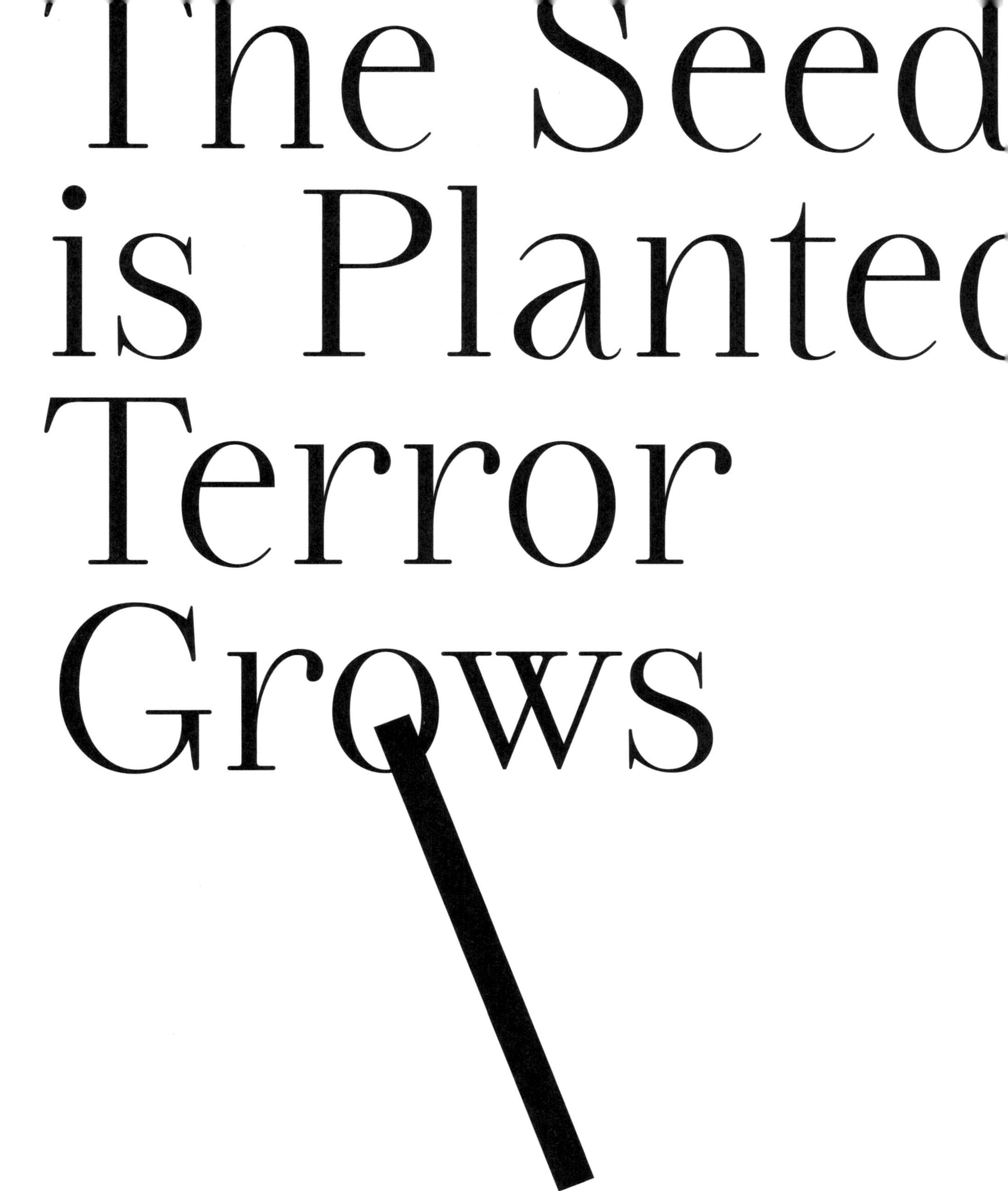
The Seed
is Planted
Terror
Grows

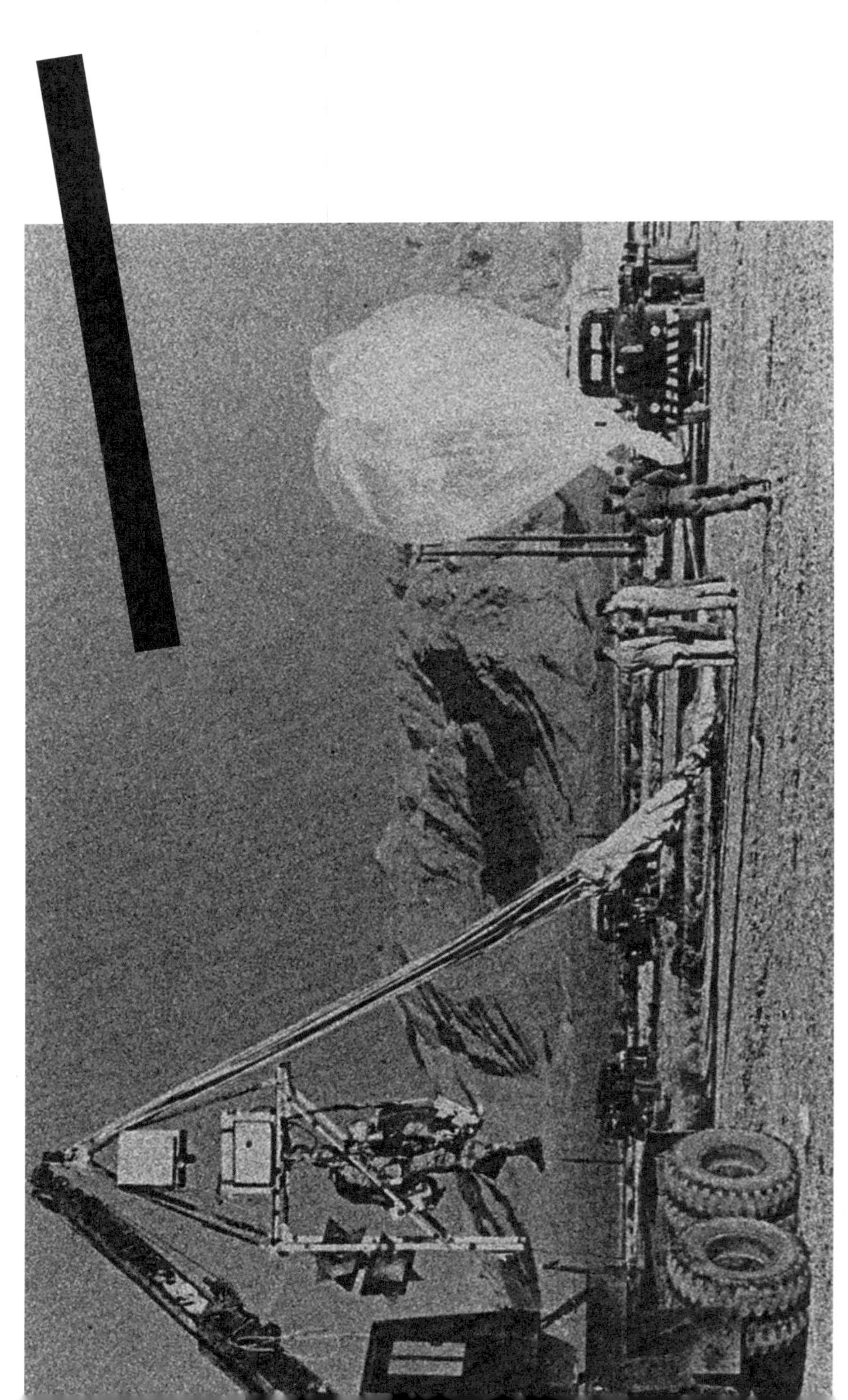

We set our alarms for 4 a.m., which should give us plenty of time. Skip is already waiting at the end of our street when I get there. Gangly, blond, Skip. A skater. We do a quick inventory check: foldable camping stools, flashlights, binoculars, first aid kit, snake bite kit, compass, strike-anywhere matches, handkerchiefs, knives, sunglasses, toilet paper, water, bottle of Coke, a loaf of sliced white bread, baloney, and mustard. We start walking through the darkness. A right on Fox Road, left on Tres Yuccas, right on MacArthur, then straight up north until the gravel turns to dirt and we continue on into the desert. We find the arroyo running northeast and follow it. Three miles in, I have to piss and do so on a fire-orange mesquite bush, its brilliant color signaling the sun's ascent over the Organ Pass. Six miles in, we pass by the family of scorched and dismembered anthropomorphic dummies, lying side by side in a shallow grave, their sun-bleached jumpsuits shredded at the edges like a child's pirate costume. We keep moving, stopping only to drink water. Two hours later we arrive at the 10-foot-tall barbed wire fence, which stretches unendingly in either direction. We have 20 minutes to spare, so to celebrate we take turns masturbating. We then set out the stools, grab our binoculars, and wait.

Skip sees it first and points in its direction. A bright spherical light a few thousand feet up in the sky, perhaps five miles east of our location, framed by beautiful pink clouds of dawn. The light remains in place for a while, hovering, shimmering, oscillating, before rushing westward toward us with a frightening velocity. Another light surfaces from the ground, travels perfectly vertically and collides with the sphere.

For a few seconds, the world's chromatic spectrum is inverted.
Red sky, blue desert, black sun.
Skip and I grin at each other, exposing dark green teeth.

We pack our bags and follow the arroyo back into town, in time for the first period of school.

A woman (her is name is Frau Luna) is sitting naked on a large paper crescent moon, her high-heeled feet dangling above a few token stars. She seems at ease, even smiling. Clearly blind to her fate. Her mood changes when she hears a hideous hissing sound, followed by an immense rush of heat. This can't be good. She tries to jump off the paper moon but it's too late. She is propelled 40,000 feet into the air in a matter of seconds. Am I going to the real moon? Where's my coat?

I was preoccupied with flipping through comic books at the checkout, so didn't hear the conversation that preceded the incident. What I did hear was the sound of my mother's palm hitting the cashier girl's face, and the slew of expletives (half English, half Lithuanian) which she supplemented it with. We were not-so-calmly escorted out of the Piggly Wiggly, sans groceries.

ERMAN V-2 ROCKET
ORDNANCE DEPT.
ITE SANDS PROVING GROUNDS
NEW MEXICO

This from a leaked memo circulating at the Missile Range in 1979, later printed in the September 8 edition of the *Las Cruces Sun* by the journalist and family friend Peter Goldman, who was subsequently fired a month later:

To the employees and active duty members stationed at WSMR, it has been brought to our attention by the DOD that two confirmed cells are operating in the Las Cruces Metropolitan area, with possibly another operating between the Sierra, Otero and Doña Ana counties. Failure to notify INSCOM about possible disclosures in violation of clauses 12.1–12.4 may result in suspension, and/or expulsion and/or imprisonment. If you are approached and/or encouraged to reveal anything about your duties and/or research, contact the MP immediately. Be discreet, vigilant, dutiful and patriotic. Remember, the consequences of wh█ you say or do here can endanger the free worl█

[Signed by Chief of Staff Glen Ada█s]

Phillip Kaufman's remake of The Body Snatchers *came out and my parents crammed me and three of my friends into the car and drove to El Paso for a matinée screening. It scared the hell out of all of us, in different ways and for different reasons. The film's atmosphere didn't evaporate when we left the theater. On the contrary, the dread and claustrophobia seemed to spore and splatter itself across the highway back to Cruces, in the gouged-out looks of pedestrians that crossed in front of the car, even permeating the viscous leftovers in our fridge.*

It didn't help that my father looked like Donald Sutherland.

There will be no Witnesses

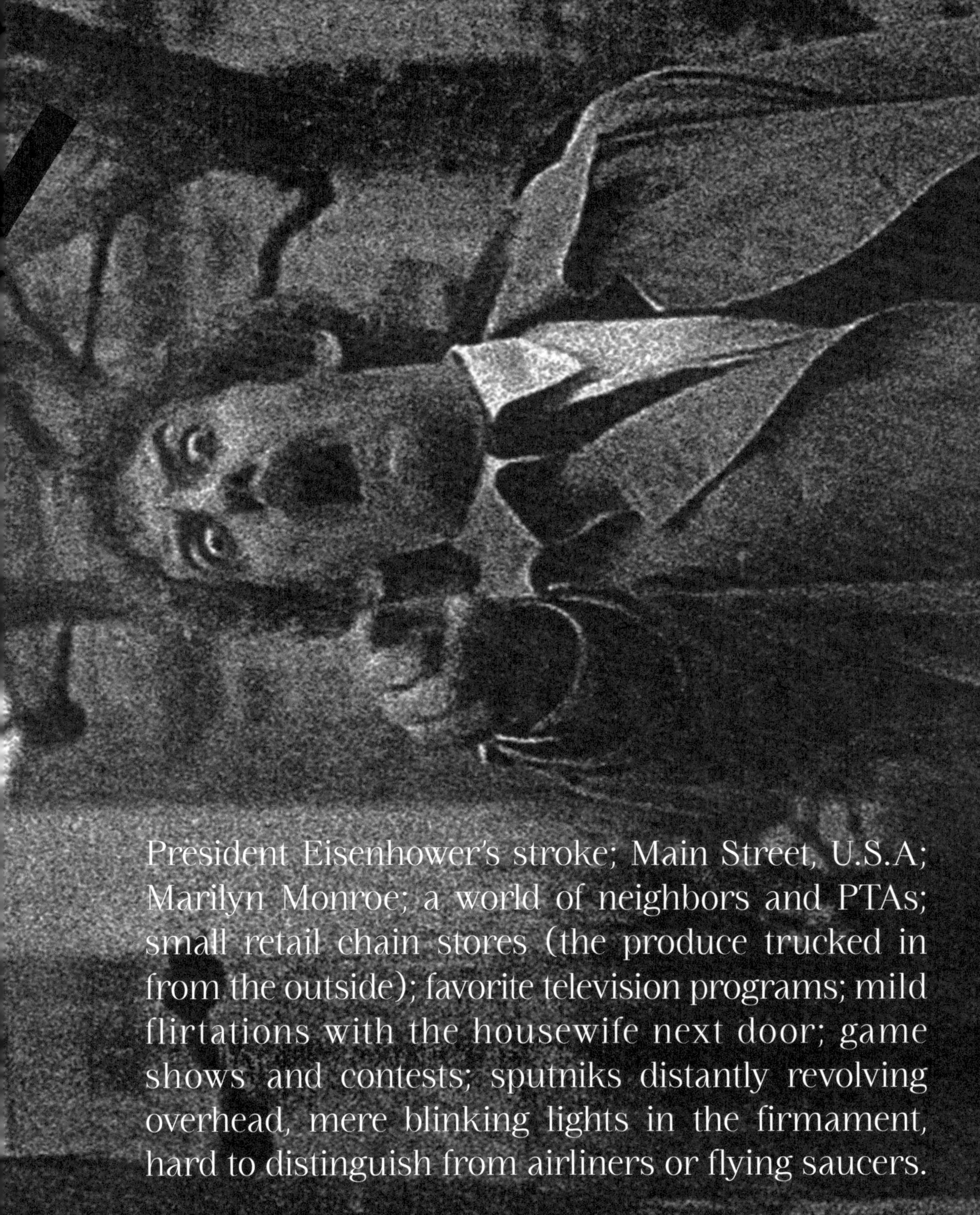

President Eisenhower's stroke; Main Street, U.S.A;
Marilyn Monroe; a world of neighbors and PTAs;
small retail chain stores (the produce trucked in
from the outside); favorite television programs; mild
flirtations with the housewife next door; game
shows and contests; sputniks distantly revolving
overhead, mere blinking lights in the firmament,
hard to distinguish from airliners or flying saucers.

– From <u>Time Out of Joint</u>, Philip K. Dick, 1959

One weekend, as an escape, we drove up to the Robledo Mountains for a picnic. My parents got high and we all stumbled around, it was fun. Then we found fossils: dinosaur footprints and imprints from ancient marine animals, residuals of a primeval time and place. My father started to trip out, and my mom followed. Drugged as they were, the Paleozoic sea rose from the foothills and threatened to swallow them. I watched them like one watches actors in a play. They finally sobered up, and we ate the food and drove back home in silence.

Here, far from the sea,
this house is steady. It does
not rock and that noise is
thunder, not gunfire. It is
peaceful here. Say it again.
Peaceful. One has only to stay
awake, not dream, the faces of dreams
cannot touch, dreamed blood stains
only the bedsheet sails of haunted ships.

– from <u>Ballad of a Sailor</u>,
by the Las Cruces poet Keith Wilson

The alien, from its invisible flying saucer high above, adjusting something like its cornea onto this parcel of land, does not see one thing at one time but everything at once and from every point in time. It sees schools of ammonite filtering plankton into their mouths, sees the family having its picnic, sees the radioactive dust from the first atomic detonation settle onto the desert floor, sees the dust rise from a Mogollon family on an excursion, sees the earth's crust burst and pus lava, sees it drown, sees it ice up, sees it dry up, sees the gypsum, and silver, and gold, and salt being formed, sees it being extracted, sees graves being filled and graves being emptied, sees nothing here. It sees into my brain.

This sandwich is dusty, I think.

My mother returned home visibly scared, wet-faced. She then screamed at my father for having brought us here, this middle-of-nowhere place, for his stupid self-interests, his imagined ambitions. I joined in, called him a really bad word for the first time. It was exhilarating. Overexcited, I ran outside and kicked at a stumpy, toothless cactus until it burst.

The following week, they purchased a gun and a box of ammunition, and preemptively scolded me for even thinking about ever trying to find it, and the horrible repercussions if I did. I of course became obsessed with finding it, which was disappointingly easy: yet another example of the stupidity of adults and the worlds they make.

The gun's heaviness shocked me, the weight alone testifying to a very real violence which now seemed unassailable, predestined.

Describe your routine.

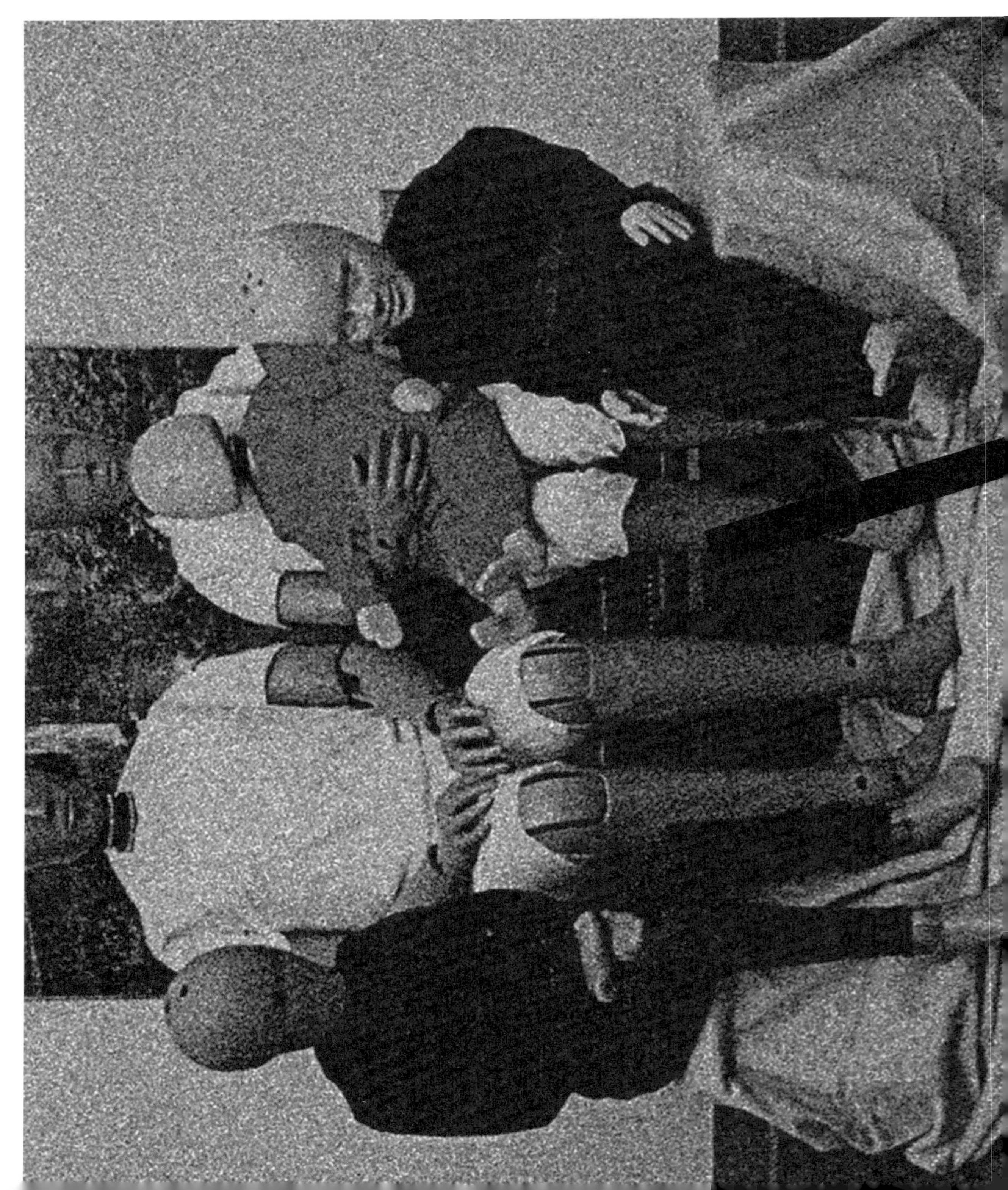

The shuttle arrives outside my house at 6 a.m. There are already three women on board. We then pick up two more. We're all computer operators, which sounds sophisticated but it really isn't. We get out of town on Route 70. Sometimes the Organ Mountain Pass is closed because of snow and sometimes I see double rainbows over the mesa. I think of it as a good omen. When we get to the gate, we have to show our passes and go directly to our assigned location. It's a strict military zone, and you can't roam around. The computer is housed in a big hangar. It's kept very cold because of the heat the computer generates, and we all keep our coats and scarfs on for the entire day. The hangar has several workstations with tape ports and disk storage drives. As a computer operator, I get messages of tasks I have to perform in order to run a job. Basically I go to an adjacent room to get a certain tape or disk from a huge library of discs and load it on the appropriate drive, input the code, and let it run. The discs spin around, back and forth, for about five minutes or so, then it's finished and I take it out and return it back to the library, and then wait for another task message. The discs are about a foot in diameter. I have no idea what's on them.

There is one officer who comes occasionally to check that all is running well and to report malfunctions. She is skinny and stern, and she has a crush on our supervisor. Sometimes in order to sync information with another base we "converse" through the computers with fellow operators in other states. It's just amazing, you can go to a terminal, type a message on a keyboard, and almost immediately get a response from another operator, even someone in Alaska! At lunch we all go to a big mess hall. There is no on-site cafeteria, so you have to bring your own food and drink. Then we go back to work. We finish at 6 p.m., board the shuttle, and go back home.

It's boring as hell.

I don't think I'll last long. I'm pregnant and don't think this is a good environment.

Noam Toran

All the Mystery, and Fear, and Terror that Love Can Hold

2020

Graphic consultant: Jeanne Pasquet
Dedicated to Orville "Bud" Wanzer (1930–2019)

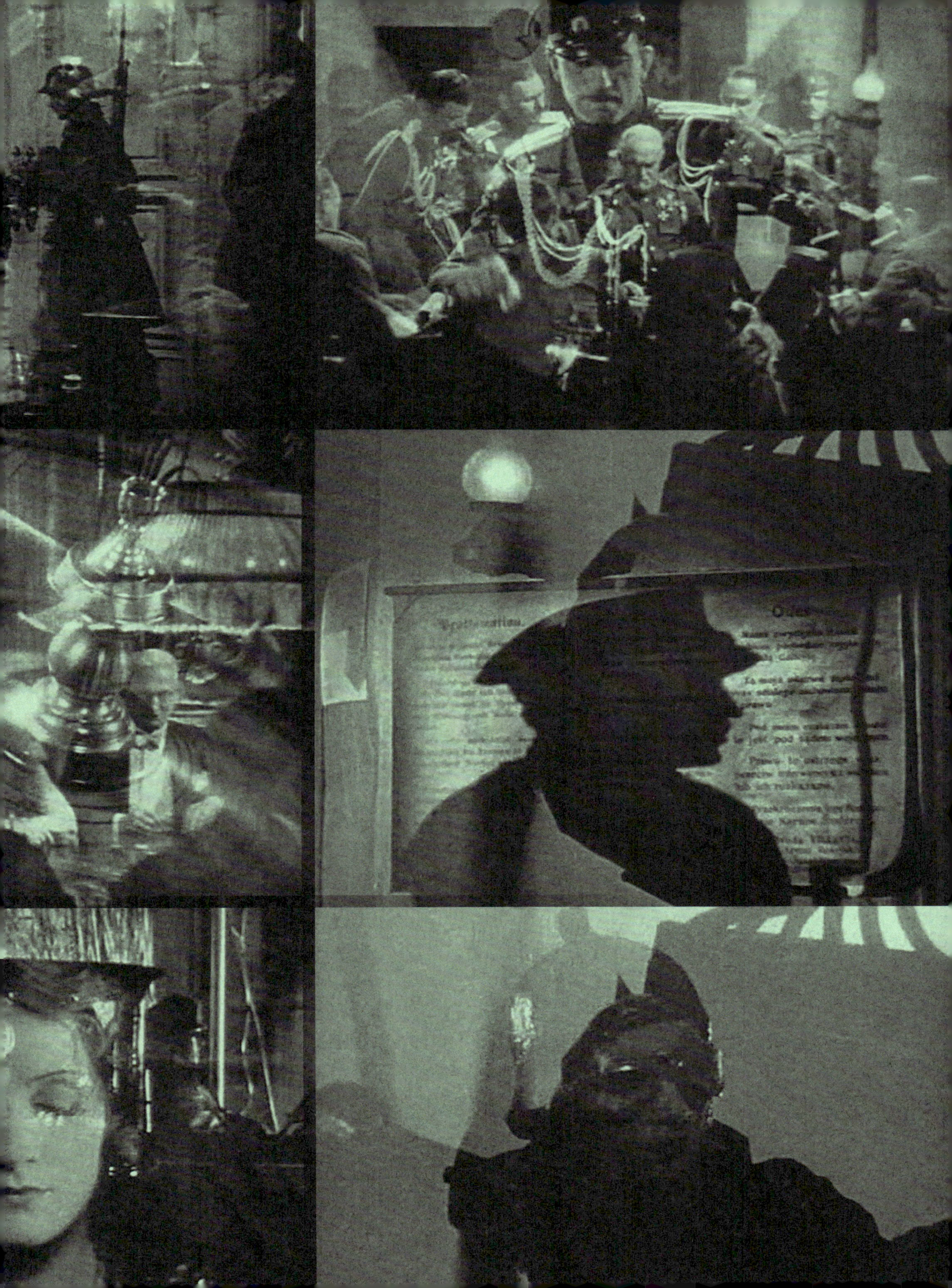

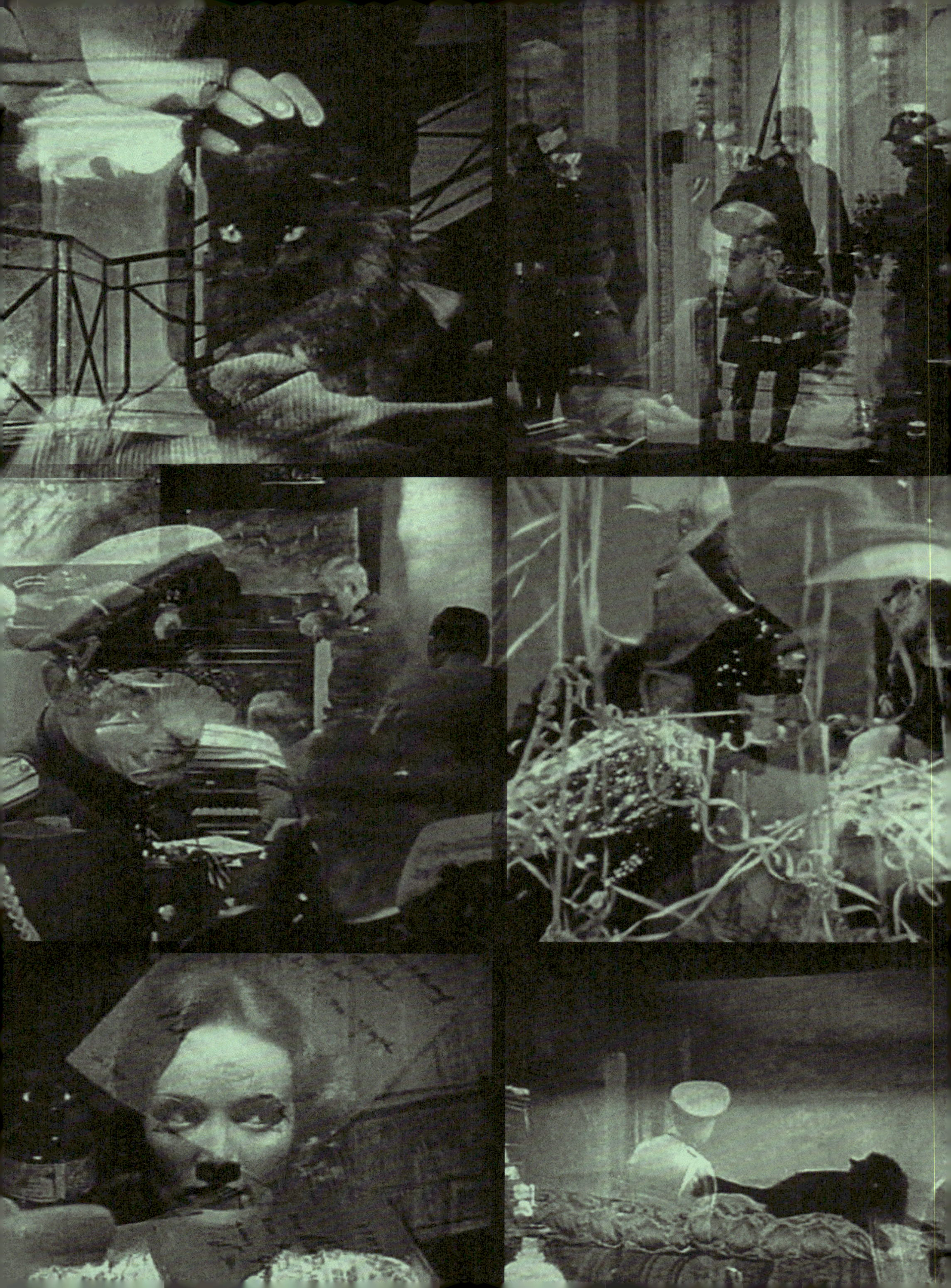

The Agent in Plain Sight
Wladimir Velminski

1. Covert Operations

The power of the agent unfolds in covert action at the point when the agent turns into a medium.[1] As a medium, the agent creates their own world, own reality, seemingly detached from actual reality. But such an appearance is deceptive, since this is precisely where the agent's true potential lies: at any given moment they have at least two moves in mind with which they can manipulate reality. Viktor Pivovarov has explored such nuances. His 1994 work *Operation "Dual Glow"* is one of twenty secret operations carried out in fjords by an agent (fig. 1),

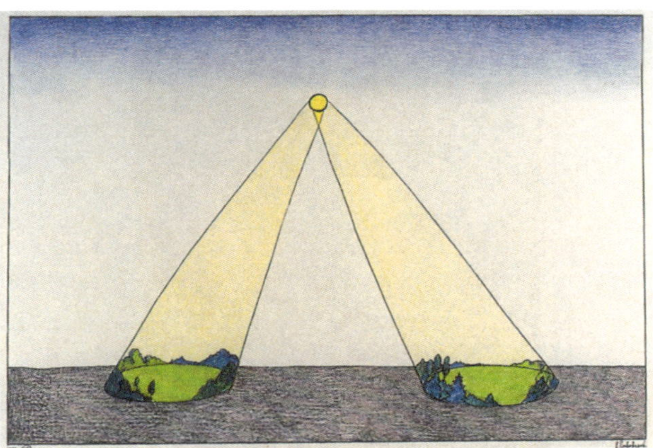

Fig. / Abb. 1: Viktor Pivovarov, *Operation "Dual Glow"* / *Operation „Doppeltes Scheinen"*, 1994

together with the covert group Glowing Flower. They are part of the cycle *Agent in Norway*, which Pivovarov divides into the sections "secret devices" and "mystical projects," "encrypted messages" and "covert groups," thus defining the agent's area of interest. Unlike a "classic" agent who, as a master of disguise, strives to remain covert in order to be effective, the agent in Norway pursues the goal of exposing his or her covert nature in order to be suggestive.[2] The overall view of the material reveals that it is not about military bases or secret weapons, but about "the private and creative lives of the intellectuals that the agent had been tailing."[3]

Such an aesthetic form of concealment, quite common in literature, had been adopted by the artists of both Sots Art and Moscow Conceptualism from the 1970s onward. At this point, it is worth mentioning the fictional works of Nikolai Buchumov,[4] created by Komar & Melamid, and the invented life and work of Charles Rosenthal,[5] originated by Ilya Kabakov. However, Pivovarov always adds an additional layer. The cycle *Agent in Norway* thus deals with the materials the agent has collected, rather than the personal work of the fictitious agent. While the face of the agent remains hidden, the activity of agenthood comes to light in order to initiate the viewer into the game of the covert, to infect them, to lure them onto their side, and thus to form an aesthetic collective body, a fifth column of art.

This is a procedure that Pivovarov has applied in his most recent book *Svidetel'stvo sovremennikov / Reports of the Contemporaries*, in which the album of the same name is published.[6] It is pointed out right at the beginning that the album is actually the collection of the bibliophile and future publisher Sergei Nitotschkin:

> It was a folder in which an anonymous collector put memories of various people, usually common persons, about Lenin and Stalin. These memories drastically contrasted with those published in millions of copies in the Soviet Union. It was not surprising that the collection had been unknown. The texts were illustrated with drawings probably made by the collector.[7]

Pivovarov undermines the form of public expression propagated in the Soviet Union when it came to the opinions of workers who, as Lenin had wished, wrote "about their everyday life, their interests and their work" and then published these texts in daily newspapers as so-called letters of the workers.[8] As soon as the readers of the album decide to play the game, they become an investigator who has to put together the scattered pieces of the puzzle to obtain full insight into the memories of Lenin and Stalin.

The complex process of nesting that Pivovarov applies to the content and form of the album is reflected both in the image-text reference and the narrative gesture that has shaped the artist's work for decades. The co-founder of Moscow Conceptualism has often pointed out that the image was reformed in Russia, while Western conceptual artists rejected it in its form as outdated. In Russia, therefore, the image absorbs didactic and propagandistic non-artistic forms.[9] Although Pivovarov was not forced to produce ideological posters and street signs in the Soviet Union,

he, too, led a double life, since his official occupation was as an illustrator of books and magazines. His 1979 typeface for the children's magazine *Vesëlye kartinki* (Funny Pictures), which still today graces the cover of the magazine, and his illustrations of Hans Christian Andersen fairy tales both have cult status in Russia. The clandestine agent is the most powerful. With regard to the image reformed by conceptual thinking, Pivovarov writes: "It became not only visible but also audible, acquired a voice, began to speak, first individual words, later sentences, then extensive texts."[10] With the creation of conceptual albums and picture cycles, the image has taken on the function of a conceptual agent and as such has completely explored all manner of text forms, both short stories and novels as well as bureaucratic documents.[11] Kabakov, who together with Pivovarov introduced the album as a genre, notes in this context that the image even acts as a "field of consciousness."[12]

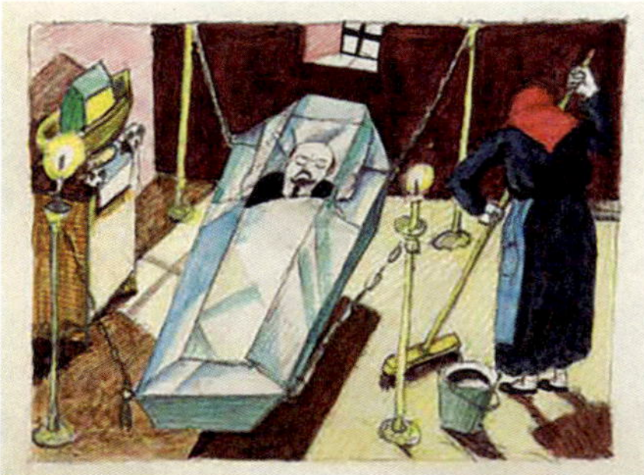

Fig. / Abb. 2: Viktor Pivovarov, *Morning in the Mausoleum / Der Morgen im Mausoleum*, 1988–2001

Pivovarov's *Svidetel'stvo sovremennikov / Reports of the Contemporaries* (1988–2001) also forms part of this tradition. Seventeen short texts are juxtaposed with seventeen images, and at the end with a cultural-historical commentary accompanied by numerous photographs. Several actors are thus involved, one

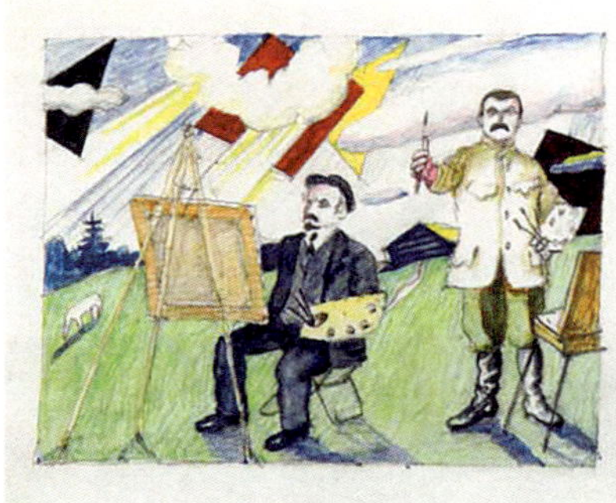

Fig. / Abb. 3: Viktor Pivovarov, *Lenin and Stalin on a Sketching Session in Nemchinovka / Lenin und Stalin während der Malstudien in Nemčinovka*, 1988–2001

referring to the other and vice versa. One member of the security staff, M. I. Potapova, for instance, reports on her former neighbor Mariya Evdokimova, who worked at the mausoleum as a cleaning lady (fig. 2):

> She would come there in the morning, she said, to put out the candles, to wipe the crystal coffin and the gold chains with a special solution, put the Tabernacle of the Covenant in the cupboard, mop the floors. A lot of work to do but the money was good and you could get a free lunch at the canteen for veteran Bolsheviks.[13]

The accompanying commentary indicates that the narrator may have confused things. So she speaks of *mishkan*, a transportable temple which the people of Israel took with them on their journey through the desert after their exodus from Egypt, its most important sacral function being the preservation of the Ark of the Covenant. But since the annotation refers to the image that clearly depicts the Ark of the Covenant, the confusion is lifted.[14] However, even this explanation is deceptive, since the images are said to have been created on the basis of the texts. This conceptual ensemble of perplexities, which obviously also uses elements of Sots Art, possesses

by means of its obfuscating poetry an efficacy that enables it to conduct a covert investigation of Russian culture.[15] This process becomes much more obvious in the example of "Lenin and Stalin on a sketching session in Nemchinovka" (fig. 3), which goes back to the report by driver E. K. Liepa:

> On a Sunday, Vladimir Ilyich and Josef Vissarionovich would go down to Nemchinovka to do sketches. Lenin drew trees inflated with wind, ragged clouds, tossing rye. Stalin preferred "ambience" landscapes— *Early Mist, Autumn Lands, Daylight Falling.*[16]

It is stated in the annotations that the picture accompanying the short text anticipates the theses of the cultural studies of the 1990s, which identified Lenin, rather more so than Stalin, as the continuation of the Russian avant-garde.[17] The surroundings are not a coincidence, either, as Nemchinovka is a place close to Moscow, and the place where Kazimir Malevich was buried. In addition to such playful elements, the completely fictional narrative also illuminates actual fragments of the past, which in everyday Russian life today not only rumble tacitly in the unconscious but also come to the surface and find admirers.

2. Patterns of Deception

During his time as prime minister, Vladimir Putin had already tried his hand in the field of art. At the Christmas market in St. Petersburg in 2008, he demonstrated his talent as a draftsman, creating, in icy cold weather, a picture on the theme of "patterns" (fig. 4). Such "artistic actions" have a long tradition

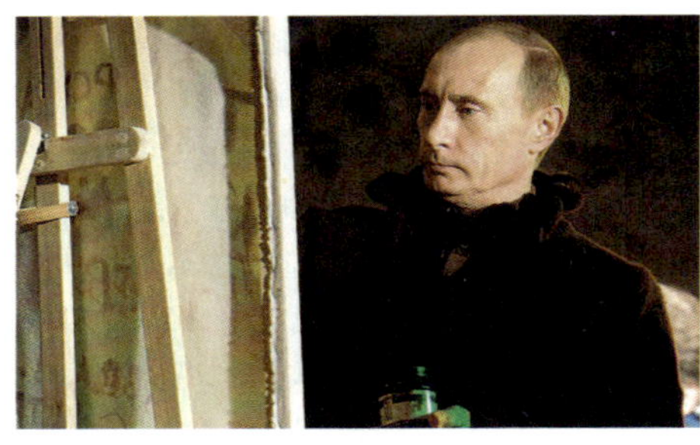

Fig. / Abb. 4: Vladimir Putin during painting classes
in St. Petersburg / Wladimir Putin während der Malstudien
in St. Petersburg, 2008

in Russia. Time and again, "personalities
of the country" are invited on the night
before Christmas, according to the title
of a story by Nikolay Gogol, to draw
alphabet pictures, which are meant to
correspond to the classic story in terms
of content. Putin was given the Russian
letter У (U) and drew his variation of Узор
(uzor, which means "pattern," fig. 5).
Two weeks later, the painting *Pattern
on Frozen Window* was sold at auction for
37 million rubles (then about 900,000

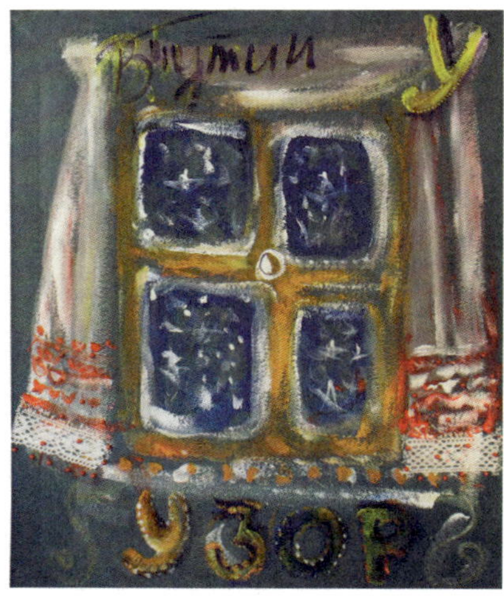

Fig. / Abb. 5: Vladimir Putin, *Pattern / Muster*, 2008

euros). A Moscow gallery by the name of
Our Artists, specialized in "true Russian
art," acquired the painting of the "young
artist."[18] News circulated in the press
that Putin's painting was more expensive
than Malevich's *Black Square*, which
was allegedly acquired for the Hermitage
in 2002 for 32 million rubles.[19] There

is something more to this obscure comparison. Malevich himself promoted
his *Black Square* as an icon of modernism.
Putin's pattern was immediately per-
ceived as an icon and ritualized (fig. 6).

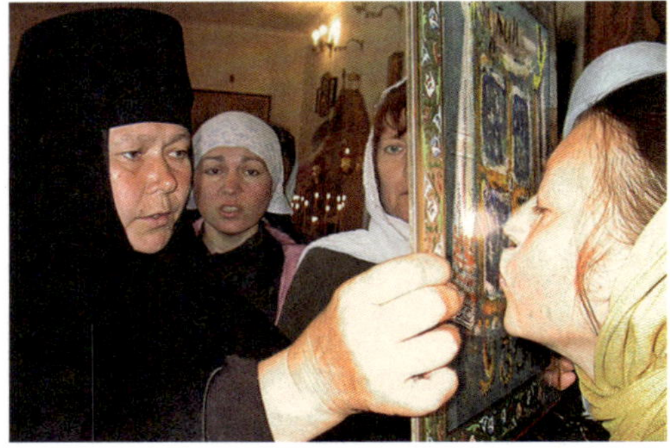

Fig. / Abb. 6: Icon worship in Russia / Ikonenverehrung
in Russland, 2009

Clear evidence of this is found in the kiss-
ing of the raised and still unprotected
"holy image"—which in the Orthodox
Church is accompanied by two signs of
the cross and a bow before the rever-
ently performed kiss, and a subsequent
sign of the cross and a bow at the end.

As a reelected president, Putin still
remained committed to art. During a
visit to a school in Kurgan at the beginning of the 2013 school year, supported
by the state treasury, the "young artist"
showed his skills when a teacher introduced him to a new interactive board.
While the obviously tense teacher
explained the advantages of the whiteboard, writing the date September 1
on it with a special pen and stressing
that the board is particularly exciting
for the students because they can write
on it with only one finger, the president
approached the whiteboard. With his
finger, he drew a funny picture, which he
began with a phallic column. Though
the class was quiet, the teacher had to
suppress her hysterical laughter. After
Putin had finished, he stepped back
from the whiteboard with the words "For
you as a souvenir." When asked by the

class what the drawing was meant to represent, Putin held his right hand up to his mouth and said: "A cat from behind." The president left the room amid the laughter of all present.[20]

Without doubt, such "artistic" demonstrations of power by a showman may be interpreted from a number of perspectives. At this point, however, the focus should be directed once again at Crimea, the place where Putin concentrated his artistic strategy. While masked "little green men" spread throughout the island and the Russian president was confronted with this fact, he behaved like the members of Pussy Riot once did when they were interrogated; he, too, claimed to have nothing to do with the action. The masked men were not Russian soldiers and had nothing to do with any military action, since the men were friendly and polite. While Putin's *fifth column*—these highly armed agents (fig. 7), who due to their masks

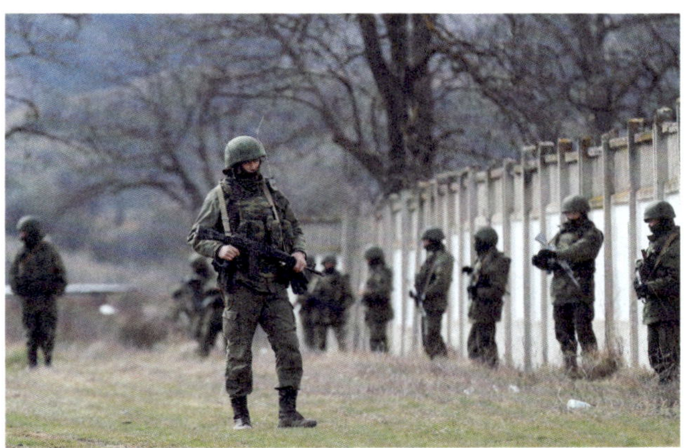

Fig. / Abb. 7: Yuri Kochetkov, *On a Secret Mission, Crimea / In geheimer Mission, Krim*, 2014

all looked the same and thus resembled an agent Smith virus, having infected the entire Matrix—occupied Crimea, there was nothing left for the West, not to mention Ukraine, but to behave like a teacher in front of the whiteboard. The "secret operation" Crimea was a perfect example.

3. The Agent's Joke

In 2014, people in Russia began to once again tell Stierlitz jokes. Agent Stierlitz is the heroic figure in a series of spy stories written between 1921 and 1967 by Yulian Semyonov, rumored to be a KGB employee himself. The adventures of Maksim Maksimovich Isaev, alias Max Otto von Stierlitz, during the Second World War in Berlin were featured in a Soviet television series *Semnadtsat' mgnoveniy vesny* (Seventeen Moments of Spring), which forms part of the Russian film canon; the jokes refer exclusively to the television series. Said joke describes a celebration of German Obersturmbannführers, with the Russian spy Stierlitz in attendance. The SS officers raise their glasses to the toast: "To victory!" Before everyone toasts, the Standartenführer Stierlitz adds: "To *our* victory!" The Soviet agent's trick is not only to distance himself from the toast of the SS officers by adding the possessive pronoun, but also to make the Nazis toast to their own demise.

This possessive pronoun *our* (*svoy, svoya* or *nash, nashe*) has been omnipresent in Russia for years. There is *Our Radio, Our Kitchen, Our Cinema, Our People*, the party youth movement *Ours!*, and, last but not least, the gallery Our Artists. The possessive pronoun had been used in relation to Crimea before and after the annexation: *Our Crimea*. From the masked agents on the island— soldiers without badges, initially dismissed as "little green men"—a battalion was created to support the *our* status. Patches were put into circulation which the "green men" in Crimea were supposed to use to identify themselves (fig. 8). A cat with its paw raised sits next to a soldier with a Kalashnikov rifle. Above the depiction is written "Polite

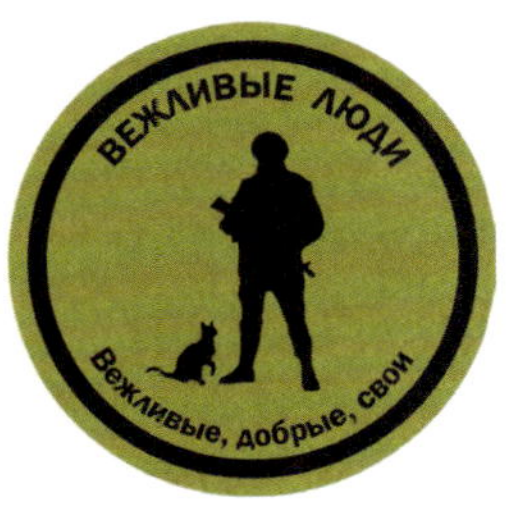

Fig. / Abb. 8: Polite People / Höfliche Menschen

People," and below that "polite, good, *ours*."

On April 10, 2014, an ensemble of the Russian army performed in Crimea; the newly composed hymn to the "Polite People" was part of their repertoire.[21] The T-shirts and protective sleeves for smartphones sold as of August 2014 show the image of the agent behind the agents, "The most polite of all people," as the caption below the image states (fig. 9).

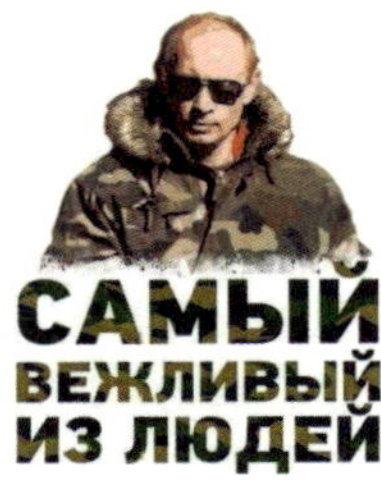

Fig. / Abb. 9: The most polite of all people / Der höflichste aller Menschen

It is nothing new that language is one of the agent's most important weapons. Since the emergence of the intelligence services, the aim has been to obtain information about both enemy and friend in order to gain an advantage and manipulate the other side. The revelations of Edward Snowden have made it clear that each of us is a potential enemy. Barack Obama confirmed this in his cultural-historical address on espionage, making it clear to all who had been outraged following Snowden's revelations:

Now let me be clear: our intelligence agencies will continue to gather information about the intentions of governments—as opposed to ordinary citizens—around the world, in the same way that the intelligence services of every other nation does. We will not apologize simply because our services may be more effective.[22]

This rhetorical demonstration of imperial power that dwarfed all military parades had to be countered by the former agent in Dresden. While Putin faced the people on April 17, 2014, during the traditional question and answer session on Russian state television, and admitted that he had deliberately operated undercover in Crimea, the American secret service agent who had gone into hiding in Russia was present via live video feed. Snowden's question as to whether Russia, just like America, employed comprehensive surveillance of its citizens' communication was answered in the negative by Putin with reference to strict regulations. But before he gave this answer, the former head of the Russian secret service made a brief statement: "Dear Mr. Snowden! You're a former agent. I, too, have some experience in espionage." While the audience in the studio laughed and applauded, the Russian president added, before answering his colleague's question in English: "So we both speak a professional language."[23] It is a language that is only spoken by agents, with techniques that are also applied in rhetoric aimed at the public. Stierlitz, Snowden, and Putin master it to perfection; there is no such thing as "former" agents. All others feel foreign in this terrain. When Angela Merkel, after her telephone conversation with Putin before the Crimea referendum, claimed that the Russian president is living in his own world, she is right, but in doing so she highlighted her own unfamiliarity with this world dominated more than ever by shrewd agents. A new language has to be learned in order to navigate this world, and to be able to get the jokes.[24]

4. Imperial Realism

One page in Pivovarov's album *Svidetel'stvo sovremennikov / Reports of the Contemporaries* has the title *Stalin i mysh* (Stalin and Mouse). The drawing depicts Stalin with his eyes either completely closed or downward looking at a small gray mouse that he, the uniformed generalissimo, holds in his fist (fig. 10).

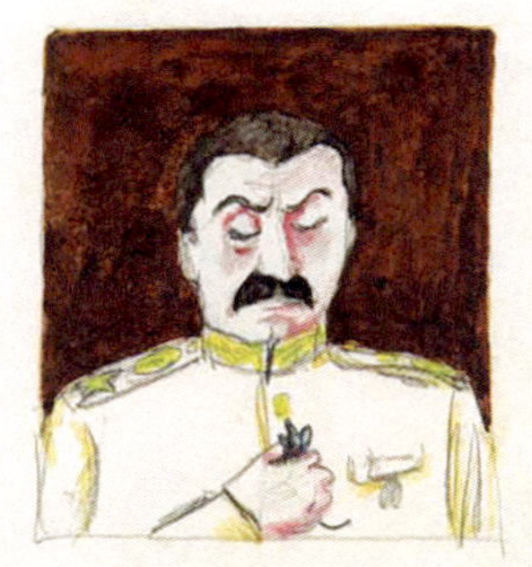

Fig. / Abb. 10: Viktor Pivovarov, *Stalin and Mouse / Stalin und Maus*, 1988–2001

A note by a certain N. Osipov, who in turn was the son of an officer from Stalin's personal bodyguard service, states:

> Stalin carried a mouse in his pocket to the Politburo sessions. If there arose some complicated issue calling for immediate solution, Stalin would retire to the back-room, take the mouse out and consult with it. When he was angry with someone, he would take the mouse out of his pocket and slightly squeeze it in his fist. The mouse squeaked and suddenly there was deathlike silence in the room.[25]

In the accompanying commentary, reference is made to the role of the mouse in mythology and its ability to foresee turbulent weather.[26] The mouse was therefore Stalin's think tank, the task of which was not only to anticipate "thunderstorms" and to develop military strategies accordingly—the main task of think tanks during the Second World War—but primarily to find out how to overcome any rejection by the population of such a commitment. In Russia, this strategy has been accompanied by the establishment of a new ideological style. Obviously, Russian think tanks are increasingly appropriating concepts from those Russian artists who once struggled under the Soviet regime and Socialist Realism. The mouse speaks of "Imperial Realism." It is the symptom of the Crimea virus.

In contrast to Socialist Realism, conceived by Stalin and based on the future aims of the avant-garde, Imperial Realism steps back into the realm of history. It needs the past in order to construct an illusion of the future. Like the game character Pac-Man, who munches his way through the labyrinth, Imperial Realism also needs "power pills" every now and then in order to keep on feeding. With the pills of Socialist, Religious, and Capitalist Realism inside it, it devours all of the "monsters" of protest, such as Activism, Sots Art, and Conceptualism.

With regard to today's Russia, the perfidious effect of Imperial Realism lies both in the elimination of irony from public perception and in the expulsion of all forms of protest, which from now on no longer need to be politically suppressed, for the masses have assumed the role of the judge. In the Russian President's question and answer session on September 18, 2014, the editor-in-chief of the magazine *New Literary Observer*, Irina Prokhorova, sister of the former presidential candidate Mikhail Prokhorov, diagnosed a "hunt for

107

representatives of other positions, condemnation of artists expressing criticism and the development of a new ideological style" in her assessment of the cultural situation in Russia. Without hesitation, the former agent said in no uncertain terms: "I do not *feel* any particular change in our country."[27] Putin may even be right in this spiritualist perception; the change is not entirely new. The outbreak of the Crimea virus only added to the fact that under the new constellation many people, including creatives and artists who thus far had publicly criticized Putin, not only endorsed the actions of the president, but were actually proud of their country. The few who now criticize something are either devoured by the masses or by Imperial Realism. Putin is anything but broken.[28] "Putin is *our* everything!" is the popular motto in Russia.

The use of pictorial recollections related to Crimea creates a new ideological identification of the Russian people and obscures the outlook for political alternatives within the country. The reference to Russia's own history with regard to Crimea serves as justification and is an attempt to authenticate the annexation of Crimea. This strategy leads to different strata of society expressing their solidarity with one another and disputing factions that are joining forces in their views to bring about political decisions in the interest of the nation. With the return of Crimea, the healing sense of belonging, which had been lost, was now spreading among the Russian people.[29] The trancemedia agent Putin—under this constellation, which is new to him as well—can assert without hesitation that the pro-Russian separatists, who act in the Ukrainian Donbass apparently without orders from above, are only "simple folk" who

want to defend "their" country, which was once the Stakhanovite working class heart of Russia (fig. 11). Just as Putin did with Crimea. So here, too, a *fifth column* is at work, one that exposes its clandestine nature and, precisely because of that, appears suggestive. Here, too, the aim is not to annex Donbass directly, but to get the population to agree to the construction of New Russia. Here, too, the agents have been very successful.

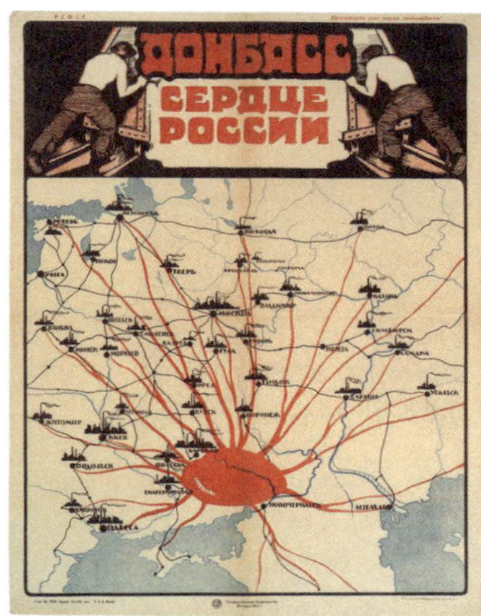

Fig. / Abb. 11: Donbass – The Heart of Russia / Russlands Herz, 1921

The symptom of the Crimea virus, however, has not only spread throughout Russia. International politics has also been infected and is in a state of profound upheaval since the annexation of the peninsula. Objective reporting is crumbling, the few critical voices are being lost in the masses, and Europe's think tanks are preparing the public for rearmament: Germany's "increased power" is closely linked to "new German responsibility," according to a paper by the Stiftung Wissenschaft und Politik (German Institute for International and Security Affairs).[30] According to Joachim Gauck, Germany's federal president at the time, it is time to abandon the "restraint that was required

108

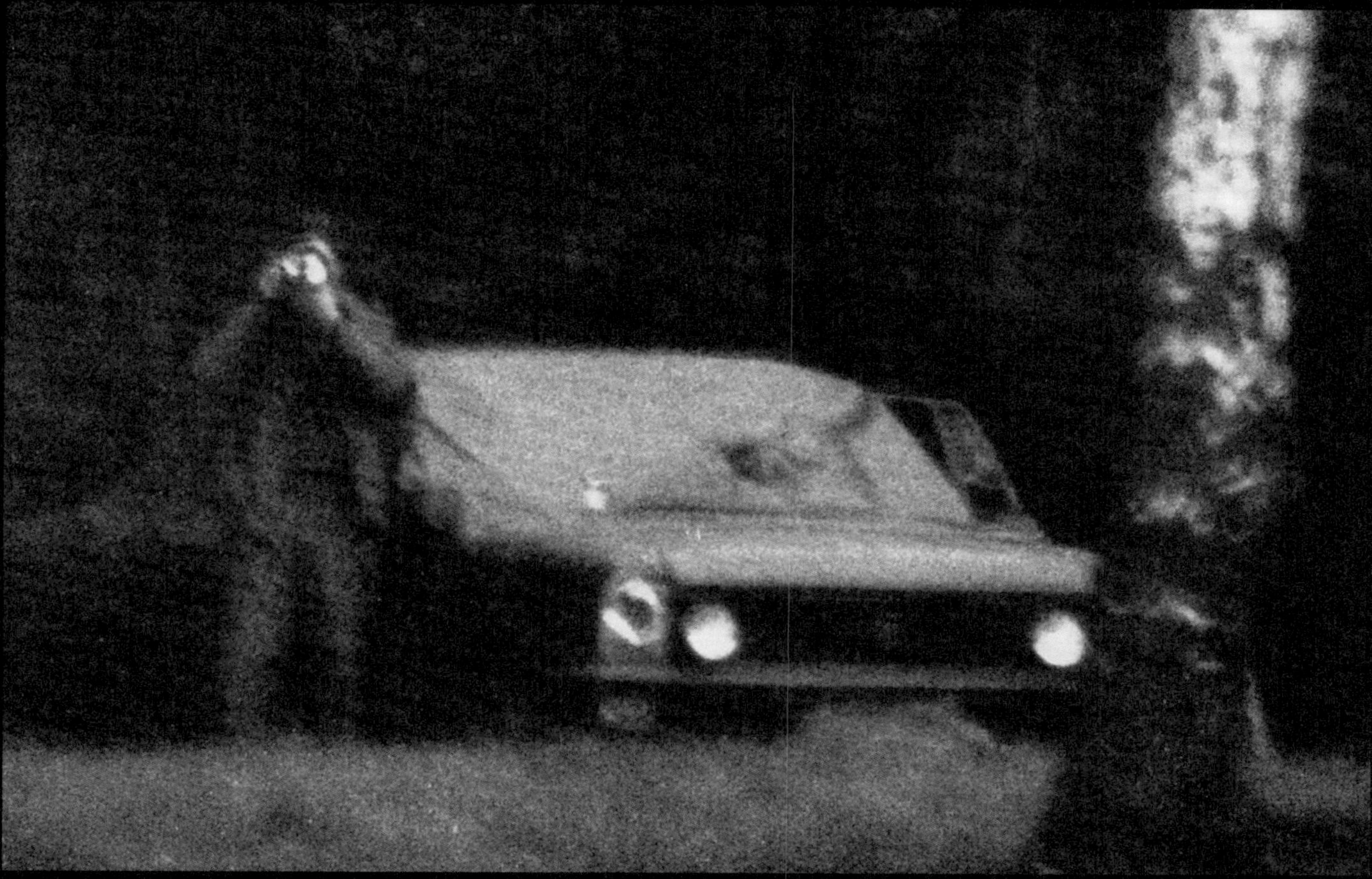

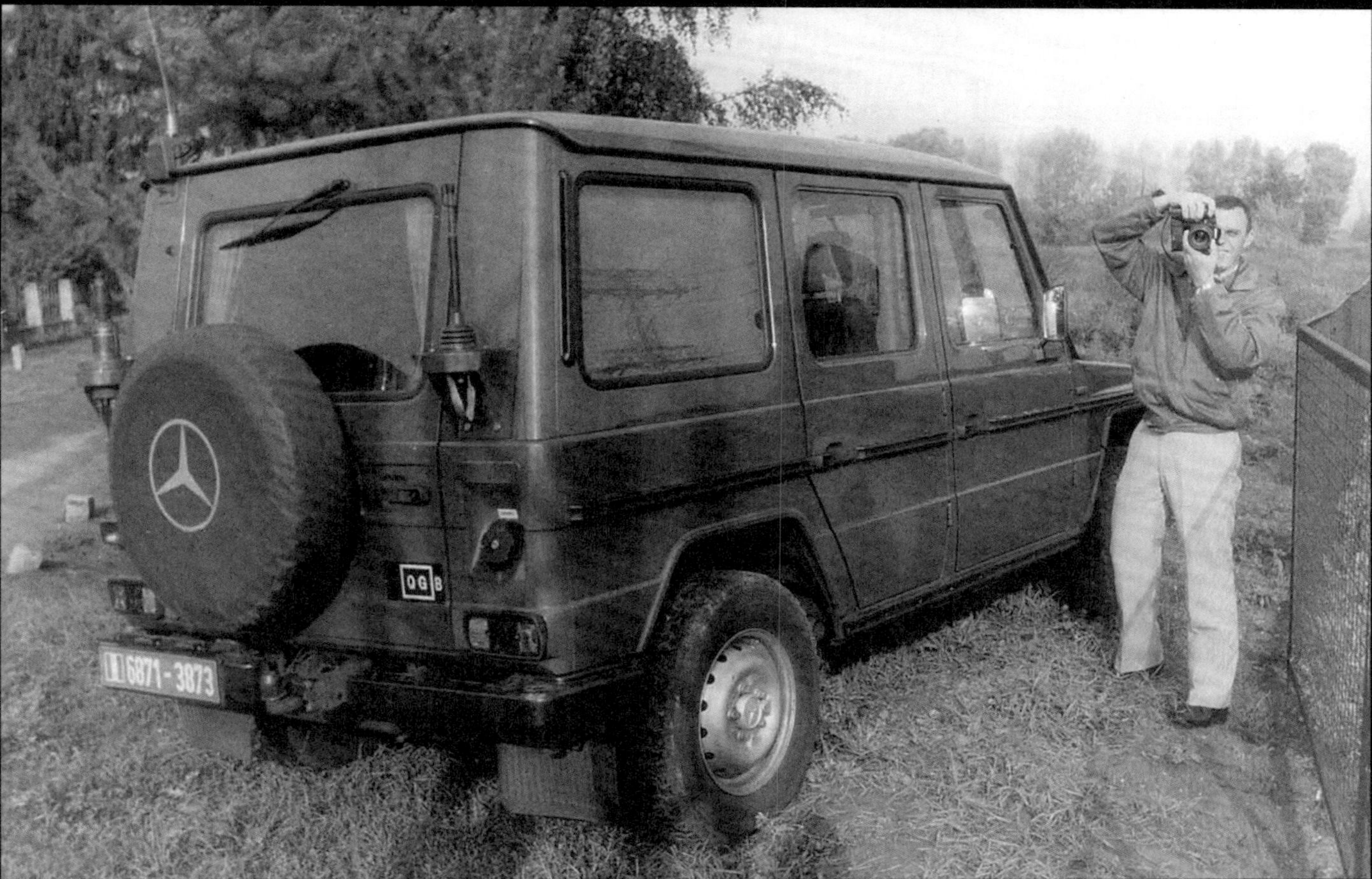

OGB
6871-3873

in past decades" and to face up to a "new responsibility"; he no longer wants to view the use of "military force" as out of the question.[31]

The strategy of Imperial Realism is accompanied by a demonstration of self-confidence in Europe, too, and particularly in Germany.[32] This self-confidence results especially from the time already lived, a time in memory mode. This is no different with regard to Russia. The difference lies solely in the way history is processed and dealt with. Whereas Germany, with the help of and under pressure from the occupying powers, began to come to terms with its history, Russia after the collapse of the Soviet Union was subjected to self-therapy. Films were an important medium of this self-therapy in the late twentieth century, most of which were shot in Crimea. It is this mediatic historiography that the political affinity of the Kremlin picks up on today, allowing the national myth to be resurrected on set, in familiar scenery. And the aim is not the creation of an "eternal return," the constantly propagated Nietzschean sense of history in Russia, but the creeping implementation of a recurring simulacrum. With the annexation of Crimea, the Russian people returned to the illusory notions of the good times, since Crimea was considered a place of recreation, an island of dreams. Without actually going on a journey, the Russian people from the spring of 2014 onward saw themselves transported by the media to Crimea, which became a place of compensation for the loss of a lost reality.

In the dissemination of the new sense of belonging to the homeland, Imperial Realism in Russia not only limits itself to the usurpation of critical art, but it also ties in with the ideals of its big brother. Heroic deeds are praised: artists and intellectuals who toe the line are honored. Even "serious" political orchestrations are the order of the day: at a new Yalta conference on August 14, 2014, which was attended by all the great Russian politicians, Vladimir Zhirinovskiy distanced himself from his old proposal for a new anthem: it was originally meant to be made up of three melodies from the most favored anthems, and its lyrics were to contain modern words like "Cosmos," "Internet," and "New Russia." And of course he made a new proposal: the replacement of the Russian flag with the old black-yellow-white flag of the Russian Empire, and the introduction of the old national anthem of the Russian Empire. Between 1833 and 1917, this anthem contained the following lines:

> God, save the Tsar!
> Strong, sovereign,
> Reign for glory, for our glory!
>
> Reign to make foes fear,
> Orthodox Tsar!
> God, save the Tsar![33]

Putin took to the floor immediately after Zhirinovskiy's proposals, which were accompanied by applause, and said that they were once again "personal wishes of Vladimir Volfovich" and that they did not always correspond to the "political aspirations of the Russian Federation."[34] What does indeed not collide with the aspirations of the federation is the issuing of an anniversary ruble in "honor of the annexation of Crimea to Russia." Instead of a numerical value and the national coat of arms, two objects of desire characterize the silver-plated coin: "*our* Putin" and "*our* Crimea"—an orthodox-phantasmatic signification,[35] embodying the new social "wealth"

of Russia. As long as the people in
Russia are seduced by this politically
controlled fetish, by this symbol
without content, and as long as this
symbol is considered legal tender,
the country can hardly come to terms
with its own past. The length of dura-
tion of this state of singularity,
which replaces history with the utterly
referenceless nature of a recurring
simulacrum,[36] depends on the effectiveness of the pills that have been gobbled up.

Originally published as: "Diagnose: Krim," in Wladimir
Velminski, *Diagnose: Krim* (Berlin: Merve Verlag, 2015),
pp. 162–86. Stylistic conventions have been adjusted to
conform to the publication at hand.

1   Eva Horn, *The Secret War: Treason, Espionage, and Modern Fiction*, trans. Geoffrey Winthrop-Young (Evanston, IL, 2013), p. 189.

2   This practice is quite common in Russian contemporary art. See Tomash Glants, "Iskusstvo kak Shpionazh," in *Mesto Pechati: Zhurnal interpretatsionnogo iskusstva; Nomer Chetyrnadtsat'* (Moscow, 2003), pp. 20–40.

3   Viktor Pivovarov, *Sonja und die Engel*, booklet 7 (Prague, 1996), p. 62.

4   Komar & Melamid, *Komar & Melamid's American Dreams* (Philadelphia, 2000), pp. 68–71.

5   Ilya Kabakov and Emilia Kabakov, *An Alternative History of Art: Rosenthal, Kabakov, Spivak* (Berlin, 2005).

6   Viktor Pivovarov, *Svidetel'stvo sovremennikov / Reports of the Contemporaries* (Prague, 2013).

7   Ibid., p. 21.

8   See Heike Winkel, "Schreibversuche: Kollektive Vorlagen und individuelle Strategien in den 'Briefen der Werktätigen,'" in *Die Musen der Macht: Medien in der sowjetischen Kultur der 20er und 30er Jahre*, ed. Jurij Murašov and Georg Witte (Munich, 2003), pp. 59–79, p. 63.

9   Viktor Pivovarov, *O lyubvi slova i izobrazheniya* (Moscow, 2004), p. 49.

10 Ibid.

11 Ibid.

12 Kabakov 2005 (see note 5), p. 18.

13 Pivovarov 2013 (see note 6), chapter "Morning in the Mausoleum."

14 Ibid., p. 62.

15 See Boris Groys, *The Total Art of Stalinism: Avant-Garde, Aesthetic Dictatorship, and Beyond*, trans. Charles Rougle (Princeton, NJ, 1992); Vladimir Paperny, *Kul'tura dva* (Moscow, 1996); Viktor Tupitsyn, *Kommunal'ny (post) modernizm: Russkoe iskusstvo vtoroy poloviny XX veka* (Moscow, 1998).

16 Pivovarov 2013 (see note 6), chapter "Lenin and Stalin on a sketching session in Nemchinovka."

17 Ibid., p. 62.

18 According to the gallery's press release from January 26, 2009.

19 See the press release dated January 18, 2009. See: http://regions.ru/news/2190868/ (all URLs accessed in March 2020).

20 Putin draws a cat: http://www.youtube.com/watch?v=1_rhqmknudI.

21 See: www.youtube.com/watch?v=vYRswPspgLc.

22 President Obama's speech on NSA surveillance reform, January 17, 2014, in Washington, DC.

23 See: www.1tv.ru/news/polit/256730.

24 See Fredric Jameson, *A Singular Modernity* (London, 2012), pp. 139–210.

25 Pivovarov 2013 (see note 6), chapter "Stalin and Mouse."

26 Ibid., p. 66.

27 See: https://www.youtube.com/watch?v=Lz1B8o9p0Ts.

28 See Mischa Gabowitsch, *Putin kaputt? Russlands neue Protestkultur* (Berlin, 2013).

29 See Jean-Luc Nancy, "The Intruder," in *Corpus*, trans. Richard A. Rand (New York, 2008), pp. 161–70.

30 See "Neue Macht, Neue Verantwortung: Elemente einer deutschen Außen- und Sicherheitspolitik für eine Welt im Umbruch," a paper by the Stiftung Wissenschaft und Politik (SWP) and the German Marshall Fund of the United States (GMF) (Berlin, 2013), https://internationalepolitik.de/de/neue-macht-neue-verantwortung.

31 See Frank Deppe, *imperialer realismus?: über eliten, experten und journalisten und die "neue deutsche verantwortung"; eine flugschrift* (Hamburg, 2014).

32 See Slavoj Žižek, *Enjoy Your Symptom!: Jacques Lacan in Hollywood and Out* (1992; repr., New York, 2008).

33 The anthem was officially adopted on December 31, 1833, and existed until February 23, 1917, when Tsar Nicholas II was overthrown. The text is by Vasily Andreyevich Zhukovsky, the melody by Alexei Fyodorovich Lvov.

34 See: http://lifenews.ru/news/138403.

35 Pierre Klossowski, *Living Currency*, ed. Vernon W. Cisney, Nicolae Morar, and Daniel W. Smith (London, 2017), p. 51.

36 See Jean Baudrillard, *Impossible Exchange*, trans. Chris Turner (2001; repr., London, 2011), pp. 135–40.

Das exponierte Agententum
Wladimir Velminski

1. Geheimoperationen

Die Macht des Agenten wirkt im Verborgenen, dann, wenn der Agent zum Medium wird.[1] Als Medium kreiert der Agent seine eigene Welt, seine eigene Wirklichkeit, die scheinbar kaum einen Bezug zur Realität hat. Doch dieser Schein trügt, denn genau darin verbirgt sich das Potenzial des Agenten: Er hat immer mindestens zwei Spielzüge im Blick, mit denen er die Realität verkehren kann.

Viktor Pivovarov hat solche Nuancen erkundet. Seine Arbeit *Operation „Doppeltes Scheinen"* von 1994 ist eine von 20 Geheimoperationen eines Agenten (Abb. 1, S. 101), die dieser gemeinsam mit der verdeckten Gruppe *Scheinende Blume* in Fjorden durchgeführt hat. Sie gehören zum Zyklus *Agent in Norwegen*, den Pivovarov in die Bereiche „Geheimnisvolle Geräte" und „mystische Projekte", „verschlüsselte Nachrichten" und „verdeckte Gruppierungen" einteilt und damit den Interessensbereich des Agenten benennt. Anders als ein „klassischer" Agent, der als Verwandlungskünstler bemüht ist, seine Verborgenheit geheim zu halten, um wirken zu können, verfolgt der Agent in Norwegen das Ziel, seine Verborgenheit zu exponieren, um eben dadurch suggestiv zu wirken.[2] Aus der Gesamtschau des Materials wird deutlich, dass es nicht um Militärbasen oder Geheimwaffen geht, sondern um „das private und schöpferische Leben der Intellektuellen, die der Agent beschattet hatte".[3]

Eine solche ästhetische Form des Verborgenen, die in der Literatur recht verbreitet ist, haben sich die Künstler sowohl der *Soz Art* als auch des *Moskauer Konzeptualismus* seit den 1970er Jahren angeeignet. Verwiesen sei an dieser Stelle auf die fiktiven Arbeiten von Nikolaj Buchumov,[4] die Komar & Melamid schufen oder das erfundene Leben und Werk von Charles Rosenthal,[5] das auf Kabakov zurückgeht. Pivovarov fügt jedoch immer noch eine zusätzliche Ebene hinzu. So handelt es sich bei dem Zyklus *Agent in Norwegen* nicht um das eigene Schaffen des fiktiven Agenten, sondern um die von ihm gesammelten Materialien. Während das Gesicht des Agenten im Verborgenen bleibt, kommt die Tätigkeit des Agententums zum Vorschein, um den Zuschauer in das Spiel des Verborgenen einzuweihen, ihn zu infizieren, ihn auf seine Seite zu locken und somit einen ästhetischen Kollektivkörper zu bilden, eine Fünfte Kolonne der Kunst.

Ein Verfahren, das Pivovarov auch in seinem aktuellen Buch *Svidetel'stvo sovremennikov / Reports of the Contemporaries* (dt. Zeugnisse von Zeitgenossen), in dem das gleichnamige Album veröffentlicht ist, anwendet.[6] Gleich zu Beginn wird darauf verwiesen, dass es sich bei dem Album um den Fundus eines Bibliophilen und späteren Verlegers Sergej Nitočkin handle:

Es war eine Mappe, in der ein anonymer Sammler Erinnerungen an Lenin und Stalin verschiedenster, oft einfacher Menschen aus dem Volk gesammelt hat. Diese Erinnerungen unterschieden sich wesentlich von denen, die in der Sowjetunion in Millionenauflagen erschienen sind. Daher wundert es nicht, dass man über die Existenz dieser Sammlung nichts gewusst hat. Den Texten waren Zeichnungen zugeordnet, die der Sammler möglicherweise selbst angefertigt hat.[7]

Pivovarov konterkariert die in der Sowjetunion propagierte Form öffentlicher Meinungsäußerung von Arbeitern, die, so war es Lenins Wunsch gewesen, „über ihren Alltag, ihre Interessen und ihre Arbeit" schrieben und diese Texte dann als sogenannte Briefe der Werktätigen in Tageszeitungen veröffentlichten.[8] Insofern sich der Leser des Albums auf das Spiel einlässt, wird er zum Ermittler, der die verstreut herumliegenden Puzzleteile zusammensetzen muss, um einen vollständigen Einblick in die Erinnerungen an Lenin und Stalin zu bekommen.

In dem Verschachtelungsverfahren, das Pivovarov auf Inhalt und Form des Albums anwendet, findet sich sowohl der Bild-Text-Bezug als auch der erzählerische Gestus wieder, die das Schaffen des Künstlers seit Jahrzehnten prägen. Der Mitbegründer des Moskauer Konzeptualismus hat oft darauf hingewiesen, dass das Bild in Russland einer Reform unterzogen wurde, während es die westlichen Konzeptkünstler als in seiner Form veraltet ablehnten. In Russland saugt das Bild also didaktische und propagandistische außerkünstlerische Formen in sich auf.[9] Zwar hat Pivovarov keine ideologischen Plakate und Stra-

ßenschilder in der Sowjetunion anfertigen müssen, doch auch er führte ein Doppelleben, denn offiziell arbeitete er als Buch- und Zeitschriftenillustrator. Sein 1979 gezeichnetes Schriftbild für die Kinderzeitschrift *Vesëlye kartinki* (dt. Lustige Bildchen), das bis heute auf dem Titelblatt des Magazins steht, wie auch seine Illustrationen der Hans Christian Anderson Märchen haben in Russland Kultstatus. Im Verborgenen ist der Agent am mächtigsten. Mit Blick auf das vom konzeptuellen Denken reformierte Bild schreibt Pivovarov: „Es wurde nicht nur sichtbar, sondern auch hörbar, erwarb eine Stimme, begann zu sprechen, zuerst einzelne Wörter, danach Sätze, dann umfangreiche Texte."[10] Mit Erschaffung der konzeptuellen Alben und Bildzyklen hat das Bild die Funktion eines konzeptuellen Agenten eingenommen und als solcher alle möglichen Textformen, sowohl Erzählungen und Romane als auch bürokratische Dokumente, vollkommen durchforstet;[11] Kabakov, der zusammen mit Pivovarov das Album als Genre einführte, bemerkt in diesem Zusammenhang, dass das Bild sogar wie ein „Bewusstseinsfeld" fungiert.[12] Eben in dieser Tradition steht auch Pivovarovs *Svidetel'stvo sovremennikov / Reports of the Contemporaries* (1988–2001). Siebzehn kurze Texte stehen siebzehn Bildern und am Ende je einem kulturhistorischen Kommentar gegenüber, der mit zahlreichen Fotografien belegt ist. Es sind also mehrere Akteure im Spiel, der eine verweist auf den anderen und umgekehrt. So berichtet eine Mitarbeiterin des Bewachungspersonals, M. I. Potapova, von ihrer ehemaligen Nachbarin Marija Evdokimova, die als Putzfrau im Mausoleum gearbeitet hat (Abb. 2, S. 102):

Am frühen Morgen, wenn sie kam,
musste sie die Kerzen löschen, den
Kristallsarg und die goldenen Ketten
mit speziellem Reinigungsmittel
wischen, Mischkan in den Schrank
einräumen und die Böden putzen.
Recht viel Arbeit, doch die Bezahlung
war gut und in der Kantine war
das Essen für die alten Bolschewiki
kostenfrei.[13]

Der dazugehörige Kommentar gibt an,
die Erzählerin habe vielleicht etwas
verwechselt. So spricht sie von „Mischkan", einem transportablen Tempel, den
das Volk Israel auf seiner Wanderung
durch die Wüste nach dem Auszug aus
Ägypten mitführte und dessen wichtigste sakrale Funktion in der Bewahrung
der Bundeslade bestand. Indem der
Kommentar sich aber auf das Bild bezieht, auf dem offensichtlich die Bundeslade festgehalten ist, wird die Irritation
aufgehoben.[14] Indes auch diese Aufklärung ist trügerisch, sollen die Bilder
doch nach den Texten entstanden sein.
Dieses konzeptuelle Ensemble aus
Verwirrungen, das offensichtlich auch
Soz Art-Elemente gebraucht, verfügt
in Gestalt der Verschleierungspoesie
über eine Wirkungskraft, mit deren Hilfe
es ihm gelingt, eine verdeckte Untersuchung der russischen Kultur durchzuführen.[15] Viel offensichtlicher wird dieses
Verfahren am Beispiel *Lenin und Stalin
während der Malstudien in Nemčinovka*
(Abb. 3, S. 103), das auf den Bericht des
Fahrers E. K. Liepa zurückgeht:

Jeden Sonntag fuhren Wladimir
Iljitsch und Josef Wissarionowitsch
gemeinsam nach Nemčinovka, um
Malstudien anzufertigen. Lenin
zeichnete vom Wind durchdrungene
Bäume, zerrissene Wolken, tosenden
Roggen. Stalin bevorzugte eher

Landschaften „mit Stimmung" –
„Der frühe Nebelfrost", „Die herbstlichen Weiten", „Der Abend graut".[16]

Das dem Kurztext zugehörige Bild habe,
so wird es im Kommentar festgehalten,
die Thesen der Kulturstudien der 1990er
Jahre vorweg genommen, die Lenin
und noch mehr Stalin als Fortführer der
russischen Avantgarde auslegen.[17]
Auch die Umgebung ist nicht zufällig
gewählt, handelt es sich bei *Nemčinovka*
doch um einen Ort nahe Moskau, an
dem Kasimir Malewitsch beerdigt wurde.
Neben solchen spielerischen Elementen,
beleuchtet das völlig fiktive Narrativ
auch reale Splitter der Vergangenheit,
die im russischen Alltag heute nicht
nur stillschweigend im Unbewussten
rumoren, sondern auch an die Oberfläche
gelangen und Bewunderer finden.

2. Muster der Täuschung

Bereits als Ministerpräsident hat sich
Wladimir Putin auf dem Feld der Kunst
versucht. Auf dem Weihnachtsmarkt
in St. Petersburg im Jahr 2008 führte er
sein zeichnerisches Talent vor und
fertigte bei Eiseskälte ein Bild zum Thema
„Muster" an (Abb. 4, S. 104). Solche
„künstlerischen Aktionen" haben in
Russland Tradition. Immer wieder
werden „Persönlichkeiten des Landes"
eingeladen, in der *Nacht vor Weihnachten*,
so der Titel einer Erzählung von Nikolai
Gogol, Alphabet-Bilder zu zeichnen,
die auch inhaltlich mit der Erzählung
des Klassikers korrespondieren sollen.
Putin bekam den russischen Buchstaben
У (dt. U) und zeichnete seine Variation
von Узор ([uzor], dt. Muster, Abb. 5,
S. 104). Zwei Wochen später wurde das
Gemälde *Muster auf angefrorenem
Fenster* auf einer Auktion für 37 Millionen Rubel (damals ca. 900.000 EUR)

verkauft. Die Moskauer Galerie Unsere
Künstler, die sich auf „wahre russische
Kunst" spezialisiert hat, erwarb das
Gemälde des „jungen Künstlers".[18] In der
Presse kursierten Nachrichten, Putins
Bild sei teurer als Malewitschs *Schwarzes
Quadrat*, das angeblich im Jahr 2002
für 32 Millionen Rubel für die Ermitage
erworben worden war.[19] Dieser obskure
Vergleich hat etwas in sich. Malewitsch
hat sein *Schwarzes Quadrat* selbst als
eine Ikone der Moderne beworben. Putins
Muster wurde sofort als Ikone wahrge-
nommen und ritualisiert (Abb. 6, S. 104).
Das Küssen des hochgehaltenen und
noch ungeschützten „heiligen Bildes" –
das in der orthodoxen Kirche mit zwei-
maligem Bekreuzigen und einer Verbeugung vor dem ehrfürchtig vollzogenen
Kuss, sowie anschließendem Bekreuzigen
und einer Verbeugung zum Abschluss
einhergeht – ist ein deutlicher Beleg
dafür.

Auch als wiedergewählter Präsident
bleibt Putin der Kunst treu. Als er
2013 zu Beginn des Schuljahres eine aus
der Staatskasse unterstützte Schule
in Kurgan besucht und ihm eine junge
Lehrerin eine neue interaktive Tafel
vorstellt, zeigt der „junge Künstler" sein
Können. Während die offensichtlich
angespannte Lehrerin die Vorteile des
Whiteboards erklärt, mit einem speziel-
len Stift *1. September* darauf schreibt
und betont, die Tafel sei für die Schüler
besonders spannend, weil sie auch
mit nur einem Finger darauf schreiben
könnten, tritt der Präsident an die
Tafel. Mit seinem Finger zeichnet er ein
lustiges Bildchen, das er mit einer phal-
lusartigen Säule beginnt. Während
in der Klasse Ruhe herrscht, muss die
Lehrerin ihr hysterisches Lachen unter-
drücken. Nachdem Putin fertig ist,
tritt er mit den Worten „Für Sie zur
Erinnerung" von der Tafel zurück. Auf

die aus der Klasse gestellte Frage, was die
Zeichnung denn darstellen solle, hält
Putin die rechte Hand neben den Mund
und verrät: „Eine Katze von hinten".
Unter dem Lachen der Anwesenden ver-
lässt der Präsident den Raum.[20]

Zweifelsohne lassen sich solche
„künstlerischen" Machtdemonstrationen
eines Selbstdarstellers aus vielen Perspektiven deuten. An dieser Stelle soll es
aber darum gehen, den Fokus noch
einmal auf die Krim zu richten, den Ort,
an dem Putin seine künstlerische Strategie bündelte. Während sich die maskierten „grünen Männchen" auf der Insel
verbreiteten und der russische Präsident
mit dieser Tatsache konfrontiert wurde, verhielt er sich wie einst die Mitglieder
von *Pussy Riot*, als sie verhört wurden;
auch er behauptete, mit der *Aktion*
nichts zu tun zu haben. Die maskierten
Männer seien keine russischen Soldaten,
und überhaupt habe das mit einer Mili-
täraktion nichts zu tun, die Männer
verhielten sich doch freundlich und seien
höflich. Während sich Putins *Fünfte
Kolonne*, diese hochgerüsteten Agenten
(Abb. 7, S. 105), die aufgrund ihrer
Maskierung alle gleich aussahen und,
ähnlich einem Agent Smith-Virus, der
die gesamte *Matrix* infizierte, die Krim
okkupierten, blieb dem Westen, von der
Ukraine ganz zu schweigen, nichts anderes übrig, als sich wie die Lehrerin vor
der Tafel zu verhalten. Die „Geheimope-
ration" Krim war ein *Muster*beispiel.

3. Der Witz des Agenten

Im Russland des Jahres 2014 erzählen
sich die Leute wieder einen Stierlitz-
Witz. Der Agent Stierlitz ist die heroische
Figur einer Reihe von Spiongeschichten,
die Julian Semënov, gerüchteweise
selbst ein KGB-Mitarbeiter, in den Jahren
1921–1967 verfasste. Die Abenteuer von

116

Maksim Maksimovič Isaeev, alias Max Otto von Stierlitz, während des Zweiten Weltkriegs in Berlin gingen in einer sowjetischen Fernsehserie *Semnadcat' mgnovenij vesny* (dt. Siebzehn Augenblicke des Frühlings) auf, die zum russischen Filmkanon gehört; die Witze beziehen sich ausschließlich auf die Fernsehserie. Besagter Witz beschreibt eine Feier der deutschen Obersturmbannführer, bei der auch der russische Spion Stierlitz zugegen ist. Die SS-Offiziere heben ihre Gläser zu dem Toast: „Auf den Sieg!" Bevor alle anstoßen, fügt der Standartenführer Stierlitz hinzu: „Auf *unseren* Sieg!" Die List des Sowjet-Agenten besteht nicht nur darin, sich durch die Hinzufügung des Possessivpronomens von dem Toast der SS-Offiziere zu distanzieren, sondern zusätzlich darin, die Nazis dadurch auf ihren eigenen Niedergang zum Anstoßen zu bringen.

Dieses Possessivpronomen *unser* (rus. svoj, svoja bzw. naš, naše) ist in Russland seit Jahren omnipräsent. Es gibt *Unser Radio, Unsere Küche, Unser Kino, Unsere Leute, die* Parteijugend *Unsere* und nicht zuletzt die Galerie Unsere Künstler. Auch in Bezug auf die Krim vor und nach der Annexion wurde das besitzanzeigende Fürwort verwendet: *Unsere Krim*. Aus den maskierten Agenten auf der Insel, Soldaten ohne Abzeichen, die anfangs eher abwertend als „grüne Männchen" bezeichnet wurden, schuf man eine Kompagnie, die den *Unser*-Status unterstützen sollte. Aufnäher wurden in Umlauf gebracht, mit denen sich die „grünen Männchen" auf der Krim identifizieren sollten (Abb. 8, S. 106). Mit angehobener Pfote sitzt eine Katze neben einem Soldaten mit einem Kalaschnikow-Gewehr. Über der Darstellung steht „Höfliche Menschen", darunter „Höfliche, nette, *unsere*".

Am 10. April 2014 trat ein Ensemble der russischen Armee auf der Krim auf; die neu verfasste Hymne an die „Höflichen Menschen" war Teil des Repertoires.[21] Die ab August 2014 verkauften T-Shirts und Schutzhüllen für Smartphones zeigen das Bild des Agenten hinter den Agenten, den „höflichsten aller Menschen", wie die Unterschrift unter dem Bild besagt (Abb. 9, S. 106).

Es ist keine Neuigkeit, dass die Sprache eine der wichtigsten Waffen des Agenten ist. Seit der Entstehung der Geheimdienste geht es darum, Informationen über Feind und Freund zu gewinnen, um sich einen Vorteil zu verschaffen und die Gegenseite zu manipulieren. Die Enthüllungen von Edward Snowden haben deutlich gemacht, dass jeder von uns ein potenzieller Feind ist. Barack Obama hat dies in seiner kulturhistorisch angelegten Rede über die Spionage bestätigt und allen, die sich seit Snowdens Veröffentlichungen empörten, *klar* gemacht:

> Now let me be clear: our intelligence agencies will continue to gather information about the intentions of governments – as opposed to ordinary citizens – around the world, in the same way that the intelligence services of every other nation does. We will not apologize simply because our services may be more effective.[22]

Dieser rhetorischen Demonstration imperialer Macht, die alle Militärparaden in den Schatten stellt, musste der ehemalige Agent in Dresden etwas entgegensetzen. Als sich Putin am 17. April 2014 in der traditionellen Fragestunde im russischen Staatsfernsehen dem Volk stellte und zugab, auf der Krim bewusst verdeckt operiert zu haben, wurde der in Russland untergetauchte amerikanische

Geheimdienstler per Video zugeschaltet. Die Frage Snowdens, ob Russland, genau wie Amerika, die Kommunikation der Menschen flächendeckend überwache, verneinte Putin mit der Berufung auf strenge Regularien. Doch bevor er diese Antwort gab, holte der ehemalige Leiter des russischen Geheimdienstes kurz aus: „Lieber Mister Snowden! Sie sind ein ehemaliger Agent, auch ich habe mit Spionage gewisse Erfahrungen gesammelt." Während das Publikum im Studio lacht und applaudiert, fügt der russische Präsident hinzu, bevor er die auf Englisch gestellte Frage seines Kollegen beantwortet: „Wir beide sprechen also eine professionelle Sprache."[23] Es ist eine Sprache, die nur von Agenten beherrscht wird und deren Techniken auch in der Rhetorik für die Öffentlichkeit eingesetzt werden. Stierlitz, Snowden und Putin beherrschen sie in Perfektion, „ehemalige" Agenten gibt es nicht. Alle anderen fühlen sich auf diesem Terrain fremd. Wenn Angela Merkel nach ihrem Telefonat mit Putin vor dem Krim-Referendum behauptet, der russische Präsident lebe in seiner eigenen Welt, so hat sie recht, unterstreicht damit aber ihre eigene Unkenntnis dieser Welt, die mehr als früher von gewitzten Agenten beherrscht wird. Um in dieser Welt zurechtzukommen und den *Witzen* folgen zu können, muss eine neue Sprache erlernt werden.[24]

4. Imperialer Realismus

Eine der Seiten von Pivovarovs Album *Svidetel'stvo sovremennikov* trägt den Titel *Stalin i myš* (dt. Stalin und Maus). Auf der Zeichnung ist Stalin zu sehen, dessen Augen entweder ganz geschlossen oder nach unten gesenkt sind und eine kleine graue Maus anschauen, die er, der uniformierte Generalissimus, in seiner

Faust hält (Abb. 10, S. 107). In der Notiz eines gewissen N. Osipov, der wiederum der Sohn eines Offiziers aus dem persönlichen Leibwächterdienst Stalins war, heißt es:

Zu den Sitzungen des Politbüros brachte Stalin in seiner Hosentasche eine Maus mit. Wenn irgendeine schwierige Frage nach einer Lösung verlangte, ging Stalin in ein hinteres Zimmer, holte die Maus heraus und beriet sich mit ihr. Wenn er mit jemandem unzufrieden war, holte er die Maus aus der Hosentasche und drückte sie leicht in seiner Faust zusammen. Die Maus quietschte und im Sitzungssaal herrschte Totenstille.[25]

Im dazugehörigen Kommentar wird auf die Rolle der Maus in den Sagen und ihre Fähigkeit, Unwetter vorherzusehen, verwiesen.[26] Die Maus ist also Stalins *Think Tank*, dessen Aufgabe nicht nur darin besteht, „Unwetter" zu erahnen und entsprechend militärische Strategien auszuarbeiten, die Hauptaufgabe der *Think Tanks* während des Zweiten Weltkriegs, sondern in erster Linie zu ermitteln, wie die Ablehnung eines solchen Engagements in der Bevölkerung überwunden werden kann. In Russland geht diese Strategie mit der Begründung einer neuen ideologischen Stilrichtung einher. Offensichtlich eignen sich die russischen Denkfabriken zunehmend Konzepte derjenigen russischen Künstler an, die sich einst am Sowjetregime und am Sozialistischen Realismus abarbeiteten. Die Maus spricht vom *Imperialistischen Realismus*. Er ist das Symptom des Krim-Virus.

Anders als der von Stalin entworfene und an den Zukunftszielen der *Avantgarde* anknüpfende *Sozialistische Realismus*, tritt der *Imperialistische Realismus*

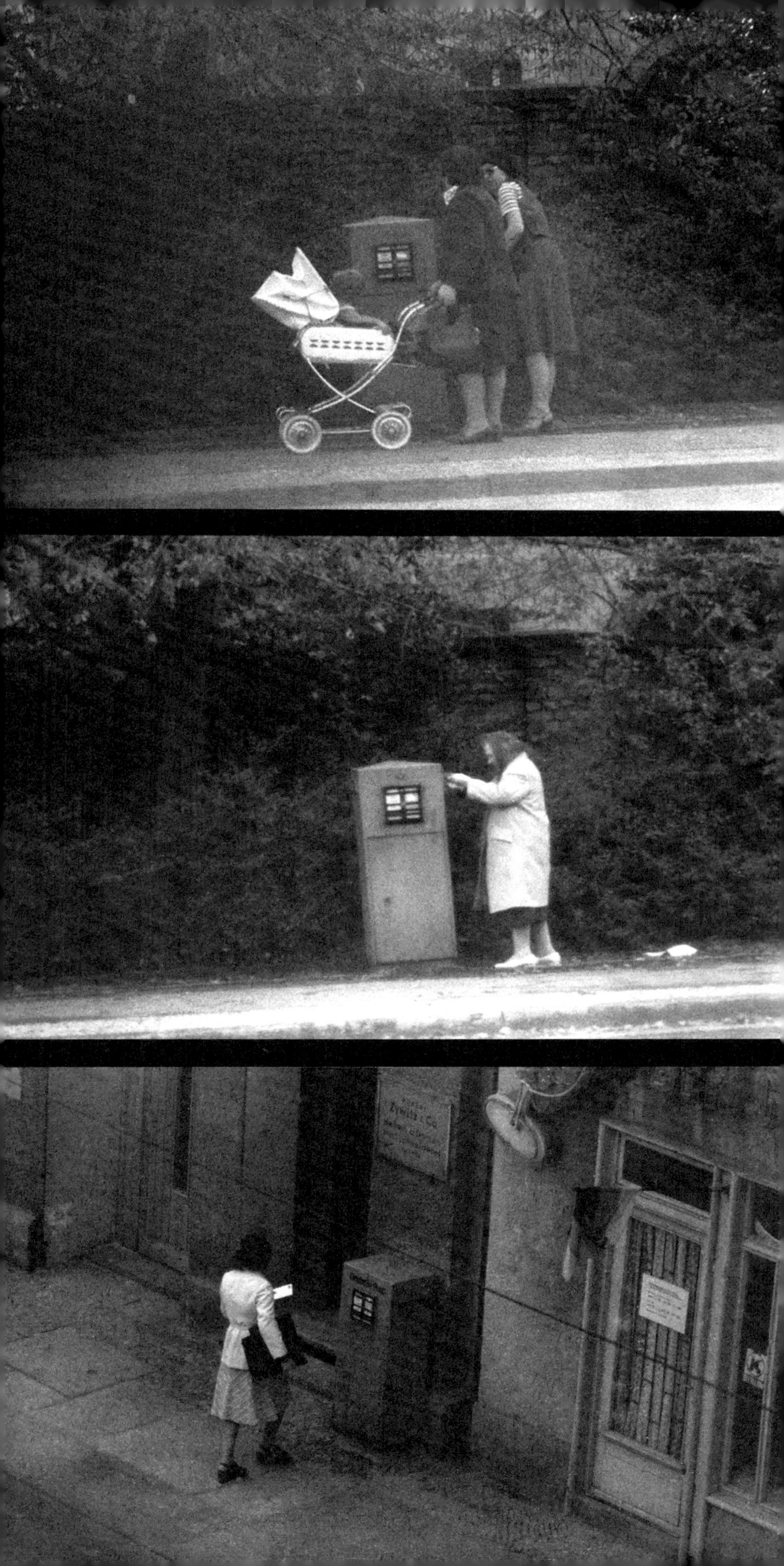

zurück in den Raum der Geschichte. Er braucht die Vergangenheit, um eine Illusion der Zukunft zu entwerfen. Wie die Spielfigur *Pac-Man*, die sich durchs Labyrinth frisst, braucht auch der *Imperialistische Realismus* immer wieder „Kraftpillen", um sich weiter durchzufressen. Die Pillen des *Sozialistischen*, *Religiösen* und *Kapitalistischen Realismus* intus, verschlingt er alle „Monster" des Protests, wie den *Aktivismus*, die *Soz Art* und den *Konzeptualismus*.

Mit Blick auf das heutige Russland ist der perfide Effekt des *Imperialistischen Realismus* sowohl die Beseitigung der Ironie aus der öffentlichen Wahrnehmung als auch die Vertreibung aller Protestformen, die fortan nicht mehr politisch unterbunden werden müssen – die Masse hat die Rolle des Richters übernommen. In der Fragerunde des russischen Präsidenten am 18. September 2014 diagnostizierte die Chefredakteurin der Zeitschrift *New Literary Review* Irina Prochorova, Schwester des ehemaligen Präsidentschaftskandidaten Michail Prochorov, eine „Hetzjagd auf Vertreter anderer Positionen, die Verurteilung von Kritik äußernden Künstlern sowie die Ausarbeitung einer neuen ideologischen Stilrichtung" bei Beurteilung der kulturellen Situation in Russland. Der ehemalige Agent sagte ohne zu zögern sehr deutlich: „Ich *fühle* keine besondere Veränderung in unserem Land."[27] Mit dieser spiritistischen Wahrnehmung mag Putin sogar recht haben, ganz neu ist die Veränderung nicht. Der Ausbruch des Krim-Virus hat nur zusätzlich dazu geführt, dass viele Menschen, darunter Kulturschaffende und Künstler, die Putin bis dahin öffentlich kritisiert hatten, unter der neuen Konstellation die Handlungen des Präsidenten nicht nur befürworten, sie sind stolz auf ihr Land. Die wenigen, die jetzt

noch etwas kritisieren, werden entweder von der Masse oder vom *Imperialistischen Realismus* verschlungen. Putin ist alles andere als kaputt.[28] „Putin ist *unser* alles!" lautet die weitverbreitete Losung in Russland.

Der Einsatz von mit der Krim zusammenhängenden Erinnerungsbildern, schafft eine neue ideologische Identifikation des russischen Volkes und verdeckt die Aussichten auf politische Alternativen im Land. Der Verweis auf die eigene Krim-Historie dient der Rechtfertigung und ist der Versuch, die Annexion der Krim zu be*glaubigen*. Diese Strategie führt dazu, dass unterschiedliche Schichten ihre Solidarität miteinander bekunden und disputierende Fraktionen sich in ihren Ansichten verbünden, um politische Entscheidungen im Sinne der Nation herbeizuführen. Durch die Rückkehr der Krim ist das fremd gewordene und zugleich heilende Gefühl der Verbundenheit in den russischen Menschen gedrungen.[29] Unter dieser auch für ihn neuen Konstellation kann der trancemediale Agent Putin ohne Zögern behaupten, dass die prorussischen Separatisten, die im ukrainischen *Donbass* scheinbar ohne Befehl von oben handeln, nur „einfache Menschen" sind, die „ihr" Land, das mal das Stachanow'sche Arbeiterherz von ganz Russland war (Abb. 11, S. 108), verteidigen wollen. Auf gleiche Weise wie Putin es mit der Krim getan hat. Auch hier ist also eine *Fünfte Kolonne* am Werk, eine die ihre Geheimhaltung exponiert und gerade dadurch suggestiv wirkt. Auch hier geht es nicht darum *Donbass* direkt zu annektieren, sondern die Bevölkerung dazu zu bringen, der Errichtung von Neurussland zu zustimmen. Auch hier verzeichnen die Agenten ihre Erfolge. Das Symptom des Krim-Virus hat sich aber nicht nur in Russland verbreitet, auch die internationale Politik ist infiziert und befindet sich seit der Annexion der Halbinsel in einem tiefgreifenden Umbruch. Die objektive Berichterstattung bröckelt, die wenigen kritischen Stimmen gehen in der Masse unter, die *Think Tanks* Europas bereiten die Öffentlichkeit auf Aufrüstung vor: Die „gewachsene Macht Deutschlands" ist eng mit „neuer deutscher Verantwortung" verbunden, heißt es in einem Papier der Stiftung Wissenschaft und Politik.[30] Nach Meinung des Bundespräsidenten Joachim Gauck ist es an der Zeit, die „Zurückhaltung, die in vergangenen Jahrzehnten geboten war", abzulegen und sich einer „neuen Verantwortung" zu stellen; den Einsatz „militärischer Gewalt" möchte er nicht mehr ausgeschlossen sehen.[31]

Die Strategie des *Imperialistischen Realismus* geht auch in Europa und besonders in Deutschland mit der Demonstration von Selbstbewusstsein einher.[32] Einem Selbstbewusstsein, das besonders aus der bereits gelebten Zeit resultiert, einer Zeit im Modus der Erinnerung. Dies ist mit Blick auf Russland nicht anders. Der Unterschied liegt allein in der Verarbeitung und im Umgang mit der Geschichte. Wo sich Deutschland mithilfe und unter dem Druck der Besatzungsmächte an die Aufarbeitung seiner Geschichte gemacht hat, war Russland nach dem Zerfall der Sowjetunion einer Selbsttherapie ausgesetzt. Wichtiges Medium dieser Selbsttherapie am Ende des 20. Jahrhunderts waren Filme, die zu großen Teilen auf der Krim gedreht wurden. An diese mediale Historiografie knüpft die politische Gewandtheit des Kremls heute an und lässt den nationalen Mythos am Set, in alter Kulisse, auferstehen. Und das Ziel dabei ist nicht etwa die Erschaffung einer „Ewigen Wiederkunft", des

in Russland immer wieder propagierten nietzscheanischen Geschichtssinns, sondern die schleichende Einrichtung eines *wiederkehrenden Simulacrums*.

Durch die Annexion der Krim kehrte das russische Volk zum Trugbild der schönen Zeit zurück, galt die Krim doch als Ort der Erholung, als Insel der Träume. Ohne eine wirkliche Reise zu unternehmen, sah sich das russische Volk ab Frühjahr 2014 medial auf die Krim versetzt, die zum Kompensationsraum für den Verlust einer verschwundenen Lebenswelt wurde.

Bei der Verbreitung des neuen Heimatgefühls beschränkt sich der *Imperialistische Realismus* in Russland nicht nur auf die Usurpation kritischer Kunst, sondern knüpft an die Ideale des großen Bruders an. Heldentaten werden gepriesen: Künstler und Intellektuelle, die der Linie treu sind, werden ausgezeichnet. Auch „ernste" politische Inszenierungen sind an der Tagesordnung: Auf einer *Neuen Konferenz von Jalta* am 14. August 2014, auf der alle großen russischen Politiker anwesend waren, hat sich Wladimir Schirinowski von seinem alten Vorschlag für eine neue Hymne distanziert. Diese sollte ursprünglich aus drei Melodien der meistfavorisierten Hymnen zusammengebastelt werden und ihr Text moderne Wörter wie „Kosmos", „Internet" und „Neues Russland" enthalten. Und natürlich hat er einen neuen Vorschlag unterbreitet: Die Ersetzung der russischen Flagge durch die alte schwarz-gelb-weiße Flagge des russischen Imperiums sowie die Einführung der alten Nationalhymne des Russischen Reiches. In der Zeit 1833 bis 1917 beinhaltete diese Hymne folgende Zeilen:

Gott, schütze den Zaren,
Den Starken, den Mächtigen,
Herrsche uns zum Ruhme,

zu unserem Ruhme.
Er herrsche zum Schrecken
der Feinde,
Der rechtgläubige Herrscher.
Gott, den Zaren, den Zaren,
Schütze den Zaren![33]

Putin meldete sich unmittelbar nach
den von Applaus begleiteten Vorschlägen
Schirinowskis zu Wort und sagte, es
handele sich bei ihnen mal wieder
um „persönliche Wünsche von Wladimir
Wolfowitsch" und diese entsprächen
nicht immer den „politischen Bestrebungen der Russischen Föderation".[34]
Was mit den Bestrebungen der Föderation
nicht kollidiert, ist aber das Stanzen
eines Jubiläumsrubels zu „Ehren
des Anschlusses der Krim an Russland".
Anstelle einer Zahl und des Staats-
wappens prägen zwei Objekte der Begier-
de die versilberte Münze: *„unser* Putin"
und *„unsere* Krim" – eine orthodox-
phantasmatische Zeichenwerdung,[35] die
den neuen gesellschaftlichen „Reich-
tum" Russlands verkörpert. Solange das
Volk in Russland von diesem politisch
gesteuerten Fetisch, von diesem Zeichen
ohne Inhalt verführt wird und solange
dieser als Bares gilt, kann das Land die
eigene Vergangenheit nur schwer auf-
arbeiten. Wie lange dieser Zustand der
Singularität anhält, der Geschichte
durch die absolute Referenzlosigkeit
eines *wiederkehrenden Simulacrums*
ersetzt,[36] liegt an der Wirkkraft der ge-
fressenen Pillen.

Ursprünglich veröffentlicht als: Wladimir Velminski,
„Diagnose: Krim", in: ders., *Diagnose: Krim*, Merve Verlag,
Berlin 2015, S. 162–186. Die Stilmaßgaben wurden denen
der vorliegenden Publikation angepasst.

1   Eva Horn, *Der geheime Krieg. Verrat, Spionage und moderne Fiktion*, Frankfurt am Main 2007, S. 211.

2   Dieses Verfahren ist recht verbreitet in der russischen Gegenwartskunst, vgl. dazu Tomaš Glanc, „Iskusstvo kak špionaž", in: // *Mesto Pečati. Žurnal interpretacionnogo iskusstva*. Nomer četyrnadcat', Moskau 2003, S. 20–40.

3   Viktor Pivovarov, *Sonja und die Engel*, Heft 7, Prag 1996, S. 62.

4   Komar & Melamid, *Komar & Melamid's American Dreams*, Philadelphia 2000, S. 68–71.

5   Ilya Kabakov, *Der Text als Grundlage des Visuellen*, Köln 2000.

6   Viktor Pivovarov, *Svidetel'stvo sovremennikov / Reports of the Contemporaries*, Prag 2013.

7   Ebd., S. 21.

8   Vgl. Heike Winkel, „Schreibversuche. Kollektive Vorlagen und individuelle Strategien in den ‚Briefen der Werktätigen'", in: Julij Murašov, Georg Witte (Hg.), *Die Musen der Macht. Medien in der sowjetischen Kultur der 20er und 30er Jahre*, München 2003, S. 59–79, hier S. 63.

9   Viktor Pivovarov, *O ljubvi slova i izobraženija*, Moskau 2004, S. 49.

10 Ebd.

11 Ebd.

12 Kabakov 2000 (wie Anm. 5), S. 18.

13 Pivovarov 2013 (wie Anm. 6), Kapitel „Der Morgen im Mausoleum".

14 Ebd., S. 62.

15 Vgl. Boris Groys, *Gesamtkunstwerk Stalin. Die gespaltene Kultur in der Sowjetunion*, München 1988; Vladimir Papernyj, *Kul'tura dva*, Moskau 1996; Viktor Tupizyn, *Kommunal'nyj (post)modernizm. Russkoe iskusstvo vtoroj poloviny XX veka*, Moskau 1998.

16 Pivovarov 2013 (wie Anm. 6), Kapitel „Lenin und Stalin während der Malstudien in Nemčinovka".

17 Ebd., S. 62.

18 So in der Pressemeldung der Galerie vom 26. Januar 2009.

19 Vgl. Pressemeldung vom 18. Januar 2009: http://regions.ru/news/2190868/

20 Putin zeichnet eine Katze: http://www.youtube.com/watch?v=1_rhqmknudI

21 Siehe: www.youtube.com/watch?v=vYRswPspgLc

22 Präsident Obamas Rede zu den Reformen der NSA-Überwachungsprogramms am 17. Januar 2014 in Washington, DC.

23 Siehe: www.1tv.ru/news/polit/256730

24 Vgl. Fredric Jameson, *Mythen der Moderne*, Berlin 2007, S. 145–216.

25 Pivovarov 2013 (wie Anm. 6), Kapitel „Stalin und Maus".

26 Ebd., S. 66.

27 Siehe: https://www.youtube.com/watch?v=Lz1B8o9p0Ts.

28 Vgl. Gabowitsch, Mischa: *Putin kaputt? Russlands neue Protestkultur*, Berlin 2013.

29 Vgl. dazu Jean-Luc Nancy, *Der Eindringling. Das fremde Herz*, Berlin 2000.

30 Vgl. „Neue Macht. Neue Verantwortung. Elemente einer deutschen Außen- und Sicherheitspolitik für eine Welt im Umbruch", in: *Internationale Politik*, Berlin 2013: https://internationalepolitik.de/de/neue-macht-neue-verantwortung

31 Vgl. Frank Deppe, *imperialer realismus?: über eliten, experten und journalisten und die „neue deutsche verantwortung". eine flugschrift*, Hamburg 2014.

32 Vgl. Slavoj Žižek, *Liebe dein Symptom wie dich selbst! Jacques Lacans Psychoanalyse und die Medien*, Berlin 1991.

33 Die Hymne wurde am 31. Dezember 1833 vereidigt und existierte bis zum 23. Februar 1917, als Zar Nikolaj II. gestürzt wurde. Der Text stammt von Vasilij Andreevič Žukovskij, die Melodie von Aleksej Fëdorovič L'vov.

34 Siehe: http://lifenews.ru/news/138403

35 Pierre Klossowski, *Die lebende Münze*, Berlin 2001, S. 93.

36 Vgl. Jean Baudrillard, *Der unmögliche Tausch*, Berlin 2000, S. 179.

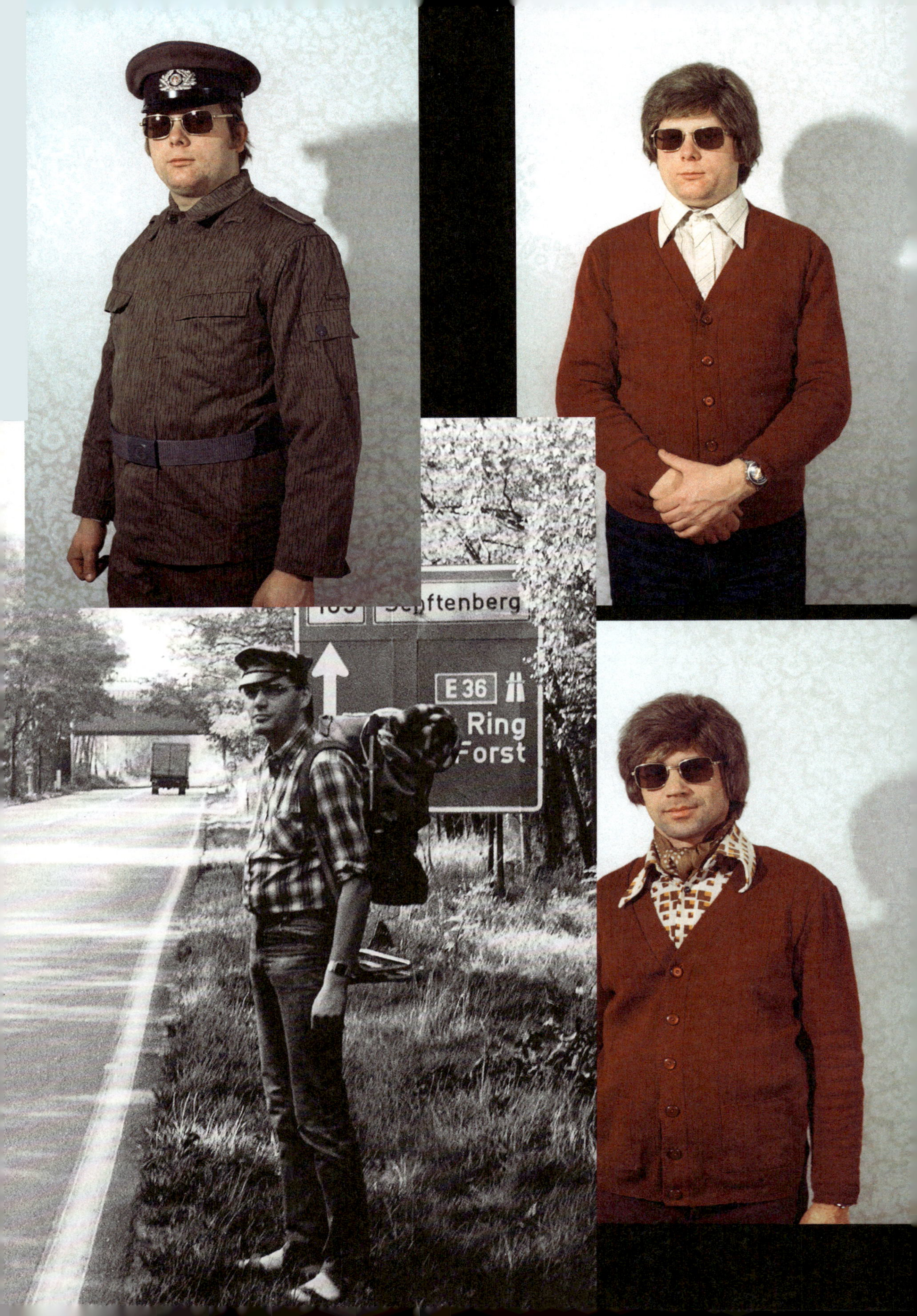

165 Senftenberg
E 36
Ring
Forst

Mask: The Political Space behind the War on Terror
Marina Otero Verzier

The laundromat in my neighborhood does something more than wash dirty laundry. It's not a case of illegal goings-on, quite the opposite. The workers at Bubbleworks, in New York's Prospect Heights neighborhood, contribute to safeguarding national security as they wash shirts.

"You work in banking?," asks the manager when I turn up there with six kilos of dirty clothes compressed into a bag advertising the country's main financial institutions. "I don't recognize your accent, where are you from?" With every transaction, he subjects me to a short interrogation. A year later he knows my address, telephone number, and credit card number; my working times, my profession, the company I work for; my underwear, nationality, type of visa, and my love life. Sometimes I discover myself dreaming about having my own washing machine. The other day, as I waited for him to return a couple of shirts to me, I looked at the framed certificates hung up behind the counter. "NYPD Operation Nexus," I read, "This business is a recognized participant in the counterterrorism program named Operation Nexus." The manager, now back with the hangers, discovers me as I try to note it down. "So, you said you were an architect, didn't you?"

In 2012, as a consequence of 9/11, the New York Police Department established Operation Nexus, a nationwide network of businesses and enterprises, including everyday local facilities such as car parks, laundromats, and stores, joining together with a common aim: the prevention of a new terrorist attack in the country. Since the launch of Operation Nexus, the police have visited over 30,000 establishments to encourage their owners and employees to use their professional experience to contribute to counterterrorism. For this, they are provided with a list of personalized protocols with which to identify "purchases, meetings or activities that may have connections with terrorism and to inform the authorities of them."[1] In exchange, they receive a framed certificate (like the one in my neighborhood laundromat) and they become the first alert mechanism to protect the City of New York against another terrorist attack.

Back at home, while I do a quick search online for Operation Nexus, I think that, perhaps, I ought to take my dirty washing elsewhere; I also think about how "security architecture" affects our relationship with the public space. In the last century, and especially in the present one, we have been witnesses to what Giorgio Agamben mentions in his book *State of Exception* as the "unprecedented generalization of the paradigm of security as the normal technique of government."[2] For the authorities, and equally for the manager at Bubbleworks, we are all a threat to the country, until proven otherwise. Observed online, at airports, and also at laundromats, the security measures established to prevent terrorist attacks have converted the presumption of innocence into the presumption of guilt. Like many of the counterterrorism initiatives established since the start of the so-called War on Terror, Operation Nexus and its general framework known as Urban Shield make us all (and especially immigrants) suspects and, also, vigilantes—"Stay alert, and have a safe day," reminds the voice on the New York subway on every journey.

The terrorist, according to the police, may be anyone who portrays themselves as "legitimate customers in order to buy or lease certain materials or equipment, or to undergo certain formalized training to acquire important skills or licenses" which subsequently could be used to facilitate an attack.[3] In this process, as we are reminded by the philosopher Étienne Balibar, the stranger is transformed into an enemy and is, all too often, subject to violent repression and institutional discrimination, or simply to continued surveillance that is a threat to privacy and freedom of expression.[4] No, I don't have anything to hide, but for months now I have been taking to Bubbleworks only what I cannot diligently wash by hand on the weekends. I understand the importance of protecting national security, but I prefer not to feel like I'm under suspicion when collecting my underwear, or when seeing what could be a friendly neighborhood chat become a police mechanism for the extraction of information about citizens.

The laundromat example is, probably, the most banal example of how current unrestricted surveillance practices, the result of alliances between the public and private sectors and the economic and political goals that they serve, violate fundamental rights and undermine democracy. Compiling data does not necessarily have to be harmful, but we must pay attention to the power techniques at play, something that reminds us of the declaration signed by academics from all over the world against mass surveillance: spying. Through this letter they request that states effectively protect fundamental rights and freedoms and, in particular, our privacy. "It is protected by international treaties, such as the International Covenant on Civil and Political Rights and the European Convention on Human Rights," they remind us, noting that "without privacy, people cannot freely express their opinions or seek and receive information."[5] And the fact is that counterterrorism tactics adopted by governments and the military ultimately illustrate the violence inherent to the exercising of power and its capacity to undertake actions designed as much for our protection as for the destruction of what makes possible our life in common, including our freedom and our political capacity.

Architecture participates in these processes. One could argue that the situation with respect to Bubbleworks would be resolved by having a washing machine at home. But in New York, their installation is often prohibited by contract and there are people who end up installing one illegally and emptying it via the bathtub. The question goes much deeper, and the solution lies not in a change of laundromats, but in political action capable of articulating, from legislation that regulates domestic architecture to technologies and "security architectures" that built the global "smart" city. The territory drawn up by the War on Terror is located at the intersection between physical and legal spaces, and it is characterized by the growing use of war technology and protocols in the civic space. Its "public security" apparatus tends to be managed by private interests.[6] Within this context, sometimes I might forget that every day I walk under the watchful eye of security cameras and urban surveillance systems, yes, that I even interiorize the choreography drawn by my body—jacket and shoes off, hands behind my head—like the security checkpoints at airports. When talking on the phone, sending messages, and using the social networks, my preferences and movements are stored in the cloud, where I share them with family and friends, and, in passing, with espionage programs and data compilation companies. My habits are analyzed by algorithms that classify me and by laundromat managers converted into police informers. Through a discursive operation, the institutions of power normalize this space of limbo between legality and illegality, law and violence, presenting it as an effective instrument in the fight against terrorism. Emergency becomes the rule, and the city a battlefield.

But if from the institutions of power legal and social hierarchies are being suspended to guarantee security, these measures are contested by opposing civic movements that employ technological innovations to construct spaces of freedom and political action: international networks of anonymous sources for the filtration of classified information; homemade drones that scrutinize the actions of the police; encryption systems for activists, journalists, and humanitarian organizations; architectural designs with Faraday-type shields; or simply actions that range from covering the computer camera with a post-it, to refusing to pass through body scanners. This is the space in which our collective coexistence develops, the city as a great celebration of anomie.

In fact, as Agamben reminds us, the term *iustitium*—the technical designation of the state of exception—constructed like *solstitium* means literally suspending the *ius*, the legal order, which connects the state of emergency with festival practices such as Carnival and other charivaric traditions.[7] "The anomic feasts dramatize this irreducible ambiguity of juridical systems and, at the same time, show that what is at stake in the dialectic between these two forces is the very relation between law and life."[8] The anomic festival is, following this argument, the space in which we have a license to suspend legal and social hierarchies and establish new orders, and in which it is possible to undertake "truly political" action, that which, as Agamben proposes, is capable of severing "the nexus between violence and law."

I didn't change laundromats. In a city like New York, you are grateful when people take an interest in you, call you by your name, ask you about your friends and family. When they miss you because you are on holiday. With every question, the Bubbleworks manager, in representation of the administration, was protecting me against the dangers of terrorism while subjecting me to a legalized and standardized violence, structured by the logic of economic neoliberalism and masked behind an informal chat. Hours before leaving the city—and the country—I decided to make my last visit to the laundromat, this time to declare my right to privacy and the danger of surveillance programs. And, deep down, to

prove myself not guilty. When I entered
I found my neighbor talking about
how he had spent the weekend. I paid for
the washing of the dirty laundry,
took a photograph of the diploma, and
said goodbye with a "see you soon."

My next house will have a washing
machine. Even if it has to be installed
illegally.

—Marina Otero Verzier. Head of Research and Development,
HNI. Chief Curator with the After Belonging Agency, OAT'16.

Originally published as: Marina Otero Verzier, "Mask: The
Political Space behind the War on Terror," *Quaderns d'arquitectura i urbanisme* 266 (January 2016), edited by Ethel
Baraona, Guillermo López, Anna Puigjaner, and José Zabala,
Association of Architects of Catalonia, 2015, http://quaderns.
coac.net/en/2016/01/mask-marina-otero/. Stylistic conventions have been adjusted to conform to the publication at
hand.

1   Operation Nexus, Police Department, City of New York
(NYPD), official website of the City of New York, http://
www.nyc.gov/html/nypd/html/crime_prevention/
counterterrorism.shtml (accessed November 12, 2014).

2   Giorgio Agamben, *State of Exception*, trans. Kevin Attell
(Chicago and London: University of Chicago Press, 2005),
p. 14.

3   Operation Nexus, Police Department, City of New York
(NYPD).

4   See Étienne Balibar, "Strangers as Enemies: Walls All
over the World, and How to Tear Them Down," lecture
at Columbia University, November 3, 2011, https://
www.francoangeli.it/Riviste/Scheda_Rivista.
aspx?idArticolo=45634.

5   "Academics Against Mass Surveillance," http://www.
academicsagainstsurveillance.net (accessed January 4,
2014).

6   Judith Butler offers reflection on the consequences of
the militarization of the police force in the United States
and the Urban Shield counterterrorism program in her
lecture "Human Shield," given at The London School of
Economics and Political Science on February 4, 2015. See:
http://www.lse.ac.uk/newsAndMedia/videoAndAudio/
channels/publicLecturesAndEvents/player.aspx?id=2859
(accessed July 2, 2020).

7   Giorgio Agamben, *State of Exception*, pp. 41 and 71.

8   Ibid., p. 73.

Maske: Der politische Raum hinter dem Krieg gegen den Terror
Marina Otero Verzier

Die Wäscherei in meiner Nachbarschaft macht mehr, als schmutzige Wäsche zu waschen. Dabei dreht es sich nicht um ungesetzliche Vorgänge, ganz im Gegenteil. Bei Bubbleworks in New Yorks Stadtteil Prospect Heights tragen die Beschäftigten, wenn sie Hemden waschen, zur Wahrung der nationalen Sicherheit bei.

„Sie arbeiten in der Bankenbranche?", fragt der Geschäftsführer, wenn ich dort mit sechs Kilo schmutziger Kleidung aufkreuze, die ich in eine Tasche gestopft habe, auf der für eines der wichtigsten Finanzinstitute im Land geworben wird. „Ihr Akzent sagt mir gar nichts, woher kommen Sie denn?" Bei jeder Transaktion unterzieht er mich einer kurzen Vernehmung. Ein Jahr später weiß er Bescheid über meine Adresse, Telefonnummer und Kreditkartennummer, meine Arbeitszeiten, meinen Beruf, die Firma, für die ich tätig bin, meine Unterwäsche, Nationalität, den Geltungsbereich meines Visums und mein Liebesleben. Manchmal erwische ich mich dabei, dass ich von einer eigenen Waschmaschine träume. Neulich, als ich darauf wartete, dass er mir ein paar Blusen zurückgab, fiel mein Blick auf die gerahmten Urkunden, die hinter dem Tresen hängen. „NYPD Operation Nexus", las ich. Und: „Dieses Geschäft ist anerkannter Teilnehmer am Terrorismus-Abwehrprogramm Operation Nexus." Der Geschäftsführer, mittlerweile mit den Kleiderbügeln zurück, trifft mich dabei an, wie ich das gerade aufschreiben will. „Ah ja, Sie sagten doch, Sie sind Architektin, nicht wahr?"

2012 baute die New Yorker Polizeibehörde als Konsequenz aus den Anschlägen vom 11. September 2001 die Operation Nexus auf, ein nationsweites Netz aus Geschäften und Unternehmen, darunter lokale Einrichtungen des täglichen Bedarfs wie Parkhäuser, Wäschereien und Lebensmittelläden, die sich einem gemeinsamen Ziel verschrieben haben: einen erneuten terroristischen Angriff im Land zu verhindern. Seit Beginn dieser Operation hat die Polizei über 30.000 Einrichtungen besucht, um deren Inhaber und Angestellte zu ermuntern, unter Nutzung ihrer beruflichen Praxis zur Terrorismusbekämpfung beizutragen. Hierfür erhalten sie eine Reihe personalisierter Protokolle, um damit „Einkäufe, Versammlungen oder Aktivitäten, die mit Terrorismus im Zusammenhang stehen könnten", zu registrieren „und den Behörden mitzuteilen".[1] Im Gegenzug bekommen sie eine gerahmte Urkunde (wie die in der Wäscherei in meiner Nachbarschaft) und werden zum Frühalarmmechanismus, der die Stadt New York vor einem weiteren terroristischen Anschlag schützen soll.

Wieder zu Hause, schlage ich schnell im Internet Operation Nexus nach und denke, ich sollte vielleicht meine schmutzige Wäsche anderswohin bringen; auch denke ich darüber nach, wie „Sicherheitsarchitektur" sich auf unser Verhältnis zum öffentlichen Raum auswirkt. Im vergangenen und zumal im gegenwärtigen Jahrhundert haben wir erlebt, was Giorgio Agamben in seinem Buch *Ausnahmezustand* „eine beispiellose Ausweitung des Sicherheitsparadigmas als normaler Technik des Regierens"[2] nennt. Für die Behörden ebenso wie für den Geschäftsführer von Bubbleworks sind wir allesamt eine Bedrohung für das Land, bis das Gegenteil bewiesen ist. Im Zuge der Überwachung im Internet, auf Flughäfen und selbst in Wäschereien haben die Sicherheitsmaßnahmen, die zur Verhinderung terroristischer Anschläge getroffen werden, die Unschuldsvermutung zur Schuldvermutung werden lassen. Wie so viele Initiativen zur Terrorismusbekämpfung, die seit dem Beginn des sogenannten Kriegs gegen den Terror ins Leben gerufen wurden, machen die Operation Nexus und ihr umfassenderes Bezugssystem – bekannt als Urban Shield – uns alle (und Einwanderer im Besonderen) zu Verdächtigen und im gleichen Zug zu Angehörigen einer Bürgerwehr: „Bleiben Sie wachsam und haben Sie einen sicheren Tag", mahnt die Stimme auf jeder Fahrt in der New Yorker U-Bahn.

Terrorist kann laut Polizei jeder Beliebige sein, der sich als „seriöser Interessent" vorstellt, „um bestimmte Materialien oder Ausrüstungen zu kaufen oder auszuleihen oder eine bestimmte formelle Ausbildung zu durchlaufen und damit wichtige Fertigkeiten oder Lizenzen" zu erwerben, die später zur Durchführung eines Anschlags genutzt werden könnten.[3] Hierdurch wird, wie Étienne Balibar in Erinnerung ruft, der Fremde zum Feind umgeformt und dabei allzu oft zum Objekt brachialer Repression und institutioneller Diskriminierung oder zum Ziel einer fortwährenden Überwachung, die die Privatsphäre ebenso bedroht wie die Freiheit der Äußerung.[4] Nein, ich habe nichts zu verbergen, aber seit Monaten habe ich zu Bubbleworks nur gebracht, was ich nicht wochenends mühsam von Hand waschen kann. Mir leuchtet ein, dass es von Bedeutung ist, die nationale Sicherheit zu schützen, aber ich möchte mich vorzugsweise nicht unter Verdacht fühlen, wenn ich meine Unterwäsche abhole oder wenn ich erkennen muss, dass das, was ein freundlicher Plausch unter Nachbarn sein könnte, zu einer polizeilichen Methode wird, Informationen über Bürger abzuschöpfen.

Die Wäschereigeschichte ist wahrscheinlich das gewöhnlichste Beispiel dafür, wie schrankenlose Überwachungspraktiken, die das Resultat von Allianzen zwischen öffentlichem und privatem Sektor sowie der ökonomischen und politischen Ziele sind, denen sie dienen, heute die Grundrechte verletzen und die Demokratie untergraben. Daten zu sammeln, muss nicht zwangsläufig schädlich sein, aber wir sollten auf die Machttechniken achten, die dabei im Spiel sind: Denken wir an die von Akademikern aus aller Welt unterzeichnete Erklärung gegen massenhafte Ausspähung. In ihrem offenen Brief fordern sie den wirksamen staatlichen Schutz unserer Grundrechte und -freiheiten, insbesondere unserer Privatsphäre. Diese sei „geschützt durch völkerrechtliche Vereinbarungen wie dem internationalen Pakt über bürgerliche und politische Rechte und die europäische Menschenrechtskonvention", bringen sie in Erinnerung; und „ohne Privatsphäre können Menschen nicht frei ihre Meinung äußern oder Informationen einholen und erhalten".[5] Schließlich verdeutlichen die von Regierungen und Militärs angewandten

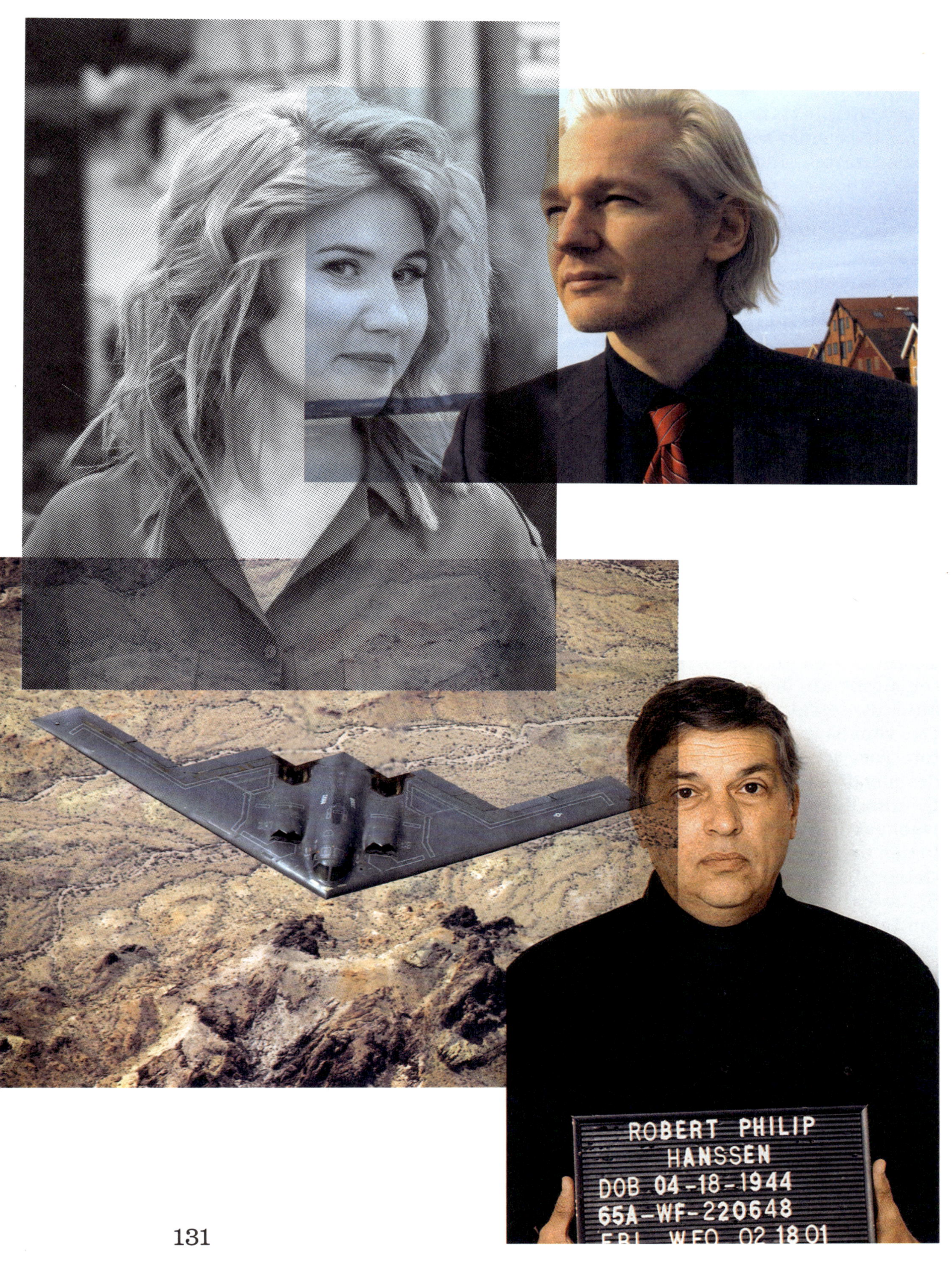
ROBERT PHILIP
HANSSEN
DOB 04-18-1944
65A-WF-220648
FBI WFO 02 18 01

Taktiken der Terrorismusabwehr die Gewalt, die der Ausübung der Macht innewohnt, und zeigen, dass Letztere sehr wohl mit Maßnahmen aufwarten kann, die ebenso sehr auf unseren Schutz zugeschnitten sind wie auf die Zerstörung all dessen, was unser Leben in Gemeinschaft ermöglicht, einschließlich unserer Freiheit und politischen Handlungsfähigkeit.

An alldem ist die Architektur nicht unbeteiligt. Was Bubbleworks angeht, könnte man anführen, ließe sich die Situation doch durch eine heimische Waschmaschine bereinigen. Allerdings sind Waschmaschinen in New Yorker Wohnungen oft vertraglich untersagt, wenngleich manche Bewohner am Ende unerlaubterweise doch eine anschließen und das Wasser über die Badewanne abpumpen. Die Frage reicht aber weit tiefer. So kann die Lösung nicht darin liegen, die Wäscherei zu wechseln, sondern nur in einem politischen Handeln, das von den gesetzlichen Vorschriften bezüglich der Wohnarchitektur bis zu den Technologien und „Sicherheitsarchitekturen", auf denen die „smarte" Stadt aufbaut, gestaltungskompetent ist. Das vom Krieg gegen den Terror errichtete Territorium liegt im Schnittfeld des physischen und des rechtlichen Raums und ist gekennzeichnet durch die wachsende Nutzung von Kriegstechnologien und -protokollen auf zivilem Gebiet. Der Apparat der „öffentlichen Sicherheit" unterliegt tendenziell privaten Interessen.[6] Unter diesen Umständen mag ich manchmal vergessen, dass ich mich tagtäglich unter dem wachsamen Auge von Sicherheitskameras und städtischen Überwachungssystemen bewege, ja könnte mir die von meinem Körper in den Sicherheitsschleusen in Flughäfen vollzogene Choreografie – Jacke und Schuhe ausziehen, Hände

hinter den Kopf – gar zur Selbstverständlichkeit werden. Wenn ich telefoniere, Mitteilungen versende und soziale Netzwerke nutze, werden meine Vorlieben und Bewegungen in der Cloud abgelegt, wo ich sie mit Familienangehörigen und Freunden teile … und ganz nebenbei auch mit Spionageprogrammen und Datensammelfirmen. Meine Gewohnheiten werden analysiert von Algorithmen und von Wäschereigeschäftsführern, die zu Polizeispitzeln geworden sind. Durch einen diskursiven Kunstgriff normalisieren die Machtinstitutionen die Grauzone zwischen Legalität und Illegalität, Gesetz und Gewalt, und präsentieren ihr Vorgehen als wirksames Instrument im Kampf gegen Terrorismus. Der Notfall wird zur Regel und die Stadt zu einem Gefechtsfeld.

Doch während die Institutionen der Macht gesetzliche und gesellschaftliche Hierarchien aufheben, um Sicherheit zu gewährleisten, treten diesen Maßnahmen opponierende bürgerschaftliche Bewegungen entgegen, die technische Innovationen einsetzen, um Räume für Freiheit und politische Tätigkeit aufzubauen: Internationale Netzwerke anonymer Quellen filtern unter Verschluss gehaltene Informationen; selbstgebaute Drohnen verfolgen Polizeiaktionen; es gibt Verschlüsselungsmethoden für Aktivisten, Journalisten und humanitäre Organisationen, architektonische Entwürfe mit faradayartigen Abschirmungen oder auch ganz einfache Maßnahmen, vom Abdecken der Computerkamera mit einem Klebezettel bis zur Weigerung, durch einen Körperscanner zu gehen. Dies ist der Raum, in dem sich unser gemeinschaftliches Dasein entwickelt, die Stadt als große Feier der Anomie.

Tatsächlich bedeutet, wie Agamben uns in Erinnerung ruft, der Terminus

iustitium – die technische Bezeichnung
für Ausnahmezustand, die nach demsel-
ben Muster aufgebaut ist wie *solstitium* –
im wörtlichen Sinn die Suspendierung
des *ius*, der Rechtsordnung, was den
Ausnahmezustand mit Feierpraktiken
wie dem Karneval und anderen chari-
varischen Traditionen verbindet.[7] „Die
anomischen Feste verschaffen dieser
unreduzierbaren Zweideutigkeit der
Rechtssysteme eine Bühne und zeigen
zugleich, daß der Einsatz im Spiel der
Dialektik der beiden Kräfte diese Beziehung zwischen Recht und Leben selbst
ist.“[8] Die anomische Feier ist demzufolge
der Raum, in dem wir den Freibrief
haben, rechtliche und gesellschaftliche
Hierarchien aufzuheben und neue
Ordnungen zu errichten und wo „wahr-
haft[es] politisches“ Handeln möglich ist,
das, wie Agamben es uns nahelegt,
„den Bezug zwischen Gewalt und Recht“
rückgängig zu machen vermag.

Ich habe die Wäscherei nicht gewech-
selt. In einer Stadt wie New York ist
man dankbar, wenn Menschen sich für
einen interessieren, einen mit Namen
ansprechen und nach Freunden und
Familie fragen. Wenn sie einen vermis-
sen, weil man im Urlaub ist. Mit jeder
Frage schützte mich der Bubbleworks-
Geschäftsführer in Vertretung der
Administration vor den Gefahren des
Terrorismus, wobei er mich einer legali-
sierten und genormten Gewalt unter-
warf, die strukturell der Logik des
wirtschaftlichen Neoliberalismus folgt
und sich hinter der Maske eines
zwanglosen Plauschs verbirgt. Ein paar
Stunden bevor ich die Stadt – und
das Land – verließ, beschloss ich, der
Wäscherei meinen letzten Besuch abzu-
statten, diesmal um mein Recht auf
Privatsphäre und die Gefahren von Über-
wachungsprogrammen kundzutun.
Und, tief im Innern, um meine Unschuld

zu beweisen. Als ich eintrat, traf ich auf
meinen Nachbarn, der davon erzählte,
wie er sein Wochenende verbracht hatte.
Ich zahlte für das Waschen der schmut-
zigen Wäsche, machte ein Foto von der
Urkunde und verabschiedete mich mit
einem „bis bald“.

Mein nächstes Heim wird eine Waschmaschine haben. Und wenn sie unerlaubt
aufgestellt werden muss.

Marina Otero Verzier. Leiterin Forschung und Entwicklung,
Het Nieuwe Instituut. Im Team der After Belonging Agency
Chefkuratorin der Oslo Architecture Triennale 2016.

Ursprünglich veröffentlicht als: Marina Otero Verzier, „Mask:
The Political Space behind the War on Terror“, *Quaderns
d'arquitectura i urbanisme 266* (Januar 2016), herausgegeben
von Ethel Baraona, Guillermo López, Anna Puigjaner und
José Zabala, Association of Architects of Catalonia, 2015,
http://quaderns.coac.net/en/2016/01/mask-marina-otero/.
Die Stilmaßgaben wurden denen der vorliegenden Publikation
angepasst.

1   Operation Nexus, Police Department, City of New York
    (NYPD), offizielle Website der Stadt New York, http://
    www.nyc.gov/html/nypd/html/crime_prevention/
    counterterrorism.shtml (Zugriff am 12. November 2014).

2   Giorgio Agamben, *Ausnahmezustand*, Frankfurt a. M. 2017
    (2004), S. 22.

3   Operation Nexus, Police Department, City of New York
    (NYPD).

4   Siehe Étienne Balibar, „Strangers as Enemies: Walls All
    over the World, and How to Tear Them Down", Vortrag
    an der Columbia University, 3. November 2011, https://
    www.francoangeli.it/Riviste/Scheda_Rivista.
    aspx?idArticolo=45634.

5   „Academics Against Mass Surveillance", http://www.
    academicsagainstsurveillance.net (abgerufen am 25. März
    2020).

6   In ihrem Vortrag „Human Shield", gehalten in The
    London School of Economics and Political Science am
    4. Februar 2015, hat Judith Butler Überlegungen zu
    den Folgen der Militarisierung des Polizeiapparats und
    zum Terrorismusbekämpfungsprogramm Urban Shield
    vorgestellt. Siehe:
    http://www.lse.ac.uk/newsAndMedia/videoAndAudio/
    channels/publicLecturesAndEvents/player.aspx?id=2859
    (Zugriff am 2. Juli 2020).

7   Agamben 2017 (wie Anm. 2), S. 52, 78.

8   Ebd., S. 87, ferner S. 104.

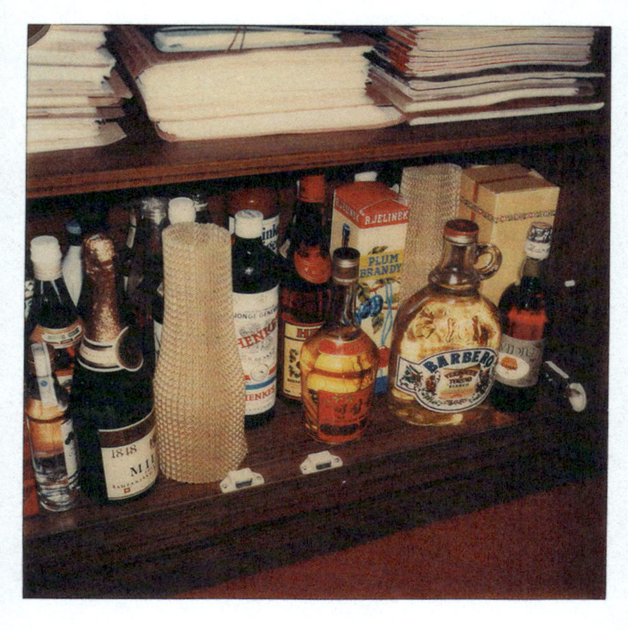
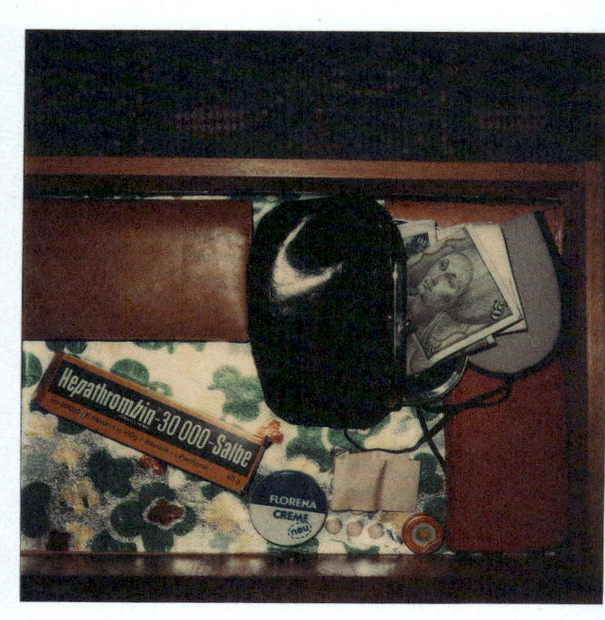
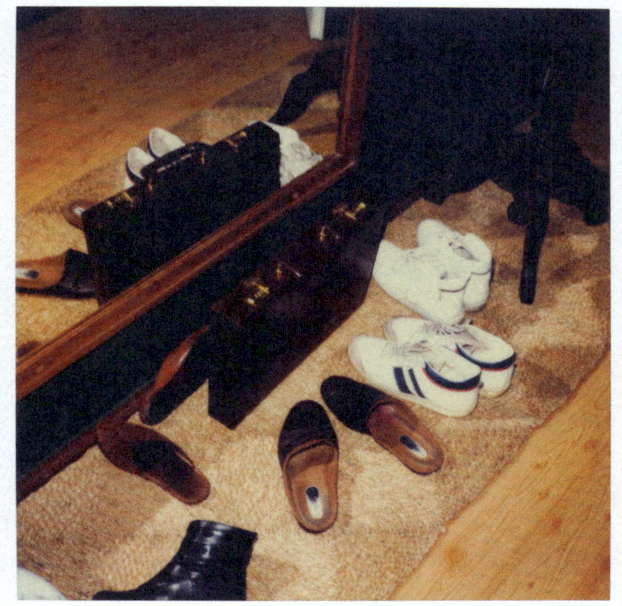
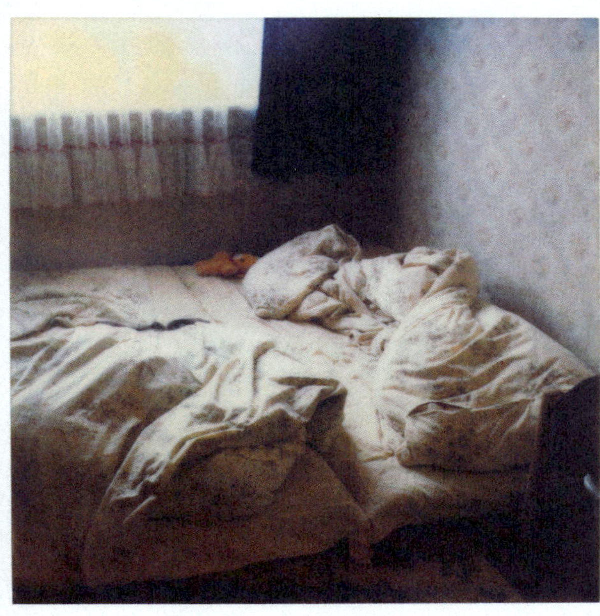

Jonas Staal
Propaganda (Art) Struggle

e-flux journal #94 — october 2018 Jonas Staal
Propaganda (Art) Struggle

Our reality is defined, in part, by a propaganda struggle. "Propaganda" here should not be understood as a singular term, since this propaganda struggle results from various competing propagandas in the plural. Various performances of power each aim to construct reality according to their interests, resulting in overlapping claims that shape the arena of the contemporary.[1] What visual forms are taken by these manifold propagandas and the realities they aim to create? What kind of artistic morphologies and cultural narratives does the propaganda (art) struggle bring about?

1. A Specter Haunting Europe (and the World)

In late July 2018, Steve Bannon – former campaign manager and advisor to Donald Trump – announced the creation of a new Brussels-based foundation that will aim to become a right-wing "alternative" to George Soros's Open Society Foundation.[2] The new foundation, which Bannon has ominously titled "The Movement," will offer polling, messaging, and data-based targeting services to the ultranationalist and alt-right parties and platforms that are trying to dismantle the European Union from within: from Geert Wilders's Freedom Party in the Netherlands and Marine Le Pen's National Rally (formerly National Front) in France, to The League in Italy and Alternative for Germany. Once again, a specter is haunting Europe – but this time, it's the specter of what DiEM25 has termed the "Nationalist International."[3]

Bannon's new organization can tell us a lot about the meaning of "propaganda" today. Essentially, propaganda can be defined as a performance of power, meaning that propaganda aims to enact infrastructures – political, economic, mass-media, and military – that shape reality according to a specific set of interests. Thus propaganda does not just aim to send a message; it aims to construct reality as such. This is what Noam Chomsky and Edward Herman, in their analysis of propaganda from the late eighties, defined as "manufacturing of consent": the process of establishing a normative reality that conforms to specific interests of elite power.[4] In this light, we can say that the Nationalist International is currently manufacturing consent both politically and culturally. The established conservative liberal parties of today speak like the extreme right of the nineties, yet this is considered the "new normal" in comparison to the even more extreme standpoints of the extreme right of the extreme right. This is how propaganda works: what is considered as the norm is reestablished. A new reality is constructed through manufacturing consent, where what was once unacceptable is

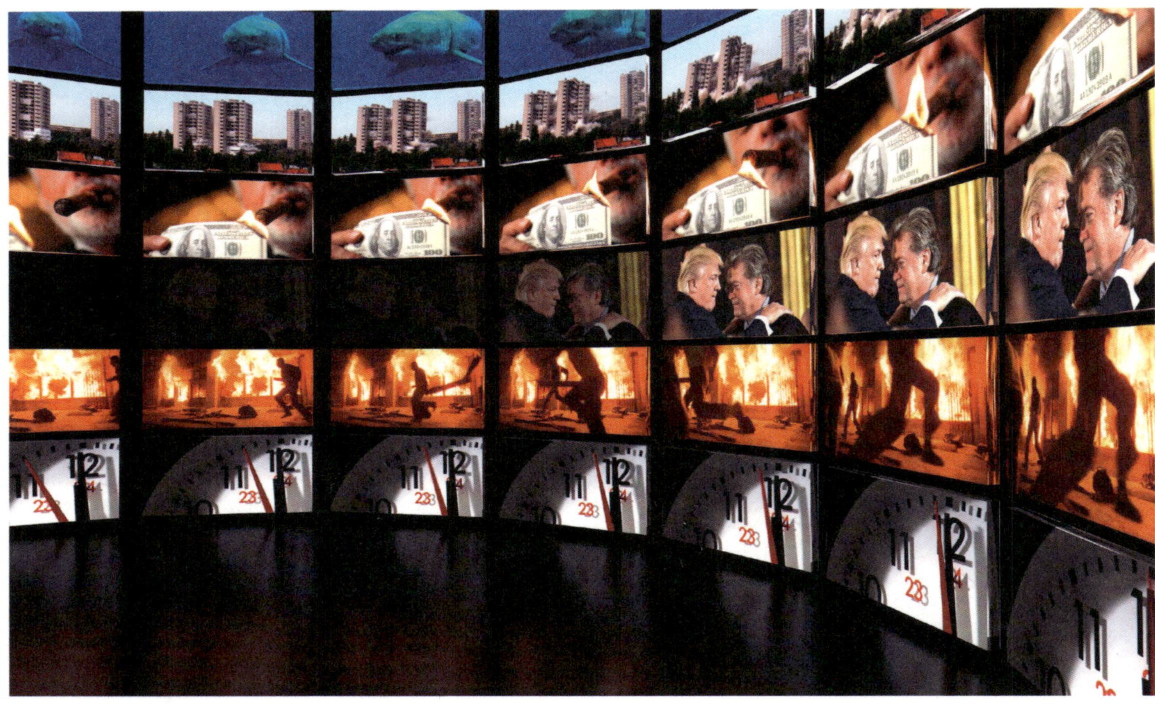

Digital study with stills from Bannon's *Generation Zero* (2010). *Steve Bannon: A Propaganda Retrospective, Study* (2018). Image: Jonas Staal and Remco van Bladel. Produced by Het Nieuwe Instituut, Rotterdam

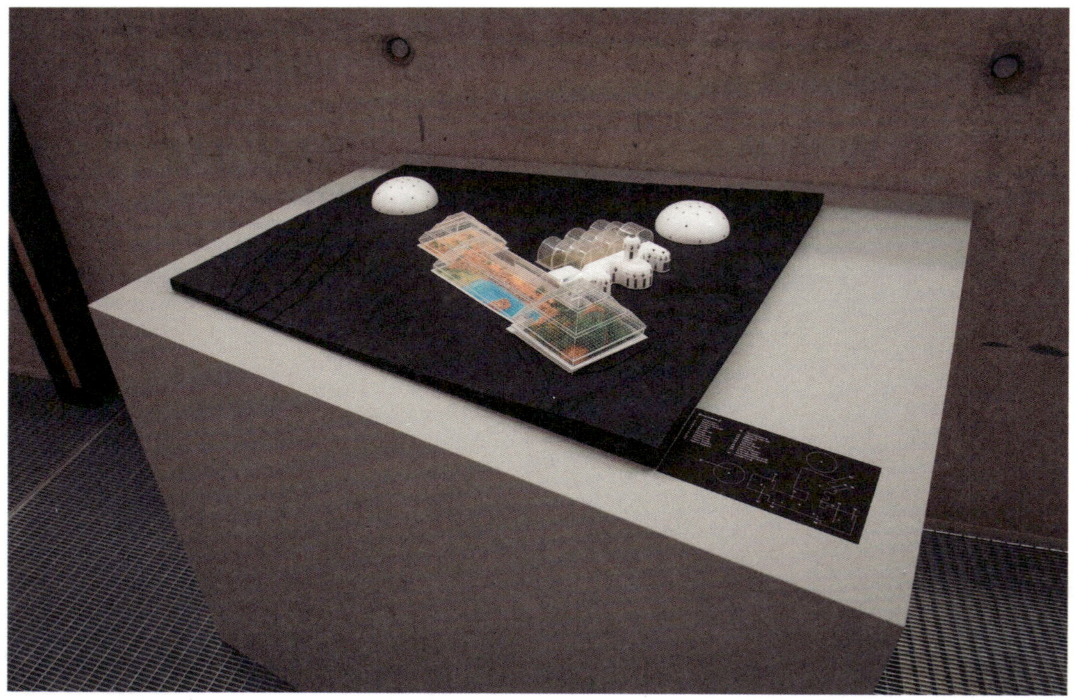

Jonas Staal, Architectural model of *Biosphere 2*, 2018. Installation view of *Steve Bannon: A Propaganda Retrospective* (2018), Het Nieuwe Instituut, Rotterdam. Photo: Nieuwe Beelden Makers.

is in sympathy with the majority of the League's objectives. Some of the proposals, i.e. those relating to the obtaining of confessions would be impracticable to implement.

now standard.

There are two crucial components to propaganda. The first is control over infrastructure; the means through which society is organized. Propaganda succeeds when the performance of power operates – from the micro to the macro scale – to construct reality in a systematic and sustained way. The second component is control over collective narratives about where we come from, who we are, and who we will become – or in the case of the Nationalist International, who we are to become *once more.* Their narratives tend to take the shape of strange retro science fictions, referring to an aspirational past "greatness" that never existed in the first place. This narrative dimension of propaganda, however obscene, cannot be underestimated, as it mobilizes a collective imagination that legitimizes the construction of a new reality. This narrative and imaginative power of art are directly visible in the domain of film.

2. Bannon's Cyclical Time

Steve Bannon himself is an example not only of a propagandist, but also a propaganda artist.[5] His work has focused on developing both the infrastructures of the Nationalist International – of which The Movement is the most recent example – and the narratives that provide purpose and unity to a growing alt-right alliance.[6]

Bannon's work in the early nineties for Goldman Sachs was foundational for his organizational work as a propagandist, as it provided him with the tools to develop various venture-capitalist and political enterprises. His role as the CEO of the Biosphere 2 project in Arizona from 1993 to 1995 revealed his obsession with closed-system technologies.[7] The largest ecosphere ever built on earth, Biosphere 2's original remit was to explore the possibilities for interplanetary colonization, but under Bannon's leadership it became a massive laboratory for researching the impacts of climate change (in sharp contrast to his later decisive role in convincing President Trump to pull out of the Paris Climate Agreement). In 2007, with funding from the ultraconservative Mercer family, Bannon cofounded Breitbart News – the self-declared "home of the alt-right" – and helped organize the anti-Obama Tea Party movement. Over time he has been instrumental in constructing, step by step, an expanding biosphere of the alt-right, with its own political, financial, and media wings – its own infrastructure.

A less discussed, albeit crucial, aspect of Bannon's oeuvre is his work as a propaganda filmmaker – as an instigator of narratives intended to unite the right. Between 2004 and 2018 he made ten documentary-style films that can be described as cultural and ideological precursors to what would later be called "Trumpism." Already in his first paleoconservative film, *In the Face of Evil: Reagan's War in Word and Deed* (2004), Bannon's obsession with strong national leadership is on display. Here, Reagan is portrayed as the sole defender of a Christian nation engaged in a battle to the death with communist evil.[8] Bannon denounces the "appeasers" – diplomats and members of the peace movement – who strive for a negotiated resolution to the Cold War. The film ends with images of the attacks on the Twin Towers; out of the rising dust and smoke, the figure of Osama Bin Laden appears. Not only is Bannon's first film a plea for a twenty-first-century Reagan-like figure to emerge and fight "Islamic Terrorism" with similar conviction; it also lays out his philosophy of the cyclical return of evil.

For Bannon, communism, Nazism, and Islamic terrorism are all successive reincarnations of what he terms "The Beast." Inspired by the fringe writings of William Strauss and Neil Howe, especially their book *The Fourth Turning* (1997), Bannon believes that time develops cyclically through four "turnings," and that every fourth generation – every fourth turning – an epic civilizational war against evil must be waged.[9] This cyclical war provides the ground for a periodic rebirth of Bannon's core ideological doctrine, which can best be summarized as "white Christian economic nationalism."

Bannon uses this theory of the cyclical return of evil to explain social upheavals in the US over the past half-century. According to Bannon, the most recent fourth turning was the Second World War, out of which the United States emerged victorious and reborn, establishing a free market within its national borders and nurturing a devout and nuclear-family-centered culture. But this glorious new turning was quickly threatened by the next turning: the rise of flower power, feminism, and progressive social movements. This turning, says Bannon, introduced a godless individualism into American society and sowed the seeds for the culture of liberal-capitalist greed, with hippies growing up to become Wall Street sharks (this ahistorical blame game has been echoed by some leftists, such as Angela Nagle, who implies that left-wing discourse on transgression gave birth over time to the alt-right).[10] In Bannon's vision, "cultural Marxists," who also emerged from the tumult of the sixties and seventies, are perpetually conspiring to take over the government and collectivize the state from within.[11]

03/11

e-flux journal #94 — october 2018   Jonas Staal
Propaganda (Art) Struggle

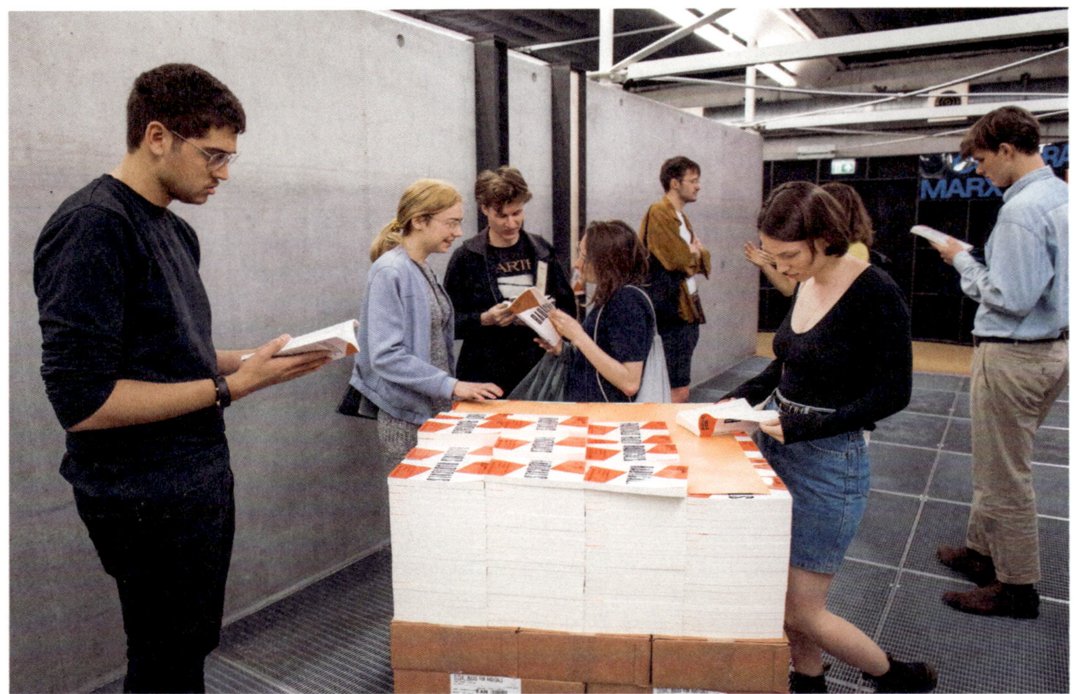

Installation view of *Steve Bannon: A Propaganda Retrospective* (2018). Free copies of Saul Alinsky's *Rules for Radicals* (1971) were gifted to visitors. Photo: Nieuwe Beelden Makers.

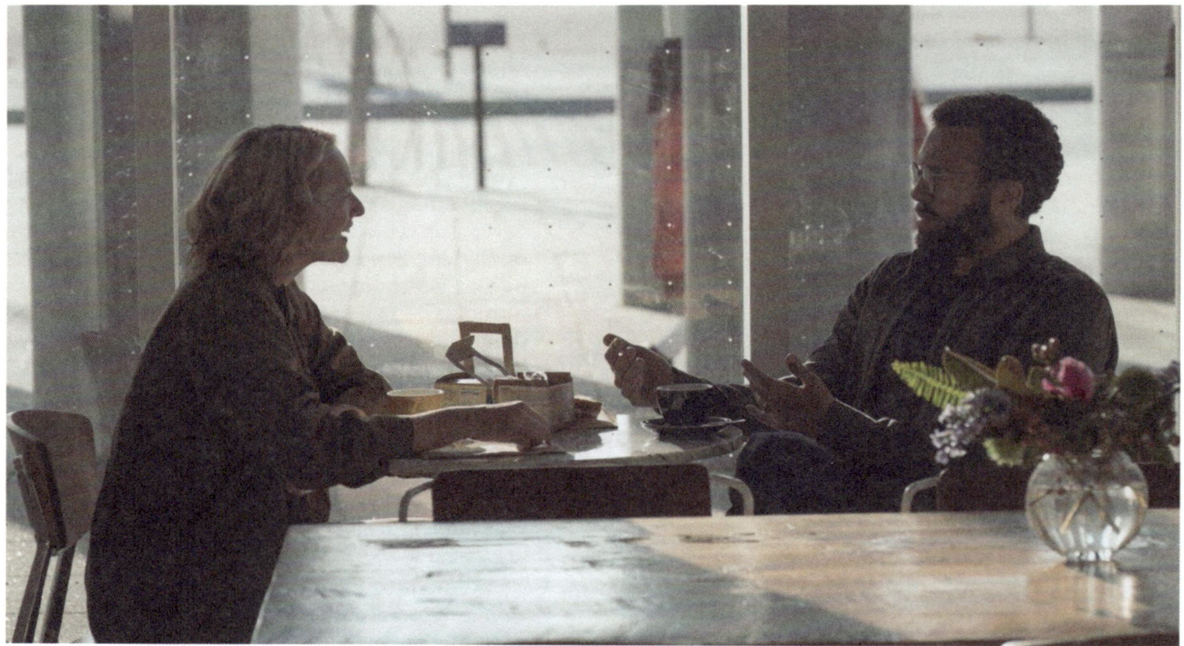

Film still from a flashback in the series *The Handmaid's Tale, Season 1, Episode 5* (2017), directed by Bruce Miller et al.

In his film *Occupy Unmasked* (2012), Bannon maps out an alleged left-wing conspiracy inspired by the writings of Jewish-American community organizer Saul Alinksy, especially his book *Rules for Radicals* (1971).[12] This conspiracy involves dark alliances between the Occupy movement, unions, and the Obama Administration. In the face of this plot, the champions of white Christian economic nationalism – from Reagan to Tea Party favorite Sarah Palin (about whom Bannon made a biopic, 2011's *The Undefeated*) to Trump and the Nationalist International today – are tasked with defending civilization. They must crush the cultural Marxists plotting to take power at universities and in the streets, the wealthy global elites who make up the "Party of Davos," and the manifold incarnations of Islamic Terrorism, from Al-Qaeda to the Islamic State.

Bannon has described his particular brand of pamphleteering filmmaking as "kinetic cinema."[13] He has also cited Leni Riefenstahl, Sergei Eisenstein, and Michael Moore as influences (the latter recently released the anti-Trump film *Fahrenheit 11/9*, around the same time that Bannon released his own pro-Trump film, *Trump@War* – both entering the propaganda fray in advance of the crucial midterm elections in the US).[14] Bannon's "kinetic" aesthetic vocabulary consists of fast-paced sequences and editing, with commentary from various "experts" providing structure to the narrative. Viewers are bombarded with thematically organized stock footage and rousing music. Images of predatory animals such as sharks represent subterranean economic forces that can rupture reality at any given moment, while burning and scattered banknotes – which appear in nearly every one of Bannon's films – exemplify the evaporation of spiritual values in a society nearing its fourth turning. "What I've tried to do is weaponize film," Bannon has claimed.[15] His films construct a "master narrative" that legitimizes the authoritarian power of strong leaders who face down the never-ending threats of a multi-headed Beast.[16] This master narrative also defines who, in Bannon's terrifying worldview, belongs with "us" and who belongs with "them" – who fights The Beast and who appeases or sides with it.

3. The Truth About Post-Truth

In Trumpism we have seen how Bannon's kinetic cinema transformed into a kinetic political campaign, twisting and turning historical narratives and symbols to the point that the very texture of what we once considered reality has been torn and reconfigured into something entirely different. When Trump was criticized for failing to denounce the alt-right in the wake of the "Unite the Right" rally in Charlottesville, Virginia, Bannon pointed the finger at the real danger: the "alt-left." In a similar vein, Geert Wilders's ideologue Martin Bosma has highlighted the bad conscience of the left, which in his reading accused his party of Nazism only to erase their own socialist stake in National-*Socialism*. Viktor Orbán, prime minister of Hungary and leader of the Hungarian Civic Alliance (Fidesz) party, has, like Bannon, perfected the "enemies outside/enemies within" narrative, warning through his state-owned media of a Muslim tsunami threatening his country's borders from without, while the pro-refugee propaganda of Jewish-Hungarian George Soros and his foundation threatens it from within.

Such narrative strategies are currently discussed as "fake news" and "alternative facts" that circulate within what is called the "post-truth era" of politics. In propaganda studies, these terms have a longer history. "Fake news" is also known as "flak," which has been defined as the covert dissemination of misinformation through proxy organizations in order to derail a dominant narrative and spread mistrust of mainstream institutions.[17] "Post-truth" is a more complex term; on one hand, we should obviously fight against misinformation, but on the other, we should also question whose truth we are supposed to "return" to and who exactly this truth – the normative idea of a pre-Trump society – serves.

The propaganda campaign of the Nationalist International has moved far beyond the reach of any fact-checking machinery. Its project is a cultural one, consisting of its own pantheon of leaders, of climate-denying and cyclical-time-promoting scientists, and of propaganda artists – like Bannon – who are capable of turning alt-reality into our new normal. Angela Nagle has argued that the Gramscians of the twenty-first century – those who make the long march through our cultural institutions in order to change politics through culture – are today on the alt-right rather than the left.[18] But by the time Nagle wrote this, the cultural long march might already have ended and turned into alt-governance. The costs of alt-right propaganda are already clear for us to see, ranging from the rise of systemic and institutional racism; the criminalization, incarceration, and murder at sea of refugees; the lawless killing of those declared to be "terrorists"; the separation of migrant children from their families; and the willingness on the part of these alt-governments to humiliate and bomb other countries.

Is there a reality that preexisted alt-reality which we would even want to return to in the first

05/11 — e-flux journal #94 — october 2018 — Jonas Staal — Propaganda (Art) Struggle

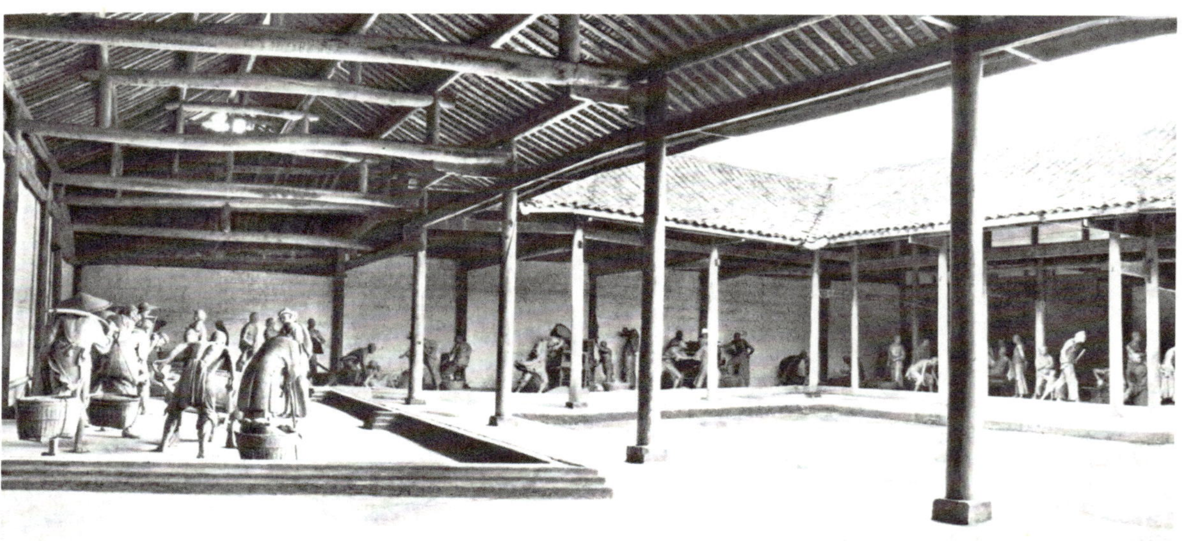

Filmstill from Adam Curtis' documentary *HyperNormalisation* (2016).

Ye Yushan et al., *Rent Collection Courtyard* (1965), Dayi County, Sichuan. Image: Ed., *Rent Collection Courtyard: Sculptures of Oppression and Revolt* (Peking: Foreign Languages Press, 1968).

place? Bruce Miller's television series *The Handmaid's Tale*, based on Margaret Atwood's 1985 novel, has recently been a hit among liberals, desperate for an end to the Trump era. The dystopian series takes place in the aftermath of a second American Civil War, when a new Christian-fundamentalist, hyper-patriarchal state called "Gilead" has risen to power. Women are not allowed to work, study, read, own property, or possess money. Instead, they are assigned to domestic work or, if declared "degenerates," sent off to brutal labor camps. The class of fertile "handmaids" plays a central role, as they are recruited to combat Gilead's infertility crises by breeding children for elite households through ritualized rape. The world of Gilead could be regarded as an example of Nationalist International retro science fiction, insofar as it imagines a mythological future-past in which modern technology goes hand in hand with symbols of traditionalist puritan culture.

A crucial component in the series are the flashbacks of its main characters, which recall the liberal-capitalist order that existed before the second American Civil War. The show's main protagonist, June, or "Offred" (read: "property of the house of Fred"), thinks back to jogging in a park, iPhone in hand, or stopping at Starbucks for a soy latte, or hanging out with her boyfriend at an über-gentrified hipster cafe. These flashbacks to a soulless consumerist world can be read as a warning to viewers: our political apathy could allow a Gileadian coup to take place. But in Miller's adaptation, which portrays Gilead's totalitarianism and its culture of rape, torture, and mutilation in brutal detail, these sepia-colored flashbacks to the capitalist-liberal order suddenly seem like the normal we long to return to.[19] A criminal mortgage system, the rise of trillion-dollar companies, global austerity and precarity: all of these suddenly seem like rather desirable problems compared to the retro-futurist horror of Gilead. In *The Handmaid's Tale*, we witness the propaganda cinema of the liberal-capitalist order staging a critique against growing authoritarianism, but only to reimpose its own normality and desirability – which, as we know, contributed substantially to the conditions that fueled the Nationalist International in the first place.[20]

When we speak of "post-truth," it is thus crucial to emphasize that there is not a "norm" to return to: there are, rather, various competing realities, past and present, each trying to impose its own set of values, beliefs, and behaviors. This is the essence of the propaganda struggle. Between alt-right propaganda and liberal-capitalist propaganda, there is admittedly a world – a reality – of difference, *but we should reject both of them*. What we need is not a return

to some past reality, but a fundamental alternative to both the Nationalist International and the liberal-capitalist regime so that, in the words of Octavia Butler's character Lauren Olamina, "Our new worlds will remake us as we remake them."[21]

4. Totalitarian Historiographies

Filmmaker Adam Curtis – who has engaged in his own version of Nagle's blame-the-right-on-the-left game[22] – has dedicated much of his work to examining the mechanisms of power and propaganda. In his most recent film, *HyperNormalisation* (2016), he traces the emergence of what he considers a "fake world" – or what Walter Lippmann in 1922 termed "pseudo-environments."[23] This "fake world," which Curtis claims has been under construction by "politicians, financiers, and technological utopians" since the 1980s, aims to bypass complex geopolitical processes and conflicts to instead construct a simple binary world that serves the interests of these powerful groups.[24] The key historical moment, in his view, was the rise of Reaganite and Thatcherite neoliberalism and the subsequent shifting of power from elected politicians to corporations and the public relations industry. This neoliberal paradigm went on to transform civic resistance into a culture of individual expression and critique: collective action was abandoned and real power was placed solely in the hands of a new managerial class, which engineers our post-political world. To ensure that resistance remains futile, a range of "global super-villains" are contrived, from Gaddafi to Saddam Hussein; these perpetual threats ensure that populations remain preoccupied with Us-vs.-Them binaries.

If Bannon is a propaganda artist of the alt-right, and Miller's *The Handmaid's Tale* embodies liberal-capitalist propaganda, then Curtis is a propagandist of the defeatist conservative left. This becomes clear when he declares that our present time has "no vision for the future."[25] Instead, he argues, the growth and popularization of cyberspace – the global technology environment – since the nineties has facilitated a cult of sovereign individualism: an online space of boundless post-political self-expression. These accumulated individual expressions, argues Curtis, do nothing but feed the algorithms of the Facebook State, strengthening the new global post-political managerialism.[26] For Curtis, the Occupy movement was a symptom of cyberspace culture: a leaderless "networked" movement that was more interested in self-expression and self-management than taking power.[27] Considering that a large portion of Occupy participants and sympathizers were people

07/11

e-flux journal #94 — october 2018   Jonas Staal
Propaganda (Art) Struggle

whose homes have been expropriated by the criminal mortgage system and whose shared precarity compelled them to gather in parks and public spaces to seek some form of desperate justice, the suggestion that it was not politicized people but algorithms that orchestrated the Occupy movement is deeply offensive.

Curtis's defeatism reaches its true cynical depths when he declares that the Tahrir uprising in Egypt was a Facebook-led revolution. In his account, corporate social media brought people into the streets to dethrone dictator Hosni Mubarak; two years later Facebook brought these same people into streets, this time to welcome back the military regime after it had deposed the democratically elected president Mohamed Morsi. Cyberspace, in Curtis's reasoning, has become a new realm of global managerialism: no matter how much we try to use it as a tool for our own ends, it is ultimately the new systems of algorithmic surveillance and management that benefit. But as Melissa Tandiwe Myambo has argued, this ideological practice of "misnaming the revolution" not only ignores the fact that in 2012 only about 8 percent of the Egyptian population was on Facebook; it also engages in the neocolonial practice of "virtual occupation."[28]

Here defeatist conservative left propaganda shows its ugly face. Curtis's determination to understand and map systems of power becomes so obsessive that even when systems are not absolute – and they never really are – he will argue that they must be, in order to bolster his narration of an all-encompassing fake world. This echoes the method employed by art historian Igor Golomstock in his major work *Totalitarian Art* (1990), where he argues that the art made in Nazi Germany, the Soviet Union, fascist Italy, and Maoist China is all part of one and the same totalitarian machinery.[29] While we can indeed witness glorified images of grand dictators, heroic soldiers, and militant peasants throughout the art produced under these regimes, major differences are present just the same, both ideologically and aesthetically.

For example, Mao Zedong's art theory, as laid out in his "Talks at the Yenan Forum on Literature and Art" (1942), promoted cooperative artistic practice between art professionals and peasant communities, with the aim of their mutual education.[30] The famous group of sculptures *Rent Collection Courtyard* (1965) resulted from such a process of co-creation and revolutionized various aspects of traditional sculpture. It rejected the pedestal as well as durable materials such as marble. Instead, the figures were created from clay and placed directly on the ground so that villagers could walk by them and scorn and spit on the

sculptural representations of the landlords that used to rule over them.[31] These specific characteristics of art production and presentation – co-creation, removal of the pedestal, and theatrical usage – were absent in Stalinist socialist realist sculpture; in the latter, monumental pedestal-facilitated figures made of solid materials, towering far above the crowd, sought to embody a sense of near eternity. So rather than describing totalitarian art, Golomstock's work represents a form of *totalizing historiography* that overlooks difference in order to find comfort and a sense of desperate control in a closed-system theory.

In the case of Curtis, his totalizing narrations are even more tragic: the Occupy movement and the uprisings gathered under the problematic term "Arab Spring," along with the manifold popular movements that have emerged around the world since, are not inventions of social media but rather the living embodied truth that there are visions and practices of alternative futures and world-making in our present. Hundreds of thousands of people did not take Tahrir Square because Facebook told them to. They put their bodies on the line not because they were controlled by a post-political managerial elite, but because they collectively reclaimed power in the face of violence, fear, pain, and death. In these rare moments of "performative assembly," as philosopher Judith Butler has termed it, in these gatherings of extremely precarious peoples, the possibility of another kind of power is enacted.[32] We might also say that in these assemblist events, the possibility of another kind of propaganda is enacted as well – another way of telling stories and proposing narratives of where we come from, who we are, and who we can *still become*.[33]

5. Towards an Emancipatory Propaganda Art

Our contemporary propaganda struggle is shaped by various performances of power, each with its own infrastructures and cultural narratives that attempt to construct reality according to its own interests. In the examples that I have discussed – the propaganda art of the Nationalist International, of liberal capitalism, and of the defeatist left – we can see that each particular structure of power performs differently as art. In other words, we can see that there is a specific, changing relationship between power and form.

Recent years have demonstrated that propaganda can set into motion vast geopolitical processes, from the Brexit vote and the election of Trump – both of which took place amidst a haze of misinformation – to more brutish examples, like the rise of the authoritarian

e-flux journal #94 — october 2018   Jonas Staal
Propaganda (Art) Struggle

regimes of Erdoğan, Modi, and Duterte. These events have shown that responding to the propaganda of the Nationalist International with mere "facts" is no solution, because facts need narratives to make them effective and affective. While it is crucial to develop a collective "propaganda literacy," understanding propaganda does not stop propaganda.

To oppose the various propagandas discussed above, we will need infrastructures and narratives that mobilize the imagination to construct a different world. To achieve this, we will need an emancipatory propaganda and an emancipatory propaganda art. There is no prior reality to which we should strive to return; there will only be the realities that we will author collectively ourselves.

✕

This text resulted from two lectures, one presented as the introduction to the conference Propaganda Art Today at Het Nieuwe Instituut, Rotterdam, on June 2, 2018, and one titled "Art and Propaganda" for Impakt Festival, Utrecht, on September 1, 2018. I want to thank architect Marina Otero Verzier, with whom I developed the exhibition-project *Steve Bannon: A Propaganda Retrospective*, for being a comrade in the process of making new propagandas a reality.

Jonas Staal is a visual artist whose work deals with the relation between art, propaganda, and democracy. He is the founder of the artistic and political organization *New World Summit* (2012–ongoing) and the campaign *New Unions* (2016–ongoing). With BAK, basis voor actuele kunst, Utrecht, he co-founded the *New World Academy* (2013-16), and with Florian Malzacher he is currently directing the utopian training camp *Training for the Future* (2018-ongoing) at the Ruhrtriennale in Germany. Exhibition-projects include *Art of the Stateless State* (Moderna Galerija, Ljubljana, 2015), *After Europe* (State of Concept, Athens, 2016) and *Museum as Parliament* (with the Democratic Federation of North Syria, Van Abbemuseum, Eindhoven, 2018). Recent publications and catalogs include *Nosso Lar, Brasília* (Jap Sam Books, 2014), *Stateless Democracy* (With co-editors Dilar Dirik and Renée In der Maur, BAK, 2015) and *Steve Bannon: A Propaganda Retrospective* (Het Nieuwe Instituut, 2018). His book *To Make a World: Propaganda Art in the 21st Century* is forthcoming from the MIT Press in 2019. Staal completed his PhD research *Propaganda Art from the 20th to the 21st Century* (2012-2018) at the PhDArts program of Leiden University, the Netherlands.

09/11

NOTE:
Inmate J-8080 refused to sign paperwork in recognized alias.
I certify that above signature belongs to Inmate J-8080, alias

1

In the words of Sven Lütticken, "The contemporary should be seen as a contested terrain, as asynchronic coexistence of different contemporalities, ideologies, and social realities." Sven Lütticken, *History in Motion: Time in the Age of the Moving Image* (Sternberg Press, 2013), 25.

2

Jamie Doward, "Steve Bannon plans foundation to fuel far right in Europe," *The Guardian*, July 21, 2018 https://www.theguardian.com/us-news/2018/jul/21/steve-bannon-plans-foundation-to-fuel-far-right-in-europe.

3

The term "Nationalist International" comes from an economic policy paper released by the Democracy in Europe 2025 movement. See DiEM25, *DiEM25's European New Deal: A Summary,* 2017 https://diem25.org/wp-content/uploads/2017/02/170209_DiEM25_END_Summary_EN.pdf.

4

Noam Chomsky and Edward S. Herman, *Manufacturing Consent* (Pantheon Books, 1988), named after the chapter "The Manufacture of Consent" in Walter Lippmann's *Public Opinion* (1922).

5

See further: Jonas Staal, *Steve Bannon: A Propaganda Retrospective* (Het Nieuwe Instituut, 2018) http://jonasstaal.nl/site/assets/files/1850/stevebannon_def.pdf.

6

The Movement is part of the second, "international" phase of Bannon's propaganda project. The first phase was the building of a powerful alt-right coalition in the United States; as David Neiwert writes, "the gradual coalescence of the alternative-universe worldviews of conspiracists, Patriots, white supremacists, Tea Partiers, and nativists occurred after the election of the first black president, in 2008. Fueled in no small part by racial animus toward Obama, the Internet and social media became the grounds on which this 'lethal union' could finally occur." David Neiwert, *Alt-America: The Rise of the Radical Right in the Age of Trump* (Verso, 2017), 231.

7

Ten years later Bannon would work on another type of biosphere, this time online. In 2005 he became involved in the Hong Kong-based company Internet Gaming Entertainment (IGE), which sold digital assets to players of the massive multiplayer online role-playing game *World of Warcraft*. These digital goods in the form of gold and weaponry, were obtained by paying Chinese workers extremely low wages to play the game in ongoing rotating shifts. This experience, according to Joshua Green, was critical to Bannon's later online mobilization of the alt-right during the Trump campaign. See Joshua Green, *Devil's Bargain: Steve Bannon, Donald Trump, and the Storming of the Presidency* (Penguin Press, 2017), 81–83.

8

The film also embodies Bannon's ideal of a right-wing Hollywood, with Reagan representing both the creative side (as an actor) and the political side (as president and an anti-communist crusader).

9

In the words of Strauss and Howe: "Turnings come in cycles of four. Each spans the length of a long human life, roughly eighty to a hundred years, a unit of time the ancients called the *saeculum*. Together, the four turnings of the saeculum comprise history's seasonal rhythm of growth, maturation, entropy, and destruction." *The Fourth Turning: An American Prophecy* (Broadway Books, 1997), 3.

10

Nagle's main target is what she calls "Tumblr-liberalism," which is preoccupied with "gender fluidity and providing a safe space to explore other concerns like mental ill-health, physical disability, race, cultural identity and 'intersectionality'" (69). Nagle argues that these concerns have resulted in a doctrine of self-flagellation in which "the culture of suffering, weakness, and vulnerability has become central to contemporary liberal identity politics" (73). In Nagle's view, Tumblr-liberalism not only gave rise to the alt-right; it also alienated the traditional working class. Angela Nagle, *Kill All Normies: Online Culture Wars from 4Chan and Tumblr to Trump and the Alt-Right* (Zero Books, 2017).

11

The term "cultural Marxism" was originally associated with the Frankfurt School and described the radical critique of standardized and commodified mass culture. The term resonates with Nazi campaign against "cultural Bolshevism" and surfaced in far-right movements in the US from the early nineties onward. The fact that the protagonists of the Frankfurt School were Jewish has made this conspiracy theory particularly popular in alt-right circles, as it encompasses both anti-Semitic and anti-left tropes. See also Sven Lütticken, "Cultural Marxists Like Us," *Afterall* 46 (Autumn-Winter): 67–75.

12

Bannon is not the first to claim that Alinsky's work serves as a handbook for the radical left-wing takeover of government and society. This conspiracy theory first emerged during Bill Clinton's presidency, as First Lady Hillary Clinton had written her 1969 college thesis on Alinsky's work. The theory rests in part on an epigraph in the book the describes the fallen angel Lucifer as "the first radical known to man who rebelled against the establishment and did it so effectively that he at least won his own kingdom." For right-wingers, this reveals not only the godless Marxist framework of Alinksy's book, but its ambition to seize control of the government. See Saul Alinsky, *Rules for Radicals: A Pragmatic Primer for Realistic Radicals* (Vintage Books, 1989).

13

John Patterson, "For haters only: watching Steve Bannon's documentary films," *The Guardian*, November 29, 2016 https://www.theguardian.com/us-news/2016/nov/29/steve-bannon-documentary-films-donald-trump.

14

Adam Wren, "What I Learned Binge-Watching Steve Bannon's Documentaries," *Politico*, December 2, 2016 https://www.politico.com/magazine/story/2016/12/steve-bannon-films-movies-documentaries-trump-hollywood-214495.

15

Keith Koffler, *Bannon: Always the Rebel* (Regnery Publishing, 2017), 48.

16

Terence McSweeney, *The "War on Terror" and American Film: 9/11 Frames Per Second* (Edinburgh University Press, 2016), 10.

17

Chomsky and Herman, *Manufacturing Consent*, 26–28.

18

Nagle, *Kill All Normies*, 40–53.

19

Of course, this does not mean that *The Handmaid's Tale*'s potent symbolism and original narrative cannot simultaneously operate to enable emancipatory politics. In fact, the red cloak and white hood worn by the handmaids in the book and TV series have shown up at protests in defense of women's reproductive autonomy and gender equality the world over.

20

See also Mihnea Mircan and Jonas Staal, "Let's Take Back Control! Of Our Imagination," *Stedelijk Studies* 6 (Spring 2018) https://stedelijkstudies.com/journal/lets-take-back-control-of-our-imagination/.

21

Octavia Butler, *Parable of the Talents* (Grand Central Publishing, 2007), 358.

22

In his four-part documentary series *Century of the Self* (2002), Curtis suggested that an obsession with individualist "self-actualization" on the part of political progressives paved the way for the resurgence of the right.

23

"In order to conduct a propaganda there must be some barrier between the public and the event. Access to the real environment must be limited, before anyone can create a pseudo-environment that he thinks wise or desirable." Walter Lippmann, *Public Opinion* (Transaction Publishers, 1998), 43.

24

Transcript from *HyperNormalisation*.

25

Transcript from *HyperNormalisation*.

26

A term borrowed from the work *Facebook State* (2016), developed by artist Manuel Beltrán and his students.

27

A partially overlapping critique, but with more depth and greater fidelity to the potentialities of the Occupy movement, is Not an Alternative, "Counter-Power as Common Power: Beyond Horizontalism," *Journal of Aesthetics & Protest* 9 (Summer 2014) https://www.joaap.org/issue9/notanalternative.htm.

28

Melissa Tandiwe Myambo, "(Mis)naming the Revolution," *Montréal Review*, January 2012 http://www.themontrealreview.com/2009/Misnaming-the-Revolution.php.

29

Golomstock goes so far as to credit totalitarianism as an *author* in and of itself: "Totalitarianism itself carried out the historian's task of sifting through sources, using the scalpel of the concept of two cultures (*Lenin's thesis calling for revolutionaries to take from each national culture only its democratic and socialist elements –JS*), of the struggle between racial and class elements, in order to split apart the living body of national tradition." Igor Golomstock, *Totalitarian Art* (Overlook Press, 1990), 155.

30

"Prior to the task of educating the workers, peasants, and soldiers, there is the task of learning from them." Mao Tse-Tung, "Talks at the Yenan Forum on Literature and Art," in *New World Academy Reader #1: Towards a People's Culture*, eds. Jose Maria Sison and Jonas Staal (BAK, basis voor actuele kunst, 2013), 51.

31

The claim that this particular case of Maoist art production

e-flux journal #94 — october 2018   Jonas Staal
Propaganda (Art) Struggle

can be conflated with Stalinist art production is strongly refuted by art historian Christof Büttner, who argues that "it is a work of art that is so convincing that many interpret it to be the simple, unimaginative depiction of a real event and held it in disdain for exactly that reason. That was all the more true when Western art historians labeled it Socialist Realism and, even worse, stigmatized it as propaganda art for the Cultural Revolution." Christof Büttner, "The Transformations of a Work of Art – Rent Collection Courtyard, 1965–2009," in *Art for the Millions*, eds. Esther Schlicht and Max Hollein (Hirmer Verlag, 2009), 38.

32
Judith Butler, *Notes Toward a Performative Theory of Assembly* (Harvard University Press, 2018). See also Jonas Staal, "Assemblism," *e-flux journal* 80 (March 2017) https://www.e-flux.com/journal/80/100465/assemblism/.

33
This is fundamentally different from the propaganda of the Nationalist International discussed earlier, which tells us who we will become *once more*.

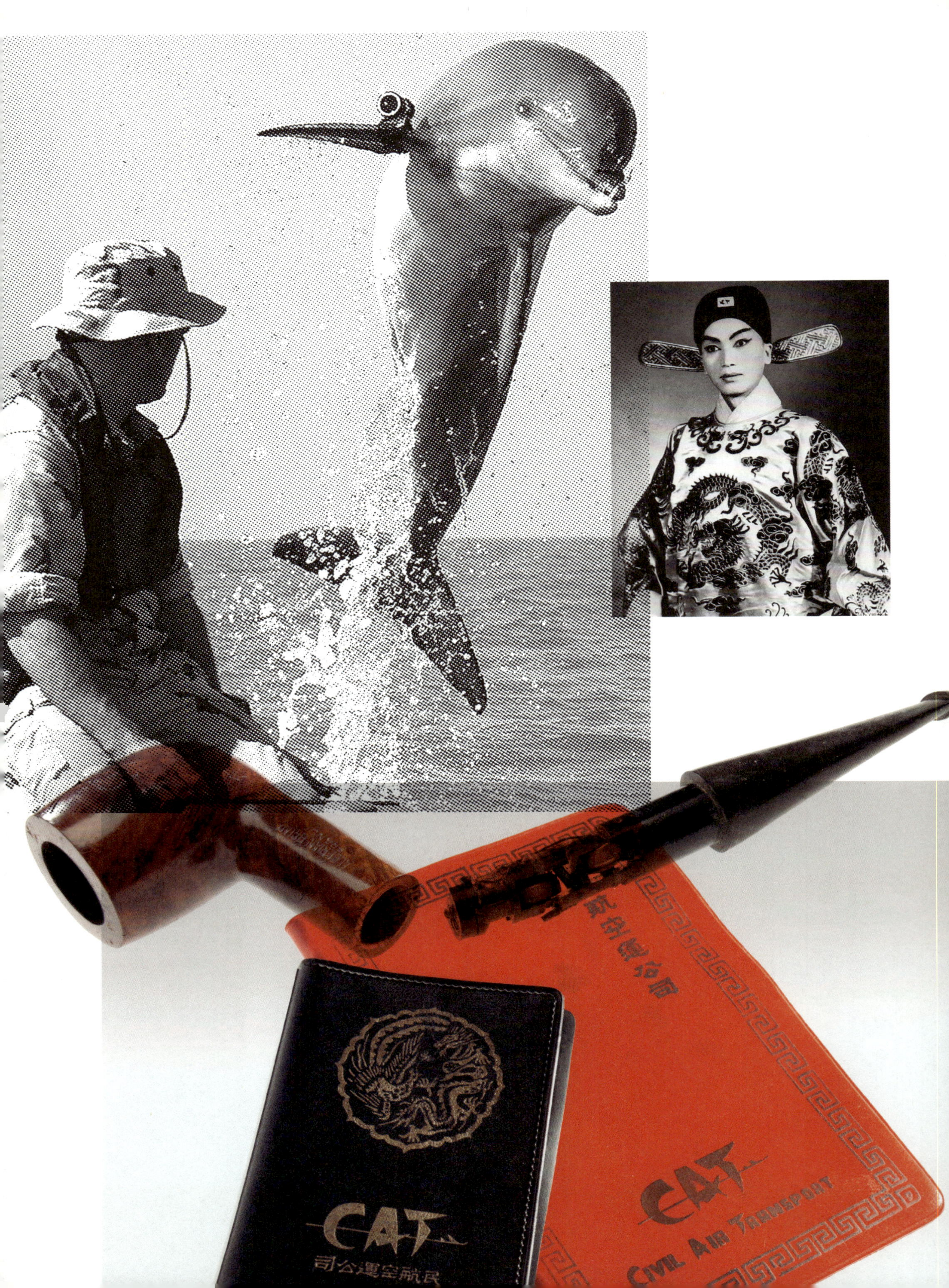

CAT
司公運空航民
CAT
CIVIL AIR TRANSPORT

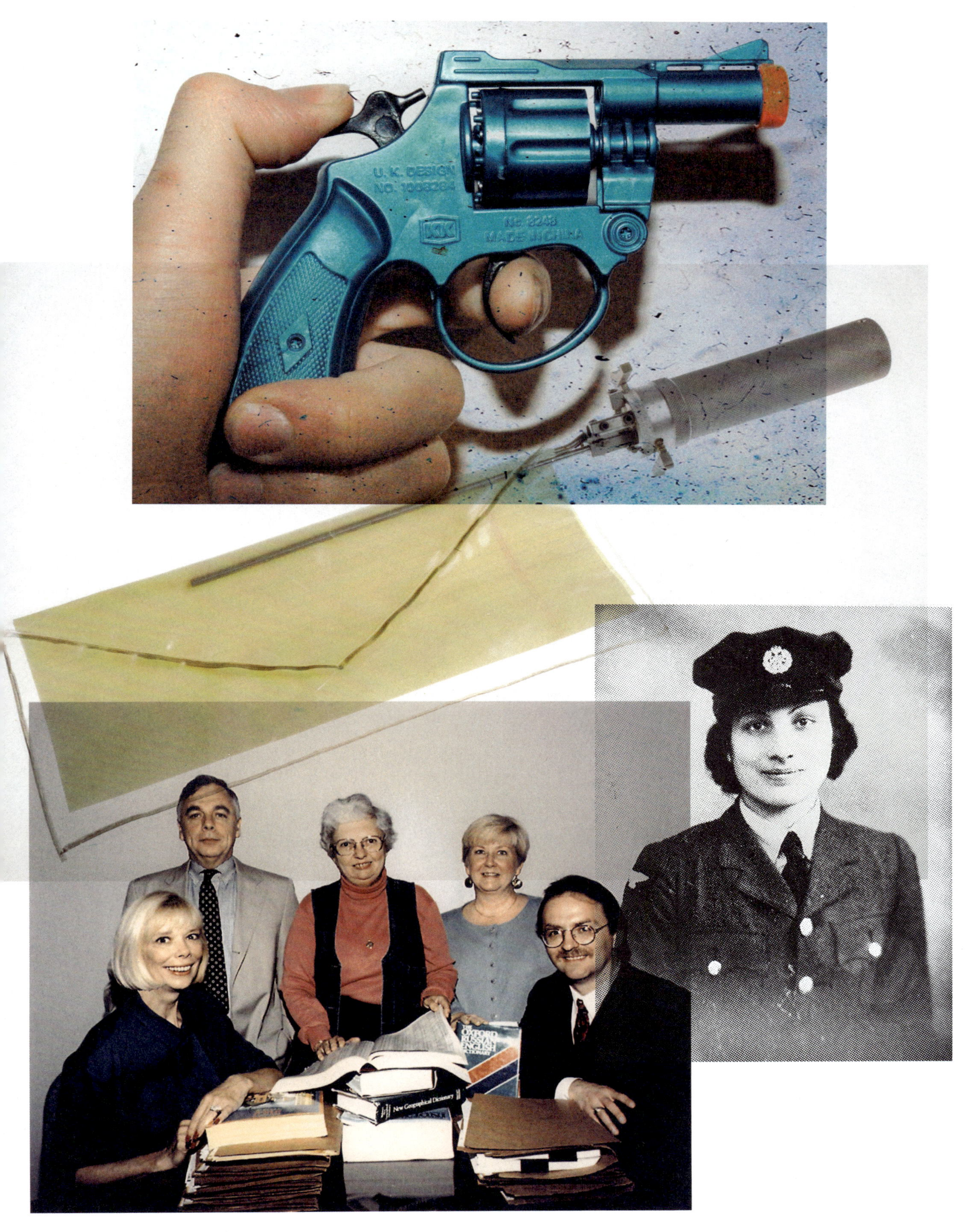

e-flux journal #37 — september 2012 Metahaven
Captives of the Cloud: Part I

Metahaven
Captives of the Cloud: Part I

We are the voluntary prisoners of the cloud; we are being watched over by governments we did not elect.

Wael Ghonim, Google's Egyptian executive, said: "If you want to liberate a society just give them the internet."[1] But how does one liberate a society that already has the internet? In a society permanently connected through pervasive broadband networks, the shared internet is, bit by bit and piece by piece, overshadowed by the "cloud."

The Coming of the Cloud

The cloud, as a planetary-scale infrastructure, was first made possible by an incremental rise in computing power, server space, and trans-continental fiber-optic connectivity. It is a by-product and parallel iteration of the global (information) economy, enabling a digital (social) marketplace on a worldwide scale. Many of the cloud's most powerful companies no longer use the shared internet, but build their own dark fiber highways for convenience, resilience, and speed.[2] In the cloud's architecture of power, the early internet is eclipsed.

A nondescript diagram in a 1996 MIT research paper titled "The Self-governing Internet: Coordination by Design," showed a "cloud" of networks situated between routers linked up by Internet Protocol (IP).[3] This was the first reported usage of the term "cloud" in relation to the internet. The paper talked about a "confederation" of networks governed by common protocol. A 2001 *New York Times* article reported that Microsoft's .NET software programs did not reside on any one computer, "but instead exist in the 'cloud' of computers that make up the internet."[4] But it wasn't until 2004 that the notion of "cloud computing" was defined by Google CEO Eric Schmidt:

> I don't think people have really understood how big this opportunity really is. It starts with the premise that the data services and architecture should be on servers. We call it cloud computing – they should be in a "cloud" somewhere. And that if you have the right kind of browser or the right kind of access, it doesn't matter whether you have a PC or a Mac or a mobile phone or a BlackBerry or what have you – or new devices still to be developed – you can get access to the cloud. There are a number of companies that have benefited from that. Obviously, Google, Yahoo!, eBay, Amazon come to mind. The computation and the data and so forth are in the servers.[5]

The internet can be compared to a patchwork of city-states, or an archipelago of islands. User

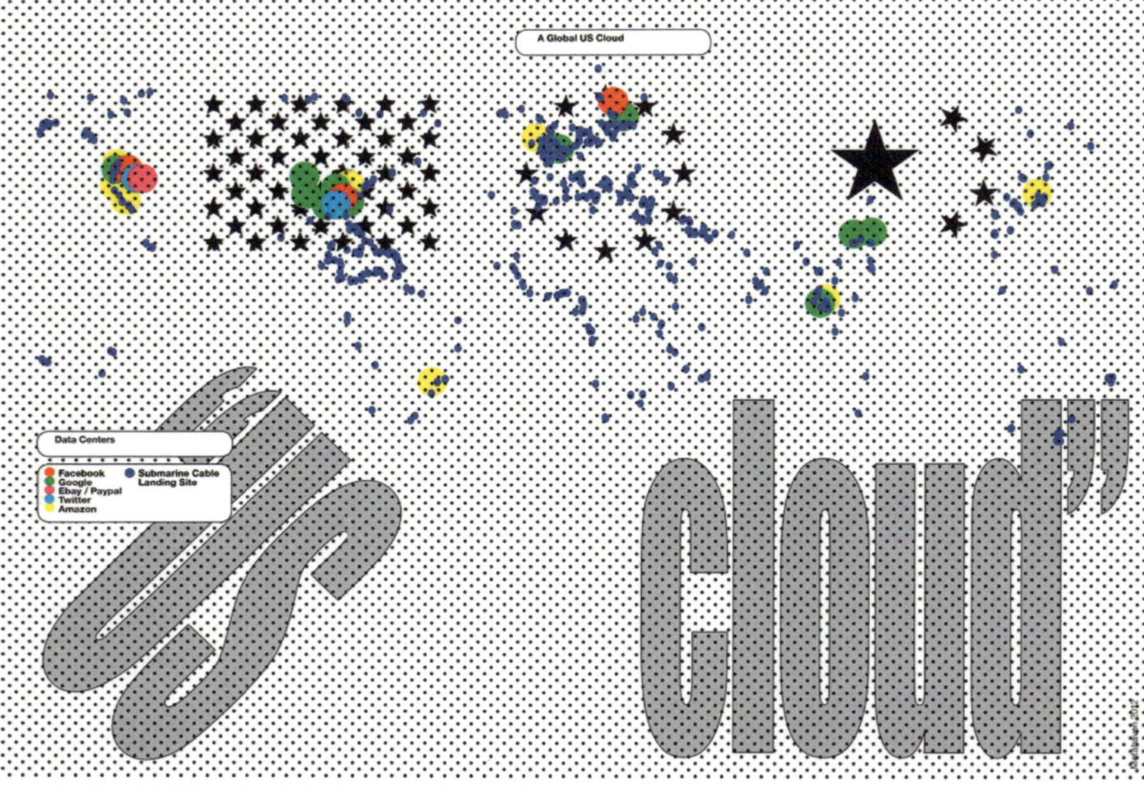

A selection of the global US social media cloud, resorting under the Patriot Act.

data and content materials are dispersed over different servers, domains, and jurisdictions (i.e., different sovereign countries). The cloud is more like Bismarck's unification of Germany, sweeping up formerly distinct elements, bringing them under a central government. As with most technology, there is a sense of abstraction from prior experiences; in the cloud the user no longer needs to understand how a software program works or where his or her data really is. The important thing is that it works.

In the early 1990s, a user would operate a "personal home page," hosted by an internet Service Provider (ISP), usually located in the country where that user lived. In the early 2000s, free online services like Blogspot and video sites like YouTube came to equal and surpass the services of local providers. Instead of using a paid-for local e-mail account, users would switch to a service like Gmail. In the late 2000s and the early 2010s this was complemented, if not replaced, by Facebook and other social media, which integrate e-mail, instant messaging, FTP (File Transfer Protocol), financial services, and other social interaction software within their clouds. Cloud-based book sales, shopping, and e-reading have brought about the global dominance of Amazon, the world's biggest cloud storage provider and the "Walmart of the Web."[6] By 2015, combined spending for public and private cloud storage will be $22.6 billion worldwide.[7] Given this transition, it is no exaggeration to proclaim an exodus from the internet to the cloud. The internet's dispersed architecture gives way to the cloud's central model of data storage and management, handled and owned by a handful of corporations.

The coming of the cloud is spelled out by Aaron Levie, founder and CEO of Box, one of Silicon Valley's fastest growing cloud storage providers. As Levie states, the biggest driver of the cloud is the ever-expanding spectrum of mobile devices – iPhones, iPads, Androids, and such – from which users tap into the cloud and flock around its server spine:

> If you think about the market that we're in, and more broadly just the enterprise software market, the kind of transition that's happening now from legacy systems to the cloud is literally, by definition, a once-in-a-lifetime opportunity. This is probably going to happen at a larger scale than any other technology transition we've seen in the enterprise. Larger than client servers. Larger than mainframes.[8]

Google, one of the world's seven largest cloud companies, has recently compared itself to a bank.[9] That comparison is apt. If data in the cloud is like money in the bank, what happens to it while it resides "conveniently" in the cloud?

The US Cloud and the Patriot Act

Where and by whom sites are registered and data is hosted matters a great deal in determining who gains access to and control over the data. For example, all data stored by US companies (or their subsidiaries) in non-US data centers falls under the jurisdiction of the USA Patriot Act, an anti-terrorism law introduced in 2001.[10] This emphatically includes the entire US cloud – Facebook, Apple, Twitter, Dropbox, Google, Amazon, Rackspace, Box, Microsoft, and many others. Jeffrey Rosen, a law professor at George Washington University, has established that the Patriot Act, rather than investigating potential terrorists, is mostly used to spy on innocent Americans.[11] But the people being watched need not even be Americans. Via the cloud, citizens across the world are subject to the same Patriot Act powers – which easily lend themselves to misuse by authorities. Matthew Waxman of the Council on Foreign Relations outlines the situation:

> These kinds of surveillance powers have historically been prone to abuse. Some of the legal restrictions on surveillance that the Patriot Act was designed to roll back were actually the direct product of abuses by the FBI, the CIA, and other government agencies. During the 1960s and '70s, national security intelligence powers were used by government agents to spy on political opposition [and] cast abusively wide nets. That legacy of abuse has raised a lot of concerns about whether there is adequate oversight with respect to these new surveillance powers.[12]

The sociologist Saskia Sassen adds to this perspective:

> Through the Patriot Act [...] the government has authorized official monitoring of attorney-client conversations, wide-ranging secret searches and wiretaps, the collection of Internet and e-mail addressing data [...] All of this can be done without probable cause about the guilt of the people searched – that is to say, the usual threshold that must be passed before the government may invade privacy has been neutralized. This is an enormous accrual of powers in the administration, which has found itself in the position of having to reassure the public that it can be 'trusted' not to abuse these powers. But there have been abuses.[13]

03/14

e-flux journal #37 — september 2012   Metahaven
Captives of the Cloud: Part I

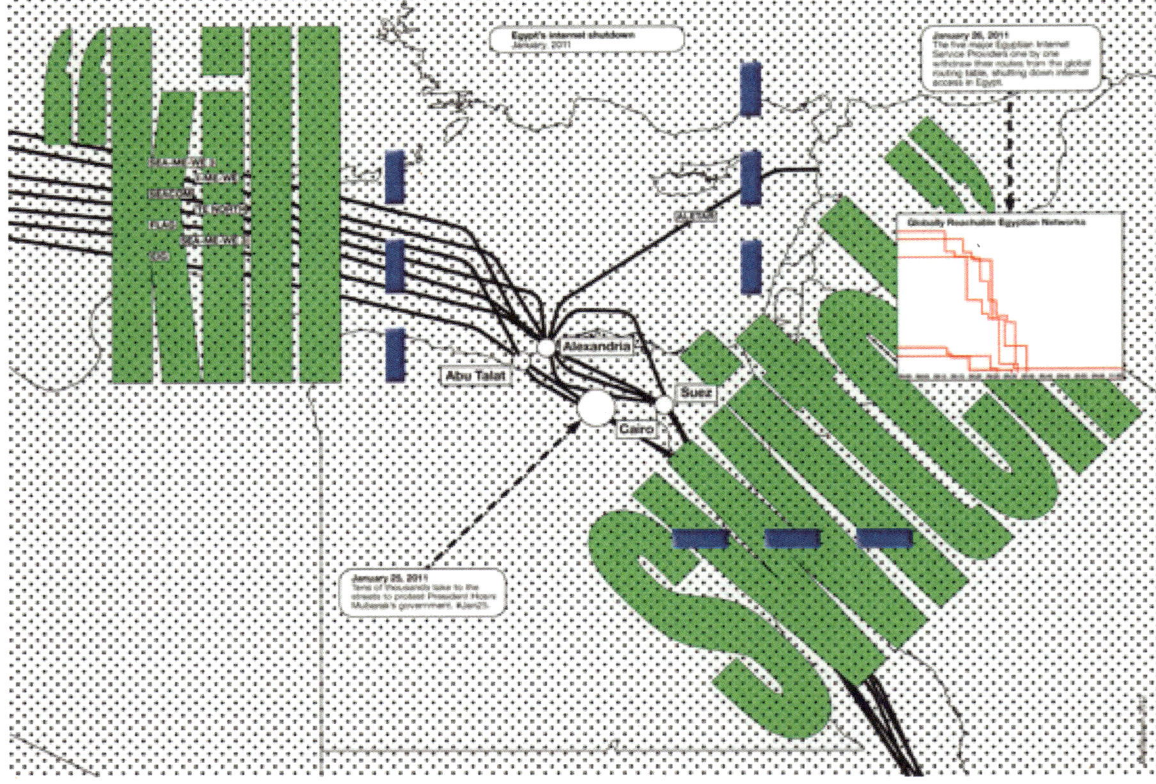

The Mubarak "kill switch" which took Egypt off the internet in January, 2011.

Microsoft was the first cloud company to publicly confirm Patriot Act access to its data stored outside the US.[14] In August 2011, Google also confirmed that its data stored overseas is subject to "lawful access" by the US government.[15] A 2012 white paper by the law and privacy firm Hogan Lovells examined these findings, concluding that while the Patriot Act does give the US government access to the cloud, many other governments enjoy similar forms of access under their own laws – and further, that using the "location" of a cloud server to determine legal protection was a mistaken idea altogether.[16] The paper noted the widespread use of so-called Mutual Legal Assistance Treaties (MLATs), which streamline the exchange between countries of data needed for investigative purposes. Apart from treaty-backed requests, "informal relationships between law enforcement agencies [...] allow for governmental access to data in the 'possession, custody, or control' of cloud service providers over whom the requesting country does not otherwise have jurisdiction." The legality of such informal relationships was not examined by the study. Neither did it backlog any recorded abuses of the Patriot Act, or discuss reports by two US Senators about a "secret interpretation" of the law, which would give the FBI far-reaching extra surveillance powers that the public is unaware of.[17]

One of the most powerful instruments the US government uses to look into the so-called "non-content information" of ISPs and cloud providers is the National Security Letter (NSL). NSLs demand specific information about users and are issued directly by the FBI. After the Patriot Act was signed into law, the number of letters issued rose exponentially: from 8,500 in 2000 to 39,346 in 2003. An NSL automatically includes a gag order that prohibits the recipient from notifying users about the request. The FBI need only assert that the information sought is "relevant" to an investigation.[18] The crucial question in the Hogan Lovells report – "Are government orders to disclose customer data subject to review by a judge?" – is answered with "yes" in Australia, Canada, Denmark, France, Germany, Ireland, Japan, Spain, the United Kingdom, and the US. However, in the US this condition is only met if the cloud provider, after receiving the NSL, first challenges its built-in gag order. Only when the NSL is unsealed by a judge can the cloud provider inform the user about the existence of the letter. For the Hogan Lovells report, this procedure counts as judicial review.

Super-Jurisdiction
In Egypt, during the revolution, Facebook and Twitter played the role of subversive, uncensorable alternative media – in part because the servers of these wildly popular services were beyond the reach of local authorities. Indeed, Hosni Mubarak's best bet to fend off the power of the internet was to switch it off entirely. To do so, "just a few phone calls probably sufficed."[19] While Mubarak's *ultima ratio* as a sovereign ruler over Egyptian soil proved sufficient to wall the country off from the network, the violent crudeness of this act also demonstrated the dictator's much more substantial *lack of power* over the network's larger infrastructure. Sovereign control over the cloud, in contrast to authoritarian power-mongering, is a sophisticated affair. One might draw a very different map here: the global spread of the US cloud, for example, results in a kind of "super-jurisdiction" enjoyed by its host country.

Super-jurisdiction can be seen in action in the 2012 seizure of Megaupload.com by the US Department of Justice (DOJ). Megaupload.com was a Hong Kong-based internet enterprise paying loving tribute to all kinds of Hollywood films (to say it politely). The site offered, according to its own self-description, "no-registration upload and sharing of files up to 1 gigabyte." It was seized in January 2012 by the DOJ and the FBI, backed by film industry copyright claimants. Megaupload.com stands accused of generating "more than $175 million in criminal proceeds" and causing "more than half a billion dollars in harm to copyright owners."[20]

The site's founder, thirty-seven-year-old internet millionaire Kim Dotcom, and three of his associates were brought to a New Zealand court to face extradition to the US. They'd been living like self-styled oligarchs. In a gesture toward transparency, they said they had "nothing to hide."[21] In particular, Dotcom himself embodies the absurd saga of a contemporary, deeply self-parodying internet hooligan – a legal black hole turned persona, unprepared in every way to be "famous," yet accepting the challenge wholeheartedly. Megaupload.com was, at least in its own self-imagination, nothing more than a technical conduit between those who upload and those who download, its content-indiscriminate policy a typical example of laissez-faire anarcho-capitalism. The US government's prosecution of the site remains highly debated, because the DOJ interpreted the site's global user base as a willful conspiracy to break US law. As Jennifer Granick at Stanford Law notes, the DOJ referenced "unknown parties" (i.e., the users of Megaupload.com) as members of a conspiracy to conduct a crime in the US. Granick notes that such users "were located all over the world, and may or may not have acted willfully." Indeed, with Megaupload.com, the government alleges "an

05/14

e-flux journal #37 — september 2012   Metahaven
Captives of the Cloud: Part I

agreement to violate a US civil law, including by many people who are not subject to US rules." As Granick then asks, "Does the United States have jurisdiction over anyone who uses a hosting provider in the Eastern District of Virginia? What about over any company that uses PayPal?"[22] Indeed, these are the sorts of questions prompted by super-jurisdiction.

Super-jurisdiction means that the law of one country can, through various forms of cooperation and association implied by server locations and network connections, be extended into and enacted in another. The US, as a result of its unique position in managing the internet's core, also has jurisdiction over all so-called top level domains, no matter where they are hosted and by whom. All top-level domain names (dot-com, dot-org, dot-net, etc.) must be registered through VeriSign, a Virginia-based company. Using its jurisdiction over the domain name registry, in 2012 the DOJ seized Bodog.com, a gambling website operated from Canada. A US Customs Enforcement spokesperson confirmed to *Wired* that the US had in a similar manner seized 750 different domain names of sites it believed committed intellectual property theft.[23] Michael Geist, an internet law professor at the University of Ottawa, observes that, indeed, "All Your internets Belong to US":

> The message from the [Bodog] case is clear: all dot-com, dot-net, and dot-org domain names are subject to US jurisdiction regardless of where they operate or where they were registered. This grants the US a form of "super-jurisdiction" over internet activities since most other countries are limited to jurisdiction with a real and substantial connection. For the US, the location of the domain name registry is good enough.[24]

Cloud Surveillance

The various technical components that enable global communication – server, network, and client – all lend themselves to surveillance. *Access Controlled,* a MIT Press handbook on internet surveillance and censorship, states that "the quest for information control is now beyond denial."[25] It mentions the so-called "security first" norm, by which the combined threats of terrorism and child pornography create a mandate for the state to police the net without restriction. As the authors assert in their conclusion, "The security-first norm around internet governance can be seen, therefore, as but another manifestation of these wider developments. Internet censorship and surveillance – once largely confined to

authoritarian regimes – is now fast becoming the global norm."[26] Indeed, if a lawsuit brought by the Electronic Frontier Foundation (EFF) against AT&T is any indication, the US government seems determined to expand its access to electronic communication. The EFF's star witness in the case was Mark Klein, a former AT&T technician who claimed to have seen, in 2002, the creation and ongoing use of a dedicated private room where the National Security Agency (NSA) had "set up a system that vacuumed up internet and phone-call data from ordinary Americans with the cooperation of AT&T."[27] Klein said the system allowed the government full surveillance of not just the AT&T customer base, but that of sixteen other companies as well.[28] The US government dismissed the case against the telecommunications provider, asserting the privilege of state secrets. The government has also dismissed cases against itself and other telecom companies that assisted with similar endeavors, including Sprint, Nextel, and Verizon.[29] If the allegations are true, according to *Access Controlled*, "they show that the United States maintains the most sophisticated internet surveillance regime."[30]

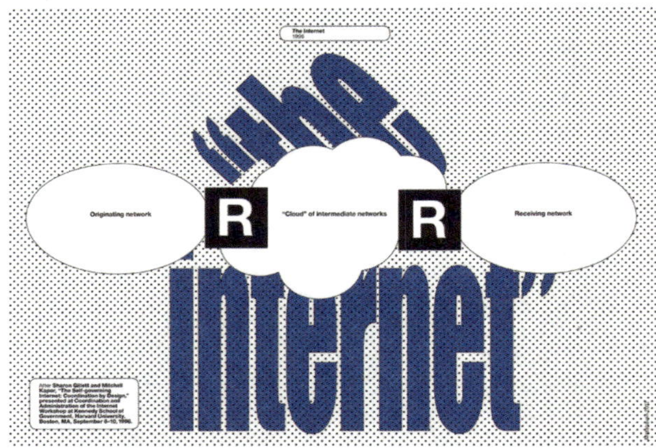

The first mention of the notion of the "cloud" was in a 1996 diagram in an MIT research paper, redrawn here.

As technologies expand, the governance, legislation, and legalities of surveillance become increasingly complicated. In May 2012, CNET reported that the general counsel of the FBI had drafted a proposed law that would require social-networking sites, e-mail and voice-over-IP (VoIP) providers, as well as instant messaging platforms, to provide a backdoor for surveillance – a demand from the US government for cloud companies to "alter their code to ensure their products are wiretap-friendly."[31] In 2012, the UK Government announced the installation – in collaboration with telecom companies and ISPs – of so-called "black boxes" which would retrieve and decrypt communications from Gmail and other cloud services, storing the non-content data from these communications.[32] But the cloud is nothing like a national telephone network. Whenever the cloud is "wiretapped," authorities listen into a global telecommunications oracle; the data of everyone using that cloud, regardless of where and who they are, and regardless of whether or not they are the suspect of a crime, is at least in principle at the disposal of law enforcement.

Most journalism routinely criticizes (or praises) the US government for its ability to spy on "Americans." But something essential is not mentioned here – the practical ability of the US government to spy on everybody else. The potential impact of surveillance of the US cloud is as vast as the impact of its services – which have already profoundly transformed the world. An FBI representative told CNET about the gap the agency perceives between the phone network and advanced cloud communications for which it does not presently have sufficiently intrusive technical capacity – the risk of surveillance "going dark." The representative mentioned "national security" to demonstrate how badly it needs such cloud wiretapping, inadvertently revealing that the state secrets privilege – once a legal anomaly, now a routine – will likely be invoked to shield such extensive and increased surveillance powers from public scrutiny.

Users' concerns about about internet surveillance increased with the proposed Stop Online Piracy Act (SOPA), which was introduced into the US House of Representatives in late 2011. How the government would police SOPA became a real worry, with the suspicion that the enforcement method of choice would be standardized deep packet inspections (DPI) deployed through users' internet service providers – a process by which the "packets" of data in the network are unpacked and inspected.[33] Through DPI, law enforcement would detect and identify illegal downloads. In 2010, before SOPA was even on the table, the Obama Administration sought to enact federal laws that would force communications providers offering encryption (including e-mail and instant messaging) to provide access by law enforcement to unencrypted data.[34] It is, however, worth noting that encryption is still protected as "free speech" by the First Amendment of the US Constitution – further complicating, but not likely deterring, attempts to break the code. One way of doing so consists

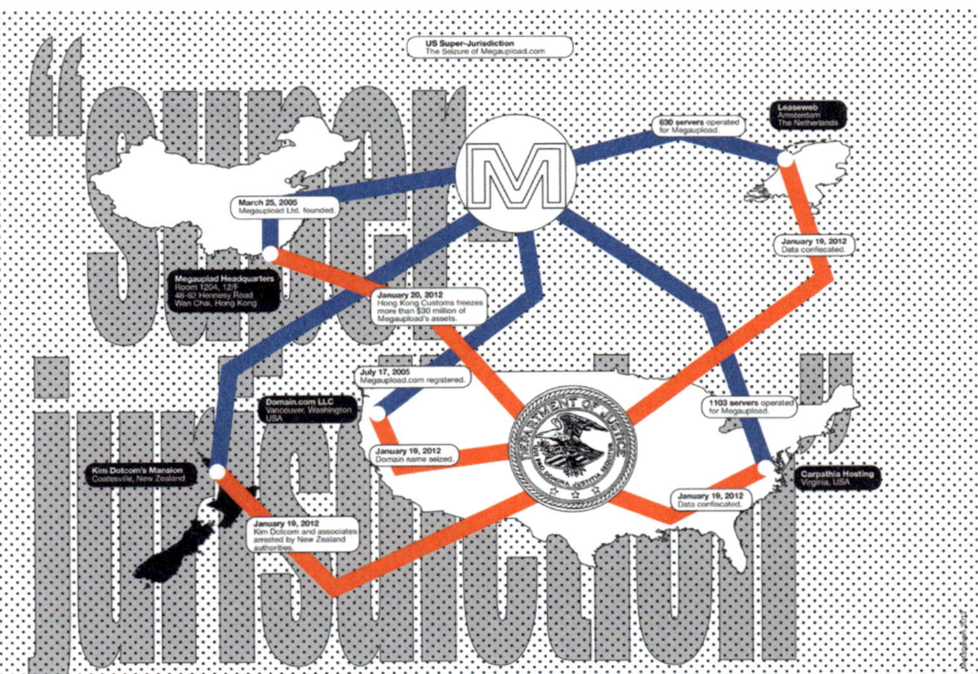

The seizure of Megaupload.com; using super-jurisdiction to allege a global conspiracy.

of surrounding encryption with the insinuation of illegality. The FBI in 2012 distributed flyers to internet cafe business owners requesting to be wary of "suspicious behavior" by guests, including the "use of anonymizers, portals or other means to shield IP address" and "encryption or use of software to hide encrypted data." In small print, the FBI added that each of these "indicators" by themselves, however, constituted lawful conduct.[35]

Coercive Paternalism

"Real name" requirements by the cloud-based social networking platforms Facebook and Google+ expressly attack anonymity and pseudonymity online, affecting the fundaments of political speech. Real name directives require users to register with a service using the name that is in their passport. The reasons given by cloud services for such real name requirements are vague – perhaps for fear of sounding too directly authoritarian. The preferred route, instead, is that of fatherly advice. Facebook claims that it has a real name policy "so that you always know who you're connecting with," while Google states that it requires real names so "that the people you want to connect with can find you."[36] These explanations gesture towards a conception of normative social arrangements – requiring that your use the same name that you'd use among your friends, family, or coworkers. Alexis Madrigal points out a certain irony in the Google+ real name requirement:

> The kind of naming policy that Facebook and Google Plus have is actually a radical departure from the way identity and speech interact in the real world. They attach identity more strongly to every act of online speech than almost any real world situation does.[37]

Cloud providers such as Amazon use real name registration as a mechanism for accountability. Though Amazon still allows users to use a "pen name," the trademarked "real name" attribution is advertised as having the ability to "potentially increase your reputation in the community" as a retailer, seller, or reviewer.[38] Some see the real name badge as a step towards "fixing their flawed [and] exploitable review system" for reviewing books – a system notoriously dominated by biased "anonymous" users, often thought to be, and sometimes proven to be, other authors, their family members, or the books' publishers.[39] Though Amazon's reasoning for promoting the use of real names is more explicit than that of Facebook and Google+, one can imagine the marketing benefits of a synchronized real name system between social media and retail websites – and the connection that such a synchronicity might have with the government. Such requirements can be seen as aligned with plans of the US government to introduce a universal "trusted identity" or "internet ID" system for US citizens, a commission the White House granted to the US Commerce Department in 2011. According to White House Cybersecurity Coordinator Howard Schmidt, the effort entails nothing less than creating an "identity ecosystem" for the internet.[40]

Cass Sunstein, the Obama Administration's chief internet advisor, has recently argued for government policy against the spread of "rumors" on the internet; as noted by the *New Yorker*, one of the most persistent of such rumors was the theory that President Obama had been born in Kenya – and thus holds his presidency illegally.[41] Sunstein believes that certain properties of the internet gear public speech toward the uninformed forwarding and circulation of rumors and conspiracy theories. In "echo chambers" and through "cybercascades," one-sided opinion would spread rapidly and widely in the network without rebuttal. Supposedly balanced reporting by professional journalists in the mainstream media now has to compete for attention with, and gets often surpassed by, every other blog post, Facebook update, or tweet. The effortless ability for all Internet users to compose and live on a "Daily Me" – a news diet catered to fit and maintain an individual, already established, self-referential set of beliefs – would result in a fragmentation of the general public into factions which no longer expose themselves to views held by other factions. Sunstein claims that under such fragmentation, "diverse speech communities" are created "whose members talk and listen mostly to one another." And,

> When society is fragmented in this way, diverse groups will tend to *polarize* in a way that can breed extremism and even hatred and violence. New technologies, emphatically including the Internet, are dramatically increasing people's ability to hear echoes of their own voices and to wall themselves off from others.[42]

Sunstein is concerned with how rumors may impair the effectiveness of government, and undermine its legitimacy. Early 2008, he and a co-author published a paper on conspiracy theories around the 9/11 attacks. In the paper, Sunstein recommended that "Government agents (and their allies) might enter chat rooms, online social networks, or even real-space groups and attempt to undermine percolating conspiracy theories by raising doubts about their

08/14

e-flux journal #37 — september 2012   Metahaven
Captives of the Cloud: Part I

factual premises, causal logic or implications for political action."[43]

Nowhere is the coercive government stance toward online rumors as clear as in China. Beijing put forth regulations requiring users to register on social medial sites with their "real name identities" by March 2012 – regulation comparable to policies already spontaneously embraced by Facebook and Google. Sites including Sina Weibo, one of the country's largest microblogging sites, have begun implementing these regulations, which also forbid users from making statements against the state's honor or statements that may disrupt civil obedience.[44] Around the same time, social media sites across the country flared up over the ouster of political leader Bo Xilai from the Communist Party. The Chinese police swiftly detained six people and shut down sixteen websites over "rumors" surrounding the incident, including claims that military vehicles were entering Beijing.[45]

Cloud as a Political Space

The increasing prominence which cloud-based internet services, social media and VoIP technologies now enjoy over legacy tools of communication shows in how they enable new, virtually cost-free forms of organization. For

09/14

social movements relying on collective action, this factor has proven to be key. Unsurprisingly, when social media platforms are suddenly "switched off," their ability to organize can be severely affected. Facebook, in the wake of nationwide anti-austerity protests in the UK in February 2011, deleted the profiles of dozens of political groups preparing to take part in further protests. In doing so, Facebook effectively disabled lawful political activism, which had, for obvious reasons, moved their coordination to the cloud. The reason for the purge is still not known and likely never will be. All the social networking behemoth could utter to justify its behavior was cryptic technospeak. Profiles had "not been registered correctly," as a Facebook spokeswoman explained.[46] In 2010, UK Prime Minister David Cameron and other Conservative politicians met in London with Facebook founder Mark Zuckerberg. Their admiration was mutual.[47]

Rebecca MacKinnon, a former CNN reporter and cofounder of the citizen media network Global Voices, asserts in her book *Consent of the Networked* that "we cannot understand how the internet is used unless we first understand the ways in which the internet itself has become a highly contested political space."[48] This applies equally, and equally urgently, to the cloud.

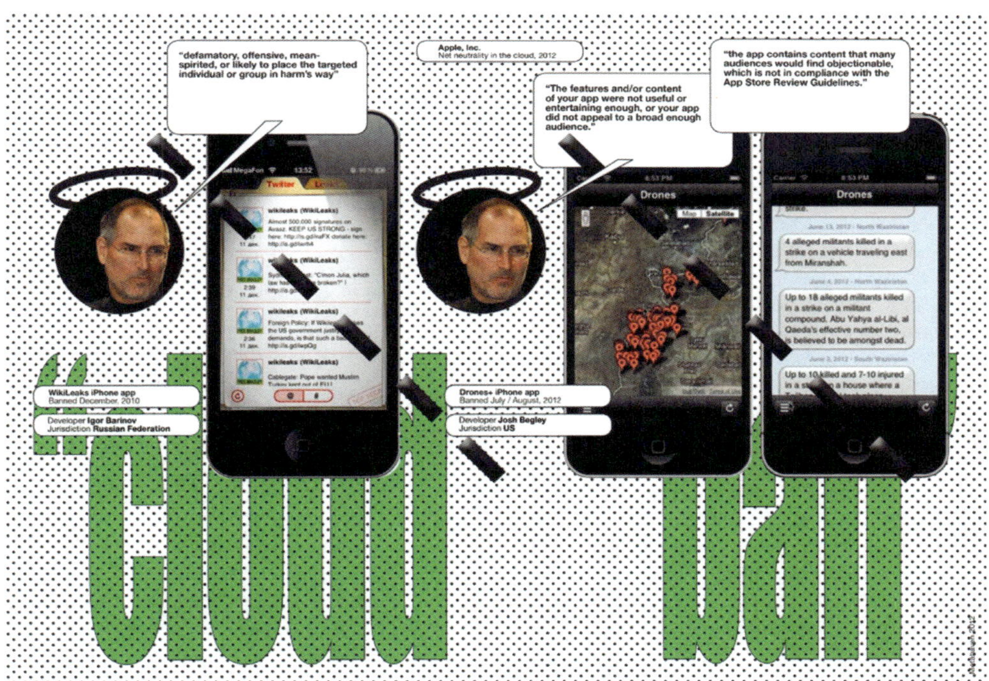

App neutrality? Apple's ban on two controversial iPhone apps in 2010 and 2012 shows a lack of network neutrality in the cloud.

The combined rights to a free flow of information, freedom of expression, and freedom from censorship, have been described as a compound right to "internet freedom." Indeed, Google's Wael Ghonim at the beginning of this story suggested that unhindered access to, and use of, the internet enables the liberation of a society.

Here, the free flow of information is blocked by clearly identifiable authoritarian despots. To not have internet freedom, one must be under the oppression of a shameless tyrant, or be living in a "closed society" where the free flow of information is not sufficiently appreciated just yet. On January 21, 2010, US Secretary of State Hillary Clinton delivered a speech on US foreign policy and internet freedom, highlighting exactly this view. Clinton assured her audience in Washington, D.C. that "As I speak to you today, government censors are working furiously to erase my words from the records of history."[49] Evgeny Morozov, a US-based, Belarusian-born internet scholar rightly criticized Clinton's "anachronistic view of authoritarianism." As Morozov explained, "I didn't hear anything about the evolving nature of internet control (e.g. that controlling the internet now includes many other activities – propaganda, DDoS attacks, physical intimidation of selected critics/activists). If we keep framing this discussion only as a censorship issue, we are unlikely to solve it." He went on to criticize the double standards the State Department advertised with regard to online anonymity:

> On the one hand, they want to crack down on intellectual property theft and terrorists; on the other hand, they want to protect Iranian and the Chinese dissidents. Well, let me break the hard news: You can't have it both ways and the sooner you get on with "anonymity for everyone" rhetoric, the more you'll accomplish. I am very pessimistic on the future of online anonymity in general – I think there is a good chance it will be eliminated by 2015 – and this hesitance by the State Department does not make me feel any more optimistic.[50]

Still, the definition of internet freedom remains relatively opaque. One example of this vagueness is provided by Internetfreedom.org, a global consortium, which aims to "inform, connect, and empower the people in closed societies with information on a free internet."[51] Savetheinternet.com, a project of Free Press, breaks down internet freedom into somewhat more clearly defined categories – "net neutrality (wired and wireless), strong protections for mobile phone users, public use of the public airwaves and universal access to high-speed internet."[52] The notion of net neutrality is as relevant to internet freedom as it is to the structure of the cloud, since the network's management is in the hands of a patchwork of government agencies and private enterprises who may (or may not) hold a bias toward certain information on the network, or a bias toward one another. Coined by the legal scholar Tim Wu in 2003, network neutrality was originally meant to benchmark and promote the open nature of the internet for the sake of innovation – an "end-to-end" infrastructure unbiased towards its content. As Wu stated, "A communications network like the internet can be seen as a platform for a competition among application developers. Email, the web, and streaming applications are in a battle for the attention and interest of end-users. It is therefore important that the platform be neutral to ensure the competition remains meritocratic."[53] Network neutrality applies to a decentralized architecture, with clearly divided roles between ISPs, broadband service providers, content providers, and services and applications on the network. It justifies a *de facto* gentlemen's agreement through a joint economic interest in innovation and fair competition. Indeed, also political speech can be considered part of a competition – one of ideas on how to (not) govern ourselves. Venture capitalist Joichi Ito expressed this view in 2003, when he wrote that such a competition of ideas "requires freedom of speech and the ability to criticize those in power without fear of retribution."[54]

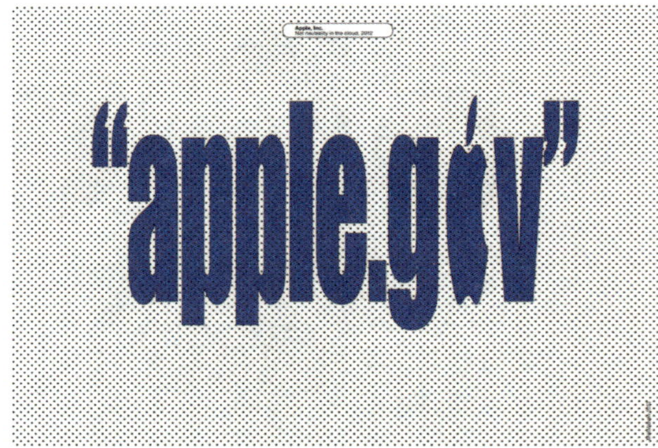

Apple.gov: governmentality in the cloud.

Insofar as the cloud's software services use the shared internet, they can be considered applications run on the network. To this end, network neutrality applies to the cloud (for example, the cloud is expected to consume more and more bandwidth in the network, possibly at the cost of other applications and services). The concept of network neutrality is more difficult to apply *in* the cloud, since some of the nominal conditions to institute neutrality are absorbed by the cloud's combination of hosting and software services within a single black box. In the cloud, there is no more principled separation between the hosting of data, software, and client-side tools through which the data is handled and experienced. Indeed, the enormous success of the cloud is that it provides for all of these things at once.[55]

The Terms of Service of any cloud-based provider are a far cry from a binding agreement to net neutrality; they allow plenty of space for "cloudy bias." For example, in August, 2012, Apple banned "Drones+" from its App Store. This app, developed by NYU student Josh Begley, provides aggregated news on US drone strikes in Pakistan, Yemen and Somalia, and it includes a Google map on which the strikes are marked. The app also prompts the user whenever a new drone strike has occurred, and says how many casualties it had produced. Crucially, the information aggregated by the app is already completely public and freely available through various other sources including *The Guardian*'s iPhone app. Apple demonstrated its cloudy parody of network neutrality in the ever-changing reasons it gave for rejecting Drones+. Apple had problems with the Google logo appearing on the Google map. In July, the company stated in an e-mail that "The features and/or content of your app were not useful or entertaining enough, or your app did not appeal to a broad enough audience." By August, Apple changed its mind. The app contained "content that many audiences would find objectionable, which is not in compliance with the App Store Review Guidelines." Indeed, the company eventually concluded that Drones+, which does not show users any images of actual drone-related bloodshed, was "objectionable and crude."[56] The *New York Times* wondered how on earth it could be that

> the material Apple deemed objectionable from Mr. Begley was nearly identical to the material available through *The Guardian*'s iPhone app. It's unclear whether Apple is treating the two parties differently because *The Guardian* is a well-known media organization and Mr. Begley is not, or whether the problem is that Mr. Begley chose to focus his app only on drone strikes.[57]

One can endlessly ponder why Apple banned Drones+ from its cloud but admitted *The Guardian,* and one will never be finished

weighing the arguments. The point is that if its cloud operated even under something remotely looking like network neutrality, Apple could not have reasonably rejected the app. The case also brings to mind Evgeny Morozov's earlier warning that government censorship of the network nowadays is more sophisticated than a crude Mubarak internet kill switch. As Rebecca MacKinnon writes,

> citizens are [...] vulnerable to abuse of their rights to speech and assembly not only from government but also from private actors. In democracies, it follows that citizens must guard against violations of their digital rights by governments and corporations – or both acting in concert – regardless of whether the company involved is censoring and discriminating on its own initiative or acting under pressure from authorities.[58]

It is highly unlikely that Drones+ was banned after direct government interference. But it isn't difficult to imagine an informal, unstated, and rather intuitive constellation of interests between Apple – universally praised by US politicians on both sides of the aisle – and the US Government. Shared interests and informal ties between private enterprise and government, based on mutual forms of "Like," rather than strict separations by Law, may account for *de facto* forms of censorship in the cloud, without the explicit order to enact it or the explicit obligation to justify it. In December 2010, Apple removed a WikiLeaks iPhone app from its store, citing its developer guidelines: "Any app that is defamatory, offensive, mean-spirited, or likely to place the targeted individual or group in harms [sic] way will be rejected."[59] Simultaneous to the WikiLeaks app being banned, other US cloud companies, including Amazon and PayPal, stopped providing services to WikiLeaks.

The political, legal and jurisdictional consequences of the cloud are slowly becoming apparent – right at the time when we are unlikely to withdraw from it. The cloud is just too good. We won't stop using our iPhones, iPads, Androids and Kindles. Paypal is still our frenemy. Happily the captives of the cloud, we will tweet our critiques of it, and Facebook-broadcast our outcries over its government back doors. But the story is not over yet. Will the anarcho-libertarian roots of the internet kick back at the cloud's centralized architecture – or are they forever overrun by it? Has the cloud assumed its final form, or is there still a time and a place for surprises?

×

Written by Daniel van der Velden and Vinca Kruk. Research

11/14

e-flux journal #37 — september 2012 Metahaven
Captives of the Cloud: Part I

assistant: Alysse Kushinski. Design assistant: Rasmus Svensson. All images courtesy of Metahaven. Metahaven 2012.

→ *To be continued in "Captives of the Cloud: Part II."*

Metahaven is an Amsterdam-based design collective on the cutting blade between politics and aesthetics. Founded by Vinca Kruk and Daniel van der Velden, Metahaven's work – both commissioned and self-directed – reflects political and social issues through research-driven design, and design-driven research. Research projects included the *Sealand Identity Project*, and currently include *Facestate*, and *Iceland as Method*. Solo exhibitions include *Affiche Frontière* (CAPC musée d'art contemporain de Bordeaux, 2008) and *Stadtstaat* (Künstlerhaus Stuttgart/Casco, 2009). Group exhibitions include *Forms of Inquiry* (AA London, 2007, cat.), *Manifesta8* (Murcia, 2010, cat.), the *Gwangju Design Biennale 2011* (Gwangju, Korea, cat.), *Graphic Design: Now In Production* (Walker Art Center, Minneapolis, 2011, and Cooper-Hewitt National Design Museum, New York, 2012, cat.) and *The New Public* (Museion, Bolzano, 2012, cat.). Metahaven's work was published and discussed in *The International Herald Tribune*, *The New York Times, Huffington Post*, *Courrier International, Icon, Domus*, *Dazed*, *The Verge*, *l'Architecture d'Aujourd'hui*, and *Mute*, among other publications. Vinca Kruk is a Tutor of Editorial Design and Design Critique at ArtEZ Academy of Arts in Arhem. Daniel van der Velden is a Senior Critic at the Graphic Design MFA program at Yale University, and a Tutor of Design at the Sandberg Instituut Amsterdam. In 2010, Metahaven released *Uncorporate Identity*, a design anthology for our dystopian age, published by Lars Müller.

1
Wael Ghonim, cited in Rebecca MacKinnon, *Consent of the Networked: The Worldwide Struggle for Internet Freedom* (New York City: Basic Books, 2012), xx.

2
Brandon Teddler, "To The Cloud!," *Ezine Mark,* February 20, 2012. See http://cloud.ezinemark.com/t o-the-cloud-7d3407dff%2043c.html.

3
Sharon Gillett and Mitchell Kapor, "The Self-governing Internet: Coordination by Design," presented at Coordination and Administration of the Internet Workshop at Kennedy School of Government, Harvard University, Boston, MA, September 8–10, 1996. See http://ccs.mit.edu/papers/CC SWP197/ccswp197.html.

4
John Markoff, "An Internet Critic Who Is Not Shy About Ruffling the Big Names in High," *New York Times,* April 9, 2001. See http:// www.nytimes.com/2001/ 04/09/ technology/09HAIL.html ? ex=1230872400&en= 5d156fc75d409335 &ei=5070.

5
Eric Schmidt, "Conversation with Eric Schmidt Hosted by Danny Sullivan," Search Engine Strategies Conference, August 9, 2006. See http://www.google.com/press/podium/ses2006.html.

6
"Amazon: The Walmart of the Web," *The Economist,* October 1, 2011. See http://www.economist.com/nod e/21530980.

7
Nathan Eddy, "Cloud Computing to Drive Storage Growth: IDC Report," *eWeek,* October 21, 2011. See http://www.eweek.com/c/a/Clo ud-Computing/Cloud-Computing -to-Drive-Storage-Growth-IDC -Report-193712/.

8
Nick Bilton, "Data storage server, and founder, move quickly." *International Herald Tribune,* August 28, 2012.

9
Barb Darrow, "Amazon Is No. 1. Who's Next in Cloud Computing?," *GigaOM,* March 14, 2012. See http://gigaom.com/cloud/amaz on-is-no-1-whos-next-in-clou d-computing/. Cade Metz, "Google: 'We're Like a Bank for Your Data,'" *Wired,* May 29, 2012. See http://www.wired.com/wireden terprise/?p=20996.

10
Zack Whittaker, "Summary: ZDNet's USA PATRIOT Act Series," *ZDNet,* April 27, 2011. See http://www.zdnet.com/blog/ig eneration/summary-zdnets-usa -patriot-act-series/9233.

11
Jeffrey Rosen, "Too Much Power," *New York Times,* September 8, 2011. See http://www.nytimes.com/roomf ordebate/2011/09/07/do-we-st ill-need-the-patriot-act/the -patriot-act-gives-too-much- power-to-law-enforcement.

12
Matthew C. Waxman, "Extending Patriot Act Powers," interview by Jonathan Masters, www.cfr.org, February 22, 2012. See http://www.cfr.org/counterte rrorism/extending-patriot-ac t-powers/p24174.

13
Saskia Sassen, *Territory, Authority, Rights. From Medieval to Global Assemblages*, Princeton and Oxford: Princeton University Press, 2006 (2008), 180.

14
Paul Taylor, "Privacy Concerns Slow Cloud Adoption," Financial Times, August 2, 2011. See http:// news.softpedia.com/news/ Google-Admits-Handing-over- European-User-Data-to-US- Intelligence-Agencies-215740. shtml.

15
Lucian Constantin, "Google Admits Handing over European User Data to US Intelligence Agencies," *Softpedia,* August 8, 2011. See http://www.hldataprotection. com/ uploads/file/Hogan%20Lov ells% 20White%20Paper%20Gover nment %20Access%20to%20Cloud% 20Data%20Paper%20(1).pdf.

16
Winston Maxwell, and Christopher Wolf, "A Global Reality: Governmental Access to Data in the Cloud," *A Hogan Lovells White Paper,* May 23, 2012. See http:// www.hldataprotection. com/ uploads/file/Hogan%20Lov ells% 20White%20Paper%20Gover nment %20Access%20to%20Cloud% 20Data%20Paper%20(1).pdf.

17 Mike Masnick, "Senators Reveal That Feds Have Secretly Reinterpreted The PATRIOT Act," *Techdirt,* May 26, 2011. See http:// www.techdirt.com/arti cles/20110525/15411414434/se nators-reveal-that-feds-have -secretly-reinterpreted-patr iot-act.shtml.

18
Kim Zetter, "Unknown Tech Company Defies FBI In Mystery Surveillance Case," *Wired,* March 14, 2012. See http:// www.wired.com/thr eatlevel/2012/03/mystery-nsl /.

19 Ryan Singel, "Egypt Shut Down Its Net With a Series of Phone Calls." *Wired,* January 28, 2011. See http://www.wired.com/threatl evel/2011/01/egypt-isp-shutd own/.

20
Claire Connelly and Lee Taylor, "FBI Shuts down Megaupload.com, Anonymous Shut down FBI," News.com.au, January 20, 2012. See http://www.news.com.au/techn ology/fbi-shuts-down-megaupl oadcom-charges-seven-with-on line-piracy/story-e6frfro0-1 226249114650#ixzz1k8bkZU4v.

21
Ibid.

22
See Jennifer Granick, "Megaupload: A Lot Less Guilty Than You Think," Center for Internet and Society at Stanford Law School, January 26, 2012. See http://cyberlaw.stanford .edu/node/6795.

23
David Kravats, "Uncle Sam: If It Ends in .Com, It's .Seizable," *Wired,* March 6, 2012. See http://www.wired.com/threatl evel/2012/03/feds-seize-fore ign-sites/.

24
Michael Geist, "All Your Internets Belong to US, Continued: The Bodog.com Case," michaelgeist.ca, March 6, 2012. See http://www.michaelgeist.ca/c ontent/view/6359/135/.

25
Ronald Deibert, John Palfrey, Rafal Rohozinski, Jonathan Zittrain (eds.), *Access Controlled: The Shaping of Power, Rights, and Rule in Cyberspace* (Cambridge, Massachusetts: The MIT Press, 2010), 6.

26
Ibid., 11.

27
Ellen Nakashima, "A Story of Surveillance," *The Washington Post,* November 7, 2007. See http://www.washingtonpost.co m/wp-dyn/content/article/200 7/11/07/AR2007110700006.html

28
Ibid.

29
Dan Levine, "US Court Upholds Telecom Immunity for Surveillance," *Thomson Reuters,* December 29, 2011. See http://newsandinsight.thomso nreuters.com/Legal/News/2011 /12_- _December/U_S__court_up holds_telecom_immunity_for_s urveillance/.

30
Ronald Deibert et. al., *Access Controlled,* 381.

31
Declan McCullagh, "FBI: We Need Wiretap-Ready Web Sites – Now," *CNET,* May 4, 2012. See http://news.cnet.com/8301-10 09_3-57428067-83/fbi-we-need -wiretap-ready-web-sites-now /.

32
Geoff White, "'Black Boxes' to Monitor All Internet and Phone Data," *Channel 4,* June 29, 2012. See http://www.channel4.com/news /black-boxes-to-monitor-all- internet-and-phone-data.

33
Alex Wawro, "What Is Deep Packet Inspection?," *PC World,* February 1, 2012. See http://www.pcworld.com/artic le/249137/what_is_deep_packe t_inspection.html.

34
Declan McCullagh, "Report: Feds to Push for Net Encryption Backdoors," *CNET,* September 27, 2010. See http://news.cnet.com/8301-31 921_3-20017671-281.html.

35
See http://publicintelligence.ne t/fbi-suspicious-activity-re porting-flyers/.

36
"Facebook's Name Policy – Facebook Help Center," facebook.com. See http://www.facebook.com/help /?faq=112146705538576&in_context. "Google-Page and Profile Names – Google+ Help," plus.google.com.See http://support.google.com/plus/bin/ answer.py?hl=en&answer=1228271.

37
Alexis Madrigal, "Why Facebook and Google's Concept of 'Real Names' Is Revolutionary," *The Atlantic,* August 5, 2011. See http://www.theatlantic.com/t echnology/archive/2011/08/wh y-facebook-and-googles-conce pt-of-real-names-is-revoluti onary/243171/.

38
"Amazon.com Help: Pen Names and Real Names," amazon.com. See http://www.amazon.com/gp/hel p/customer/display.html?ie=U TF8&nodeId=14279641.

39
Mark T. Kieczorek, "Amazon Real Name Badge," *Maktaw,* July 23, 2004. See http://www.marktaw.com/techn ology/AmazonRealNameBadge.ht ml. Amy Harmon, "Amazon Glitch Unmasks War Of Reviewers," *New York Times,* February 14, 2004. See http://www.nytimes.com/2004/ 02/14/us/amazon-glitch-unmas ks-war-of-reviewers.html?pag ewanted=3&src=pm.

40
Declan McCullagh, "Obama to Hand Commerce Dept. Authority over Cybersecurity ID," *CNET,* January 7, 2011. See http://news.cnet.com/8301-31 921_3-20027800-281.html?tag= contentMain;contentBody.

41
Elizabeth Kolbert, "The Things People Say," *The New Yorker,* November 2, 2009.

13/14   Metahaven   e-flux journal #37 — september 2012   Captives of the Cloud: Part I

See http://www.newyorker.com/arts/critics/books/2009/11/02/091102crbo_books_kolbert?currentPage=all.

42
Cass R. Sunstein, *Republic.com 2.0,* (Princeton and Oxford, Princeton University Press, 2007), 44.

43
Cass R. Sunstein, Adrian Vermeule, "Conspiracy Theories." *Harvard University Law School Public Law & Legal Theory Research Paper Series*, Paper No. 199, University of Chicago Law School, 2008, 22. See http://papers.ssrn.com/sol3/papers.cfm?abstract_id=1084585.

44
Michael Kan, "Beijing to Require Users on Twitter-like Services to Register With Real Names," *PC World,* December 16, 2011. See http://www.pcworld.com/businesscenter/article/246360/beijing_to_require_users_on_twitterlike_services_to_register_with_real_names.html?tk=rel_news.

45
Michael Bristow, "China Arrests Over Coup Rumours," *BBC News,* March 31, 2012. See http://www.bbc.co.uk/news/world-asia-china-17570005. David Eimer, "China Arrests Six Over Coup Rumours," *The Telegraph,* March 31, 2012. See http://www.telegraph.co.uk/news/worldnews/asia/china/9177717/China-arrests-six-over-coup-rumours.html.

46
Shiv Malik, "Facebook Accused of Removing Activists' Pages," *The Guardian,* April 29, 2012. See http://www.guardian.co.uk/technology/2011/apr/29/facebook-accused-removing-activists-pages.

47
Tim Bradshaw, "Mark Zuckerberg Friends David Cameron," *Financial Times,* June 21, 2012. See http://blogs.ft.com/tech-blog/2010/06/mark-zuckerberg-friends-david-cameron/#axzz1yC7waUhe.

48
MacKinnon, *Consent of the Networked,* xxii.

49
"Internet Freedom." The prepared text of U.S. of Secretary of State Hillary Rodham Clinton's speech, delivered at the Newseum in Washington, D.C. Foreign Policy, January 21, 2010. See http://www.foreignpolicy.com/articles/2010/01/21/internet_freedom?page=0,2.

50
Evgeny Morozov, "Is Hillary Clinton launching a cyber Cold War?" *Foreign Policy Net.Effect,* January 21, 2010. See http://neteffect.foreignpolicy.com/posts/2010/01/21/cyber_cold_war.

51
See http://www.internetfreedom.org/.

52
See http://www.Savetheinternet.com/.

53
Tim Wu, "Network Neutrality, Broadband Discrimiration." *Journal of Telecommunications and High Technology Law,* Vol. 2, p. 141, 2003. See http://papers.ssrn.com/sol3/papers.cfm?abstract_id=388863.

54
Joichi Ito, "Weblogs and Emergent Democracy." See http://papers.ssrn.com/sol3/papers.cfm?abstract_id=388863.

55
On a related note, cyberlaw professor Jonathan Zittrain in 2008 wrote *The Future Of The Internet — And How To Stop It*, a book focusing on the rise of the web's "tethered appliances," which, like North Korean radio sets, can be attuned to exclude or disregard certain content, and are designed not to be tinkered with by their users. Zittrain argued that such closed service appliances — emphatically including design icons like iPods and iPhones, for example — would in fact contribute to stifle the generative and innovative capacity of the web. See Jonathan Zittrain, *The Future Of The Internet — And How To Stop It,* New Haven and London: Yale University Press, 2008.

56
Christina Bonnington and Spencer Ackerman, "Apple Rejects App That Tracks U.S. Drone Strikes." *Wired*, August 30, 2012. See http://www.wired.com/dangerroom/2012/08/drone-app/.

57
Nick Wingfield, "Apple Rejects App Tracking Drone Strikes." *New York Times Blog,* August 30, 2012. See http://bits.blogs.nytimes.com/2012/08/30/apple-rejects-app-tracking-drone-strikes/.

58
MacKinnon, ibid., 119.

59
Gregg Keizer, "Apple boots WikiLeaks app from iPhone store." *Computerworld,* December 21, 2010. See http://www.computerworld.com/s/article/9201920/Apple_boots_WikiLeaks_app_from_iPhone_store.

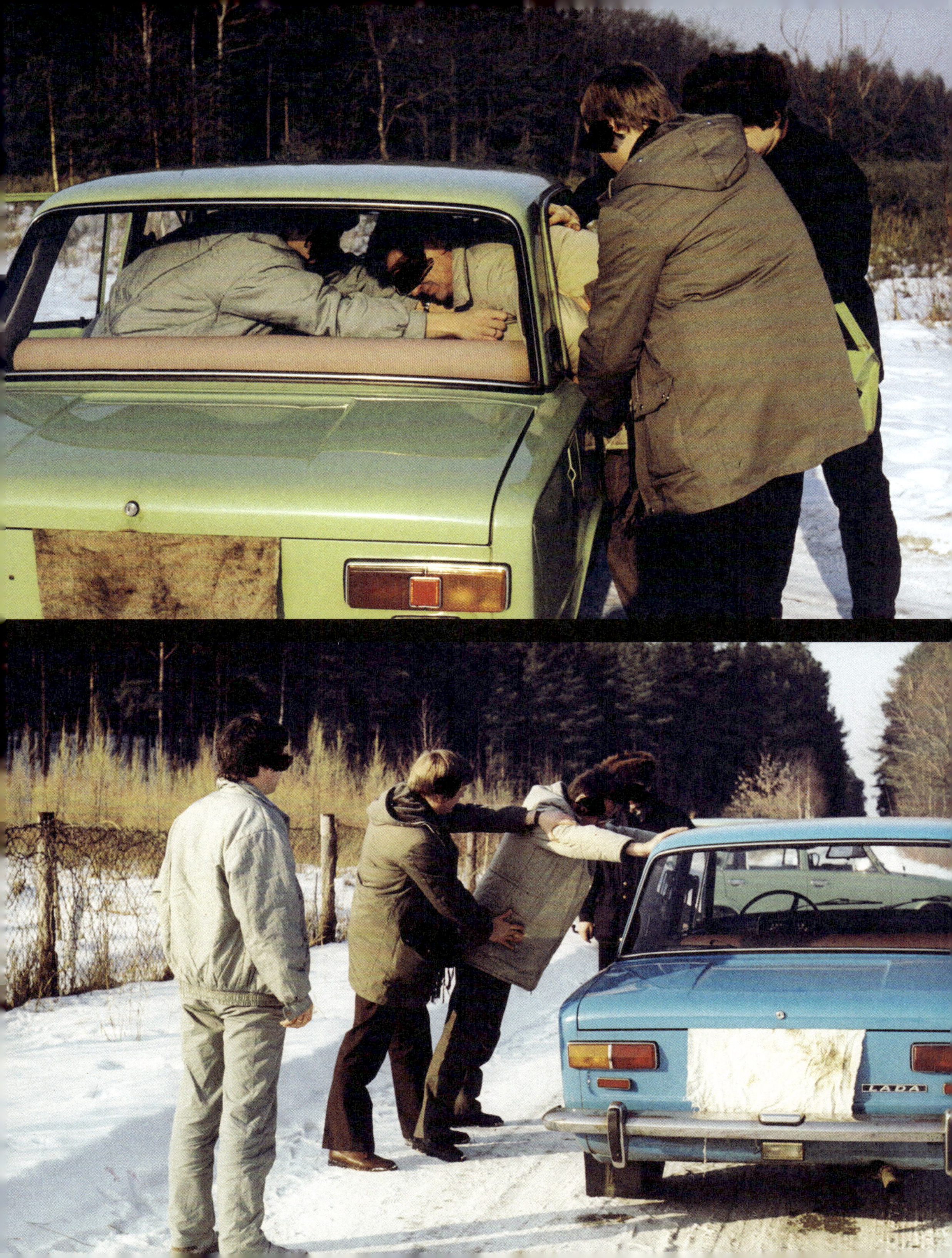

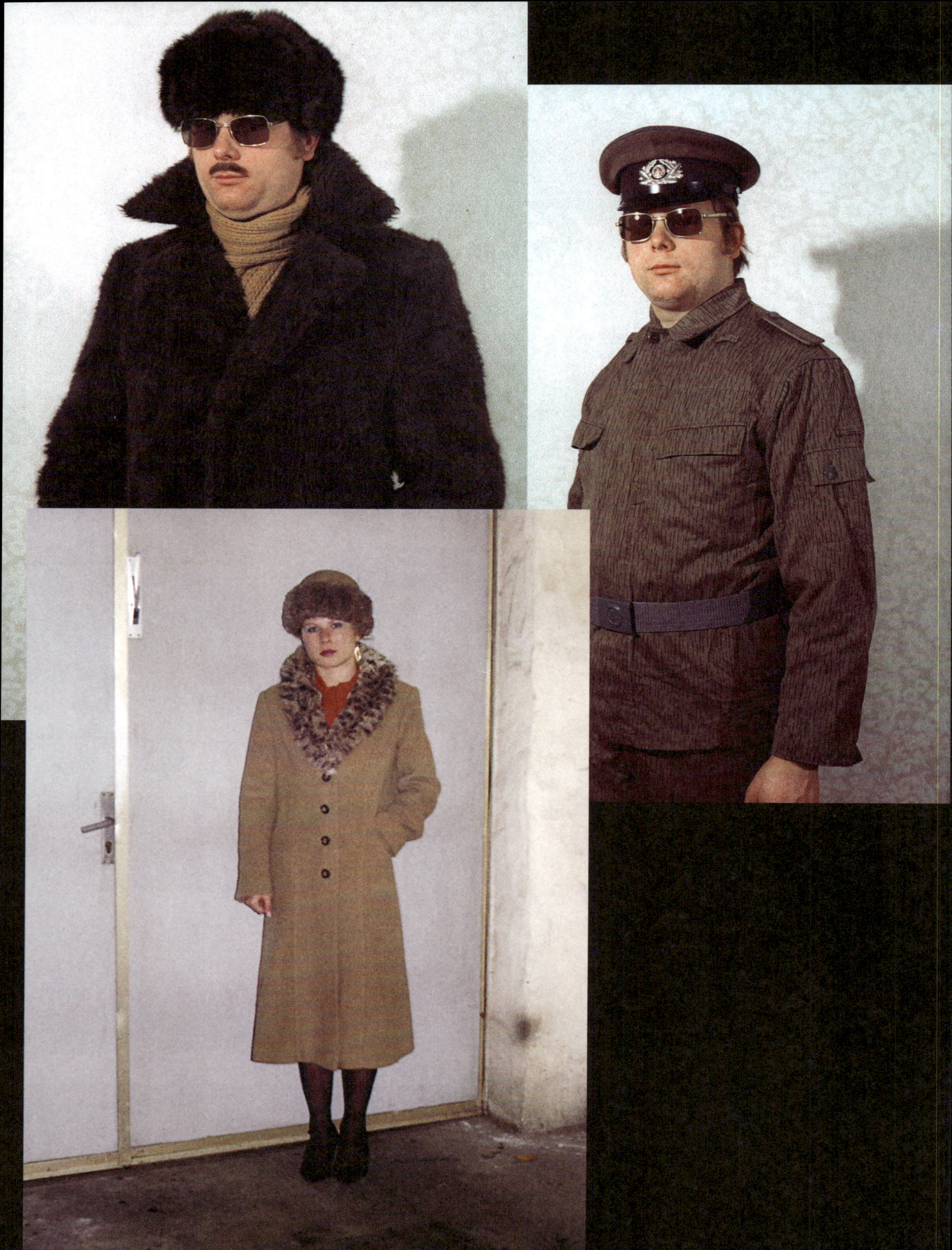

The Guardian

The artist who spied on MI6

It was a top-secret mission he couldn't refuse. Painter James Hart Dyke was assigned to shadow spooks for a year, sketchbook in hand. What did he learn about their mysterious world? View the M16 paintings

Joanna Moorhead

Mon 14 Feb 2011 08.00 GMT

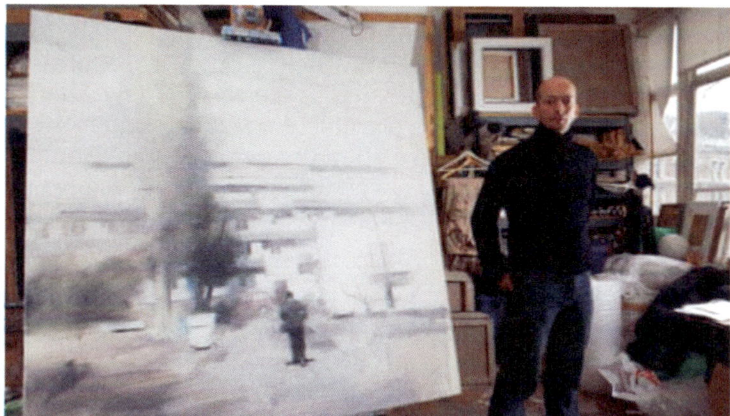

James Hart Dyke in his studio with one of his MI6 paintings, Going For a Meeting 3. Photograph: Graham Turner for the Guardian

'I'll come straight to the point," said "M", looking across the desk at his top agent. "I've got a job for you, Bond. I want you to start painting. Show the world out there what this organisation is really all about. Show them the world of spying, Bond. Show it like it is . . . put it on canvas with a brush and paints . . ."

In all his fictitious exploits, Ian Fleming's James Bond never did get to be a painter. But about 18 months ago, proving that life is often stranger than fiction, a conversation much like this really did take place. Sitting behind the desk was the then head of MI6, Sir John Scarlett - who was known, as all heads of MI6 are, not as "M" but as "C", for chief - and opposite him, a rather dapper man in his early 40s by the name of James. Not a spy called James Bond, but an artist called James Hart Dyke.

Hart Dyke, a painter who has accompanied Prince Charles as official artist on four royal tours, and been embedded as a war artist with the Grenadier Guards in Iraq and Afghanistan, suspected an elaborate joke when he was approached by MI6, the government secret service that deals with overseas intelligence-gathering. "It sounded so unlikely that I reckoned someone was having me on," he says. His first brush with the spooks was a mysterious phone call - "it was from someone I'd once worked with, I can't tell you who" - followed by a meeting over a drink in a pub. "We found a quiet corner, and he sketched out the landscape. Basically, I was being asked to infiltrate MI6 as an artist! It sounded extraordinary. I couldn't have made it up."

Meetings at MI6's fortress-like HQ in south London followed, at which Hart Dyke was told that he would have to operate within strict parameters. Hart Dyke, who trained as an architect at the Royal College of Art and made his name as a landscape painter, was given access to M16, but not paid by the service. "The chief told me that keeping identities hidden would be crucial - there was no way this project could compromise the safety of the officers or the agents. And I wasn't allowed, either, to identify the locations I visited."

But in every way they could, the bosses at MI6 allowed Hart Dyke to sample the life of an undercover agent - with sketchbook and pencil in hand. "I had a pass so I could go in and out of the HQ building, and I travelled to other MI6 centres in the UK and overseas - MI6 works in around 80 countries across the world. I saw where the officers work, how they live, and what they do. As far as possible, I was 'one of them' - I don't believe I was ever in any danger, but I know that very often the world of spying and espionage is very dangerous. And of course I often saw people wondering what I was really up to - I saw officers looking at me as I sketched away and they seemed to be thinking, oh yes - an artist, are you? A likely story …"

Suspicion, after all, is part of the psyche of the spying business: and Hart Dyke became aware of the low-level suspicion - of people and of events - that, of necessity, permeates every day for a spy. "What struck me most - and I've tried to get this across in my paintings - is the intriguing interface between the mundane and the totally unexpected. So, for example, you'll be in a totally normal setting - on a busy street perhaps, or in a hotel bar - but you're waiting for something completely out-of-the-ordinary - a tip-off or an information drop. In the midst of an entirely innocent-seeming event, something entirely 'other' is taking place."

As a result, many of the paintings depict the most everyday of settings (a street corner, a hotel bedroom, a row of parked cars) populated by ordinary-looking people (a middle-aged woman in a coat and hat, a man in a leather jacket, a smart-looking woman carrying a briefcase). It's only when you know that the exhibition that's resulted from the project - which opens to the public on Tuesday - is entitled A Year With MI6 that you think twice about his subjects' motives. Does the woman standing on the street corner have a penchant for outsize handbags, or is she carrying a sheaf of secret documents to hand over to a contact? Is that man in the leather jacket glancing over his shoulder to look out for traffic, or to check he isn't being watched? And are that man and woman sitting in a bar strangers about to fall in love, or is she an MI6 officer who's about to infiltrate the life of a "target" by chatting him up?

Nothing is as it seems in the world of MI6 - and that's what Hart Dyke has tried to convey. Some of his work seems almost surreal - but for an agent the world probably is pretty surreal. So a picture of a grey dog looking up at a ball, or a doughnut on a pink-striped tablecloth, seem random images but, says Hart Dyke, they're loaded with meaning for certain officers who have taken part in certain operations. Likewise the fact that many of the paintings are either washed entirely in green or feature a heavy use of the colour: inside MI6, "C" is the only person who writes in green ink, following a tradition established by the organisation's founder, Mansfield Cumming.

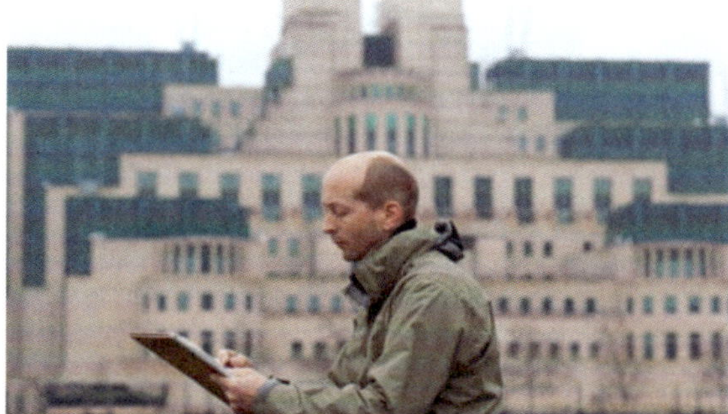

Hart Dyke with his sketchpad opposite MI6's London HQ.
Photograph: Graham Turner for the Guardian

One of the biggest revelations for Hart Dyke – and possibly the biggest "secret" his paintings reveal – is how different the reality is from the mythology. "It's not James Bond," he says. "The work real MI6 officers and agents do is nothing like as glitzy as the image. Some of it is very fast-moving and exciting, but what you don't get in fictional accounts is any sense of how much time is spent sitting around, waiting for something that might, but very often doesn't, happen."

Scarlett – now retired from MI6 and working, among other projects, as a senior adviser to Morgan Stanley – says the idea of inviting an artist in came from MI6 officers themselves, as part of the run-up to the 2010 centenary year. "We brought people together from across the service and we asked them how they thought we should mark our first 100 years," he says. "And there was a feeling that, because of the secrecy of our organisation, we've not been able to celebrate its spirit in the way that other organisations can. They said they wanted to do something that would pass the core values of the service from one generation to another – and painting, because it's such a flexible medium, was the way to capture that.

"This organisation is surrounded by myths and legends. And while that can be a good thing, it's not always." The dearth of information about the secret services has provided a vacuum that Ian Fleming, Ben Richards (the author of Spooks), John le Carré and many other writers have been only too happy to fill, but what we read, and watch, isn't the whole, or even very much of, the truth.

So, in an age obsessed with marketing and self-image, is this an attempt at PR – albeit from the last organisation likely to blow its own trumpet? No, says Scarlett. "It's because this is an important part of the machinery of government, and it's important that people understand why it's here and what it does." Until the 90s, even the chief's identity was a secret. Then,

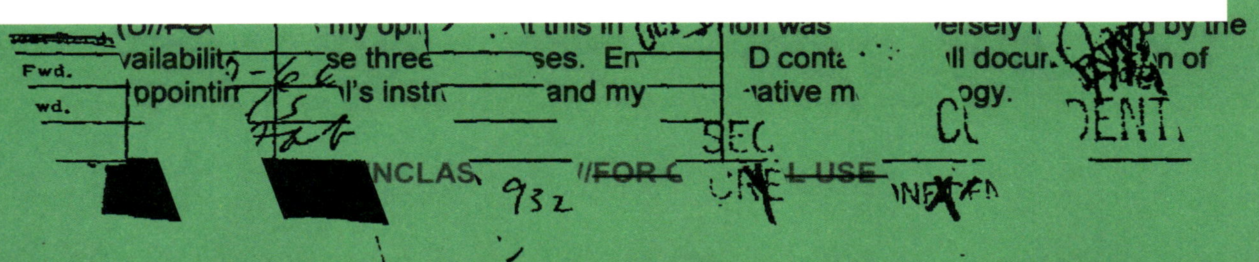

during his tenure as boss, Scarlett gave an interview, and the present incumbent, John Sawers, was the first "C" to make a speech in public. Last year also saw the publication of a history of the organisation. But Scarlett says he doesn't believe the art project is part of a gradual opening-up of the service. "It's a very unusual departure, and it's only going to happen once," he promises.

Hart Dyke's exhibition should prove an unexpected treat for that section of the British public who are endlessly fascinated by spies and their world. The show comprises around 40 paintings, 25 drawings, and prints - all for sale. MI6 did not commission Hart Dyke, but he has given it some pictures as a gift. The paintings on show have all, needless to say, been carefully vetted by the organisation - some, says Hart Dyke, have had to be altered so that sensitive information was not revealed.

For the cognoscenti, there are plenty of insider clues and tips. Scarlett praises the paintings and drawings as highly evocative of life inside MI6. "I'm hugely impressed with what he's done," he says. "It's remarkable. He's genuinely understood this place and what we're about; I'm very enthusiastic about the paintings, and I'm really pleased that some of them will remain here in our offices, so we can pass a sense of the organisation now on to future generations of staff.

"James has absolutely caught the sense of adventure amid ordinary life that is MI6. I won't be the only person here who will look at a painting set in a hotel room or on board a plane and think: I know that scene so well. And he's captured the perennial spirit of our operation - it's all about patriotism, mixed with doing our very best to protect British interests."

For his part, Hart Dyke is looking forward to ending his "spook" status. Just like a real spy, he wasn't able to tell anyone except his wife and his parents that he was working with MI6. "Living a double life was a strain," he says. "When people asked me what I was working on, I had to say something very vague or tell a cover story about doing something for the government. I'll be glad to get back to ordinary life . . . though I doubt I'll ever do anything quite as fascinating as this again."

A Year with MI6 is at the Mount Street Galleries, London W1, February 15-26. www.jameshartdyke.com

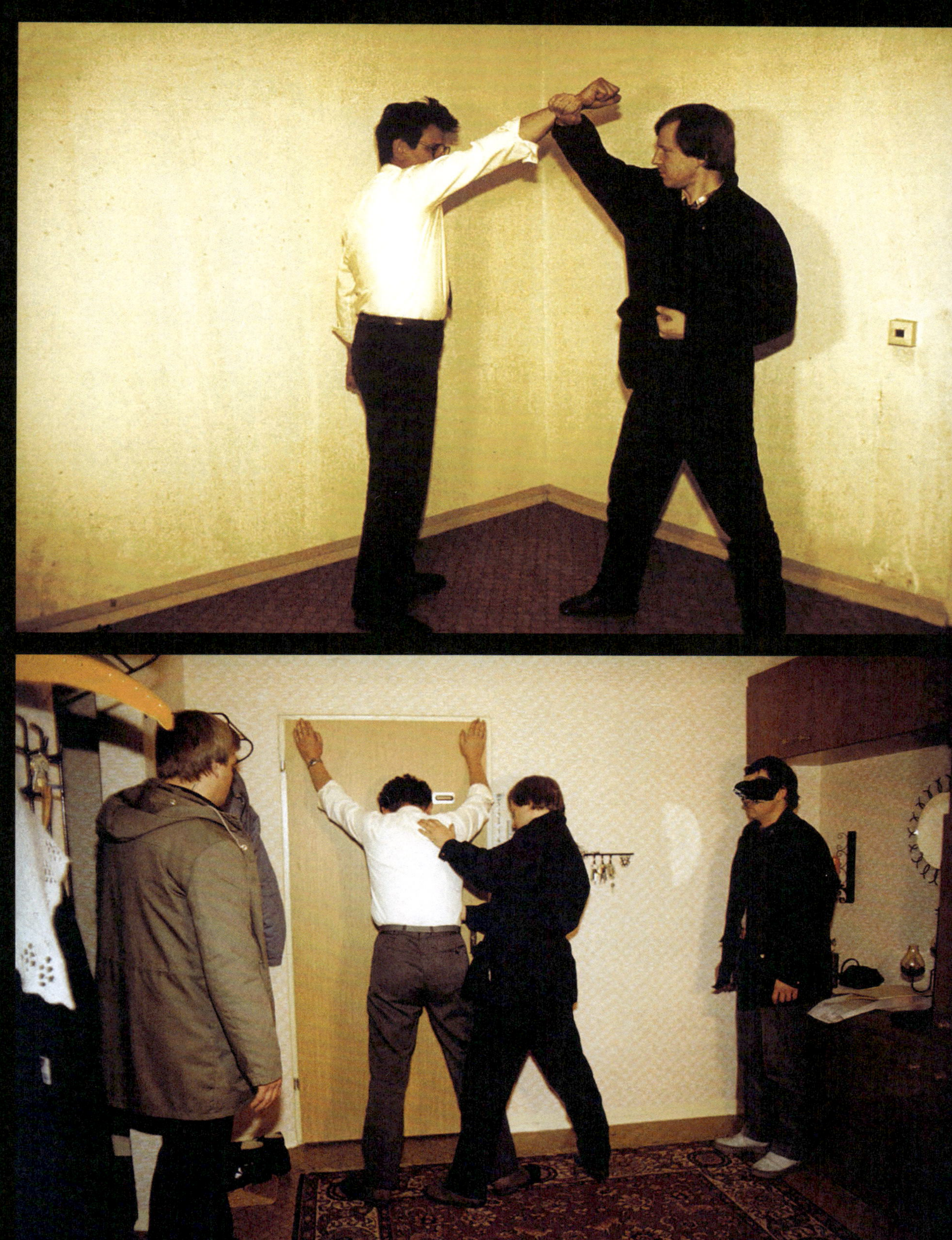

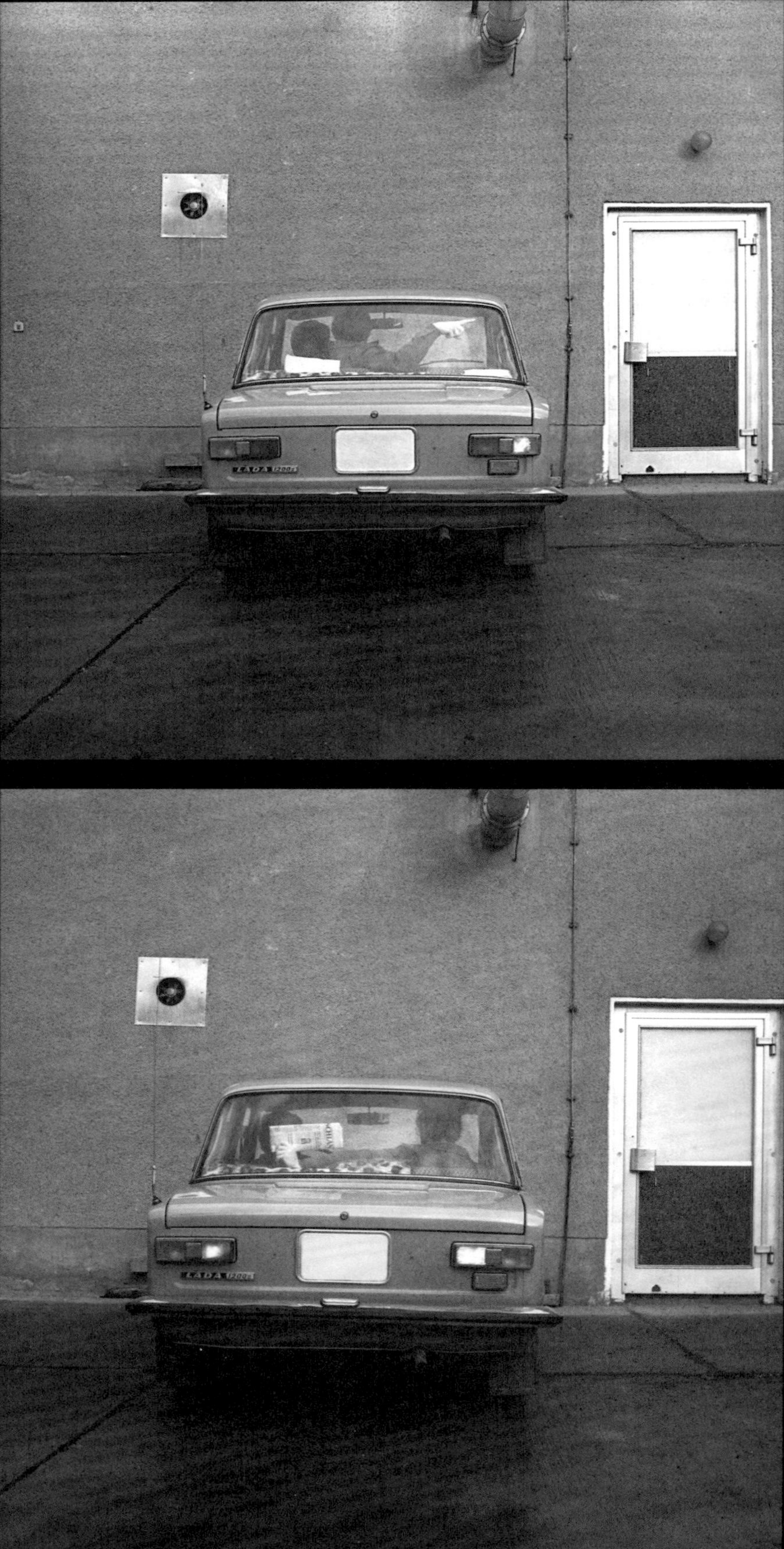

Der Spion, der sich als Künstler tarnte

Zeitgeschichte In seinem Einsatzort Brüssel erwachte in dem DDR-Agenten Horst Meier die Liebe zur Bildhauerei. Nun wird er posthum entdeckt.

Horst Meier ist vor knapp vier Wochen gestorben. Er wurde 91 Jahre alt. In den vergangenen Jahren war er ein Pflegefall, versunken in der Demenz. Er starb, wie er gelebt hat: als Geheimnis.

Niemand kannte ihn, er war nicht berühmt, doch seine Familie möchte nun, dass die Welt von ihm erfährt. Von Horst Meier, dem Spion der DDR in Brüssel, wo er sich als Künstler tarnte; von einem Menschen, der seine eigentliche Berufung erst in dieser Tarnung fand.

Der Kalte Krieg, die DDR und die Kunst – das ist das Dreieck seiner Geschichte. Eine sehr deutsche Geschichte, ohne viele Spuren, Geheimdienste verwischen ihre Spuren, und sie beginnt wie alle Geschichten des Kalten Krieges im Zweiten Weltkrieg. Meier war nach seiner Lehre als Elektriker von der Wehrmacht eingezogen und 1944 mit 18 Jahren an die Ostfront geschickt worden, noch Jahrzehnte später erzählte er vom Verwesungsgeruch. Fünf Jahre lang blieb er in Kriegsgefangenschaft, in Lagern in der Ukraine. Nahe Riga besuchte er später einige Monate lang die „Antifa-Zentralschule" – deren ideologisch geschulte Absolventen später in der DDR oft wichtige Funktionäre wurden.

Der Kriegsheimkehrer Meier, inzwischen 24, machte in Halle sein Abitur, studierte in Leipzig Journalismus, erhielt eine Stelle in Suhl, einer kleinen Bezirkshauptstadt am Rand des Thüringer Waldes. Meier hatte eine ehemalige Kommilitonin geheiratet, die beiden hatten vier Kinder.

Als Redakteur, der für Kultur zuständig war, schrieb er auch über die neue abstrakte Kunst des Westens, die er, so war es gewünscht, verdammte. Und es gibt ein Foto aus den späten Fünfzigerjahren: Meier ist da in dunklem Anzug mit weiteren Männern auf einer Tribüne zu sehen. Der berühmte Schriftsteller Erwin Strittmatter ist auch darunter. „Viel Arbeit, wenig Geld", schrieb Meier auf. Andere Notizen, die er später seiner Tochter diktierte, klingen wohlwollend. Ausflüge in den Thüringer Wald, im Winter Skifahren, er reiste mehrfach in die Sowjetunion und andere Länder des Ostblocks, auch nach Westdeutschland. Die Ehe wurde 1960 geschieden.

Ein anderes Foto, fünf Jahre später, zeigt Meier in seinem neuen Leben. Ein Freund aus der Kriegsgefangenschaft, der mit ihm auch die Antifa-Zentralschule absolviert hatte, holte ihn in die sogenannte Hauptverwaltung Aufklärung, die HVA. Diese Organisation für Auslandsspionage in der DDR wurde jahrzehntelang geführt vom legendären Markus Wolf. Klaus Rösler, so hieß der Freund, leitete bei der HVA die Abteilung XII., „Nato und EG".

Auf der Fotografie lehnt sich Meier aus der Fahrerkabine eines Lasters hinaus. Auf der Karosserie ist der Schriftzug „Ball of Toronto – Steel Drums" zu erkennen; das Gefährt gehörte offenbar einem Hersteller von Fässern und Tonnen im kanadischen Toronto. Es war Teil seiner neuen Legende. Meier, Mitte vierzig, war gerade dabei, ein anderer zu werden. Sein neuer Name: Erwin Miserre. Der echte Erwin Miserre war Jahre zuvor über die Bundesrepublik nach Kanada gezogen.

Meier reiste als Miserre in Westdeutschland ein, heuerte in seinem alten Beruf als Elektriker bei einem Großunternehmen an, ließ sich von Frankfurt nach Saarbrücken versetzen. Er lernte Französisch, weil er sich in Paris niederlassen sollte, wo das Hauptquartier der Nato angesiedelt war. Doch dann verlegte die Nato ihren Sitz nach Brüssel.

In Belgien besuchte Meier alias Miserre Abendkurse in Bildhauerei und knüpfte Kontakt zu Olivier Strebelle, einem der berühmtesten Bildhauer Belgiens. Strebelle ist heute 89 Jahre alt und kann sich gut an den Deutschen erinnern. Irgendwann in den späten Sechzigerjahren sei er plötzlich da gewesen, habe nach Arbeit gefragt, wollte ihm assistieren. Der Künstler lebt immer noch am Rand Brüssels, in dem Haus, das er damals schon bewohnte. Seine großen Plastiken fertigte er fast immer aus Bronze, manche sind wie dreidimensionale Puzzle zusammengesetzt, die Herstellung erfordert handwerkliches Geschick. Miserre konnte das. Die nächsten acht Jahre arbeitete er für Strebelle.

Der Belgier erwähnt die altmodische Mütze, die der Deutsche gern aufsetzte, fast mittelalterlich habe sie gewirkt. Sie hätten Miserre oft „Erwin Mystère" genannt, „Erwin Geheimnis", er habe wenig von sich erzählt. Miserres Französisch sei gut gewesen, man habe den deutschen Akzent gehört; dass er aus Ostdeutschland kam, wusste man nicht. Einer seiner anderen Leute, sagt Strebelle, habe aber damals gesagt, dass mit dem Deutschen etwas nicht stimme, der sei bestimmt ein Spion.

Die Hauptverwaltung Aufklärung hat in der Wendezeit alle Dokumente vernichtet. Man müsse, sagt Karl Rehbaum, Meiers einstiger Führungsoffizier und später guter Freund, denen glauben, die damals dabei waren. Rehbaum arbeitete ab 1965 bei der HVA. Sein prominentester Spion war der Westdeutsche Rainer Rupp alias Topas, der bei der Nato spionierte und 1994 wegen Landesverrats verurteilt wurde.

Meiers/Miserres eigentlicher Job war es, Informationen zwischen Agenten vor Ort und Ostberlin zu übermitteln; er nahm Fotos von Nato-Dokumenten entgegen und sorgte dafür, dass sie in die DDR gelangten; er war, so nannte man das, ein „Resident". Keiner, der selbst spitzelte, aber unverzichtbar, ein Mittelsmann, eine lebende Leitung. Es war nicht ungefährlich. „Das ist es nie", sagt Rehbaum. Die Aufgaben für die HVA seien aber eher profan gewesen, sogar unspektakulär, „das ist nicht wie im Film".

Meier jedenfalls konnte in Brüssel ein westliches Künstlerleben führen. Als Assistent bei einem berühmten Bildhauer, dorthin reisen, wo andere nie hinkamen. Weil er auch für seine alte Heimat eine Legende brauchte, konnte Meier oft nach Südostasien fliegen, denn für alle in der DDR war er ein politischer Korrespondent, der nach Asien abbeordert worden war.

Anfang der Siebzigerjahre lernte Meier eine Belgierin kennen, die deutlich jünger war als er und ihn auch auf Reisen begleitete. Sie war von Beruf Dolmetscherin. Ihrer Familie gefiel es nicht, dass ihr neuer Freund viel älter und ein Deutscher war. Sie sagt heute, dass sie lange nichts von seiner wahren Identität gewusst habe. Irgendwann seien sie nach Deutschland gereist, auch für einen Tag nach Ostberlin,

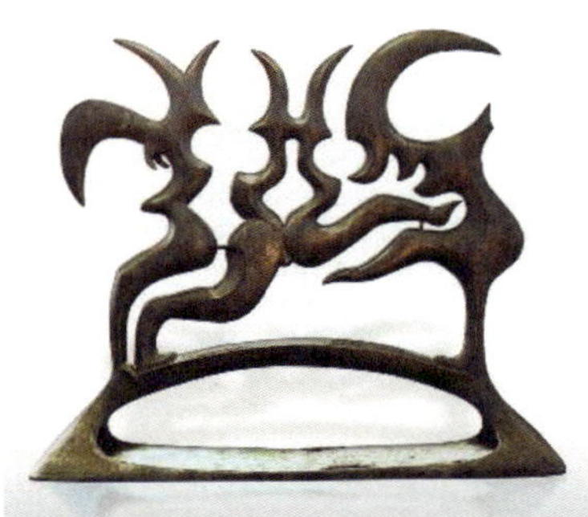

Meier-Werk „Fröhliche Maskerade", 1974/95
Gesellenstück aus Brüssel

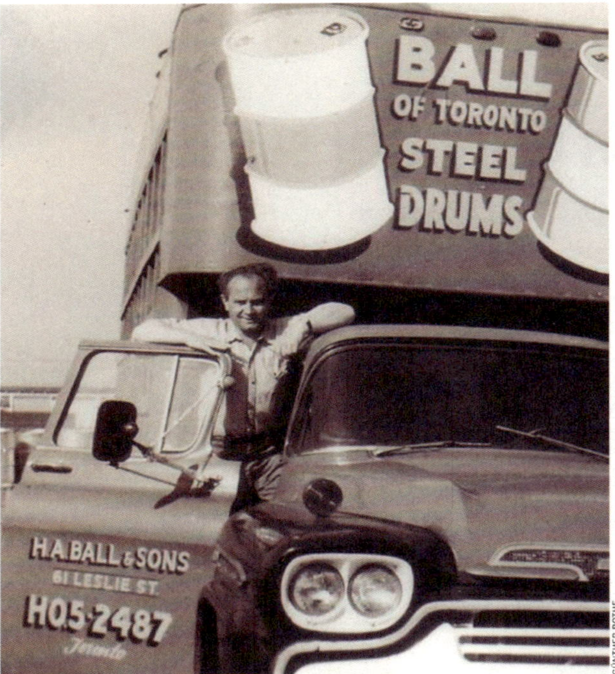
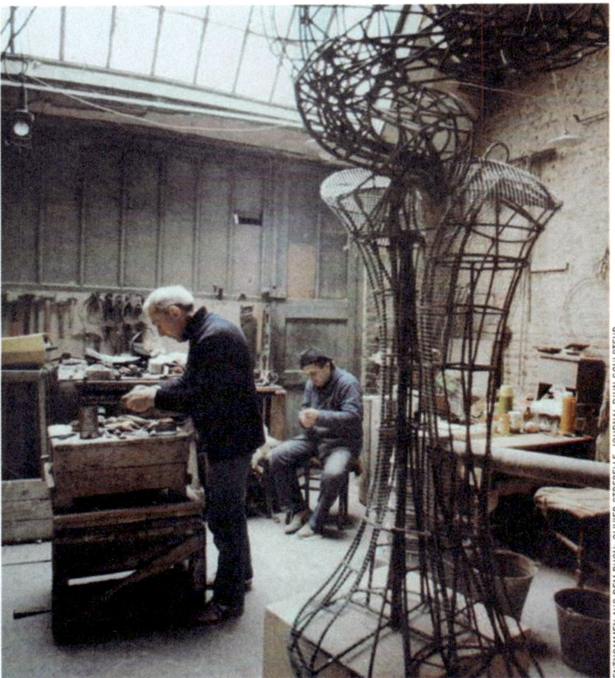

Spion Meier in Kanada 1965, Künstler Strebelle, Meier in Strebelles Atelier in Brüssel um 1975: Lebende Leitung in den Arbeiter-und-Bauern-Staat

die Sonne schien, und sie fand es dort gar nicht so schrecklich.

Abgezogen wurde Meier 1976 laut Rehbaum, weil der Verfassungsschutz der Bundesrepublik herausgefunden hatte, mit welcher „Übersiedlungsmethode" viele DDR-Agenten ins Ausland eingeschleust worden waren – dass man eben die Biografien von Auslandsdeutschen mit westdeutschem Pass nutzte. Die Gefahr, dass man Meier enttarnte, war groß.

Meier kehrte zurück in die DDR, mit seiner belgischen Freundin. Sie heirateten in Frankfurt an der Oder. Das Hochzeitsbild zeigt ein modern wirkendes Paar. Die beiden zogen aufs Land, in ein Dorf in Brandenburg, wo sie 40 Jahre lang gemeinsam lebten und zwei Kinder bekamen.

Meier beschloss, Künstler zu bleiben, niemand hatte etwas dagegen. Hinter dem Haus baute er sich schließlich ein Atelier, die HVA half mit Baumaterial aus. Und er legte sich einen großen Garten an, so wie Strebelle es in Brüssel getan hatte.

Eine Chemiefabrik beauftragte ihn damit, drei große Plastiken zu erschaffen, eine Gruppe von riesigen Windspielen, bei der Herstellung sollte eine Jugendbrigade helfen. Auf dem Gelände des Werks, das heute der BASF gehört, steht noch eine dieser Skulpturen. Ihr Titel lautet „Beflügelung", und Meier widmete sie, so schrieb er es 1982 in der Kombinatszeitung, allen sozialistischen Jugendbrigaden, denn von der Jugend erwarte er sich einen „erfolgreichen Vormarsch in die Zukunft". Wieder dieser DDR-treue Duktus. Fast klingt er wie in seinen Tagen als Redakteur des „Freien Wortes" in Suhl.

Die Plastiken, die er schuf, erinnerten an Strebelles Werk; manchmal eher etwas kitschig oder zu plump erotisch, anderes wirkt für DDR-Verhältnisse erstaunlich modern. Er war wieder Horst Meier, signierte aber weiter als „EM", als Erwin Miserre.

Er führte keine völlige Geheimexistenz mehr. Manchmal hat er zwar Werke unter der Hand verkauft, aber es muss auch weitere offizielle Verkäufe gegeben haben, etwa an eine Gewerkschaft. Noch heute steht eine seiner Skulpturen vor einer Gaststätte in der Nähe des Senftenberger Sees. Kein Schild erklärt, wie das Werk heißt, wer es hergestellt hat.

1982 entstand ein Prospekt, in dem Meiers Werke aus glänzender Bronze angeboten wurden. Zum Künstler heißt es: „Anfang der 60er bis Mitte der 70er Jahre journalistische Arbeit im Ausland. 1973 Beginn der künstlerischen Tätigkeit."

Den Prospekt gab damals Günther Rothe heraus, der, so sagt er, in der DDR ein Showorchester geleitet hatte und eine Kunstgießerei betrieb. Heute versteht er sich als Maler und Produktdesigner. Rothe ist es, der die Entdeckung Meiers vorantreibt, er hat alte Gipsmodelle in Bronze gießen lassen, sie wohl nachbearbeitet, er hat ein Buch herausgegeben*, und er will die Objekte ausstellen, erst einmal von übernächster Woche an in einem Hotel in Leipzig. Er sagt, er habe mehr als 200 000 Euro investiert. Es gibt einen Vertrag mit der Familie. Man hegt Hoffnungen.

Wer aber war nun Horst Meier? Eine Künstlerseele? Ein treuer Diener des Arbeiter-und-Bauern-Staates, der sein Leben so eingerichtet hatte, wie es der Staat wollte? Vor allem aber war er Teil der HVA-Clique und blieb es noch nach der Wende.

Seine Witwe sagt, er habe sich wirklich als Antifaschist verstanden, solche Losungen wie „Nie wieder Krieg" seien ihm wichtig gewesen. Rehbaum sagt, Meier habe mit ihm viel über die Vergangenheit geredet, den Krieg, die Gefangenschaft, die Zeit in der Antifa-Zentralschule, die frühe DDR. Meier habe doch zu der Generation gehört, die das Land mit aufgebaut hätte.

Seine Tochter aus zweiter Ehe hat er lange nach der Wende sein Leben in Stichworten aufschreiben lassen. Über seine Zeit in Brüssel ist selbst in dieser privaten Notiz nur von einer „auslandsjournalistischen Tätigkeit" die Rede. Seinen alten Freund Klaus Rösler, mit dem er Jahre der Kriegsgefangenschaft durchgestanden hatte, nennt er dort nur mit seinem HVA-Decknamen Martin.

Klaus „Martin" Rösler war es auch, der 1983 bei seinem alten Freund eine Skulptur für den Geheimdienstchef Markus Wolf bestellte. Zu seinem belgischen Lehrmeister Strebelle nahm Meier nie wieder Kontakt auf, auch nicht nach der Wende. Ein Spion bleibt immer Spion. Auch wenn er keiner mehr ist.   Ulrike Knöfel

Video: In Olivier Strebelles Atelier

spiegel.de/sp432016bruessel
oder in der App DER SPIEGEL

---

* Günther Rothe: „Meier/Miserre". Michael Imhof; 144 Seiten; 24,95 Euro.

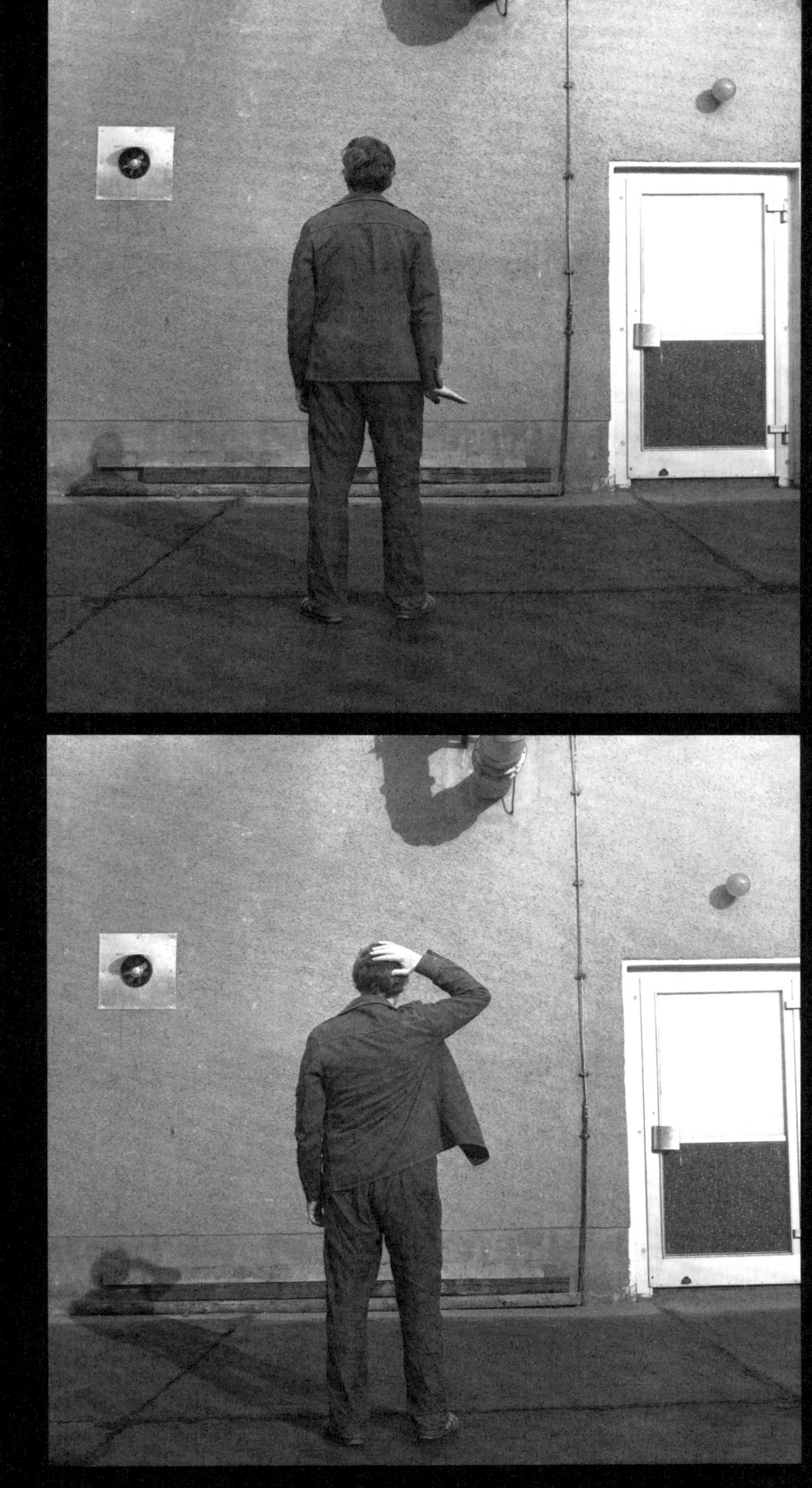

Author Biographies / Autorenbiografien

Jörg Heiser

Jörg Heiser is an art critic, university lecturer, curator, and musician. He earned his doctorate with the dissertation *Double Lives in Art and Pop Music* (published in 2015). Currently, he is a professor in the Faculty of Fine Arts at Berlin University of the Arts, where he is also dean and director of the Institute for Art in Context. For twenty years he worked as an editor for the art magazine *Frieze*.

Jörg Heiser ist Kunstkritiker, Hochschullehrer, Kurator und Musiker. Er wurde mit der Dissertation *Doppelleben Kunst und Popmusik* (erschienen 2015) promoviert, ist Professor an der Fakultät Bildende Kunst der Universität der Künste Berlin und ebendort Dekan und geschäftsführender Direktor des Instituts für Kunst im Kontext. Er arbeitete zwanzig Jahre als Redakteur für das Kunstmagazin *Frieze*.

Jelena Martinovic

Jelena Martinovic is a Swiss scholar, writer, and educator living in London. She has lectured internationally, most recently at Goldsmiths, University of London, and has developed educational projects in contemporary art. As a researcher at University College London, her work focuses on the historical relationship between art and science, and between medicine and mental health.

Jelena Martinovic ist eine in London lebende Schweizer Wissenschaftlerin, Schriftstellerin und Hochschullehrerin. Sie wirkt international als Gastdozentin, jüngst am Goldsmiths, University of London, und hat Bildungsprojekte zur zeitgenössischen Kunst entwickelt. Als Forscherin am University College London liegt ihr Tätigkeitsschwerpunkt auf der historischen Beziehung zwischen Kunst und Wissenschaft sowie zwischen Medizin und psychischer Gesundheit.

Metahaven

The work of Metahaven (b. 1980, b. 1971) consists of filmmaking, writing, and design. Solo exhibitions include: *Field Report*, RMIT, Melbourne (2020), *Turnarounds*, e-flux, New York (2019), *Version History*, ICA London (2018), *Earth*, Stedelijk Museum Amsterdam (2018), and *Hometown*, Izolyatsia, Kyiv (2018). Group exhibitions include: *Ghost:2651*, Bangkok (2018), the Busan Biennale (2018), and the Sharjah Biennial (2017). Recent publications include: *PSYOP: An Anthology* (London: Koenig Books, 2018), and *Digital Tarkovsky* (Moscow: Strelka Press, 2018).

Metahaven (geb. 1980 und 1971) arbeitet auf den Gebieten des Filmemachens, Schreibens und Designs. Einzelausstellungen unter anderen: *Field Report*, RMIT, Melbourne (2020), *Turnarounds*, e-flux, New York (2019), *Version History*, ICA London (2018), *Earth*, Stedelijk Museum Amsterdam (2018) und *Hometown*, Izolyatsia, Kyiv (2018). Gruppenausstellungen unter anderem: *Ghost:2651*, Bangkok (2018), Busan Biennale (2018) und Biennale von Sharjah (2017). Neuere Veröffentlichungen unter anderen: *PSYOP: An Anthology* (Koenig Books, London 2018) und *Digital Tarkovsky* (Strelka Press, Moskau 2018).

Marina Otero Verzier

Marina Otero Verzier is an architect based in Rotterdam. The director of research at Het Nieuwe Instituut, she leads research initiatives such as *Automated Landscapes*, *Work Body Leisure*, and *BURN-OUT: Exhaustion on a Planetary Scale*. As of September 2020, she will be head of the Master in Social Design program at the Design Academy Eindhoven.

Marina Otero Verzier ist eine in Rotterdam ansässige Architektin. Als Forschungsdirektorin am Het Nieuwe Instituut leitet sie Forschungsinitiativen wie *Automated Landscapes*, *Work Body Leisure* und *BURN-OUT: Exhaustion on a Planetary Scale*. Ab September 2020 wird sie die Leitung des Social-Design-Masterprogramms an der Design Academy Eindhoven innehaben.

Cristina Ricupero

Cristina Ricupero is an independent curator and art critic based in Paris. She has curated exhibitions worldwide and is known for her special interest in social issues and in constructing a storyline through an exhibition. This approach is evident in projects such as *Divided We Stand*, with Ricupero serving as artistic director of the Busan Biennale, South Korea (2018), *New Ways of Doing Nothing*, Kunsthalle Vienna (2014), *The Crime Was Almost Perfect*, Witte de With in Rotterdam and PAC-Milan (2014), and *Secret Societies*, Schirn Kunsthalle Frankfurt and CAPC de Bordeaux (2011–12).

Cristina Ricupero ist eine in Paris ansässige unabhängige Kuratorin und Kunstkritikerin. Sie hat weltweit Ausstellungen kuratiert und ist bekannt für ihr besonderes Interesse sowohl an sozialen Themen als auch daran, Ausstellungen entlang eines Erzählstrangs zu entwickeln. Diesen Ansatz veranschaulichen Projekte wie *Divided We Stand*, realisiert auf der von ihr künstlerisch verantworteten Busan Biennale, Südkorea (2018), *New Ways of Doing Nothing*, Kunsthalle Wien (2014), *The Crime Was Almost Perfect*, Witte de With in Rotterdam und PAC-Milan (2014), sowie *Secret Societies*, Schirn Kunsthalle Frankfurt und CAPC Bordeaux (2011–12).

Jonas Staal

Jonas Staal is an artist and the founder of the artistic and political organization *New World Summit* (2012-ongoing). He is also the co-initiator, together with the lawyer Jan Fermon, of the *Collectivize Facebook* lawsuit, which aims for users to become the cooperative owners of the Facebook platform. Staal's interdisciplinary work focuses on the relationship between art, democracy, and propaganda. His latest book is *Propaganda Art in the 21st Century* (Cambridge, MA: The MIT Press, 2019).

Jonas Staal ist Künstler und Gründer der künstlerischen und politischen Organisation *New World Summit*, die seit 2012 besteht. Auch hat er gemeinsam mit dem Rechtsanwalt Jan Fermon ein Gerichtsverfahren in Sachen *Collective Facebook* auf den Weg gebracht, das anstrebt, die Nutzerinnen und Nutzer zu genossenschaftlichen Eigentümern der Facebook-Plattform zu machen. Staal befasst sich in seiner interdisziplinären Arbeit mit der Beziehung zwischen Kunst, Demokratie und Propaganda. Zuletzt erschien sein Buch *Propaganda Art in the 21st Century* (The MIT Press, Cambridge, MA, 2019).

Noam Toran

Noam Toran's work involves the creation of intricate narratives developed as a means to disrupt hegemonic historiographies. Drawing from marginalized or neglected histories, Toran reflects upon the interrelations of memory, erasure, mythology, identity, and the essential force of storytelling as embodied in archives, films, literatures, and performances.

Noam Toran bezieht in seine Arbeit verwobene Narrative ein, die darauf angelegt sind, hegemonische Geschichtsschreibungen aufzubrechen. Aus marginalisierten oder kaum beachteten historischen Quellen schöpfend, reflektiert Toran über die Wechselbeziehungen zwischen Gedächtnis, Ausstreichung, Mythologie und Identität ebenso wie über die elementare Macht des Erzählens, wie sie sich in Archiven, Filmen, der Literatur und in Aufführungen entfaltet.

Wladimir Velminski

Wladimir Velminski studied mathematics, physics, Slavic studies, and cultural studies in Berlin and Moscow. In 2008, he received his doctorate from the Department of Art and Visual History (IKB) at the Humboldt University in Berlin. In addition to his work as founder of the Berlin-based publishing house ciconia ciconia, he heads the research area "Geschichte und Theorie medialer Regime in Osteuropa" (History and Theory of Media Regimes in Eastern Europe) at the Bauhaus-Universität Weimar. He is regularly offered visiting professorships in Germany and abroad, and he has authored numerous publications on Eastern European cultural and media history.

Wladimir Velminski studierte Mathematik, Physik, Slawistik und Kulturwissenschaft in Berlin und Moskau. 2008 wurde er am Institut für Kunst- und Bildgeschichte der Humboldt-Universität zu Berlin promoviert. Neben seiner Tätigkeit als Verleger des Berliner Verlags ciconia ciconia leitet er den Forschungsbereich „Geschichte und Theorie medialer Regime in Osteuropa" an der Bauhaus Universität Weimar, zudem werden ihm immer wieder Gastprofessuren im In- und Ausland angetragen. Er ist Autor zahlreicher Publikationen zur Kultur- und Mediengeschichte Osteuropas.

List of Works / Werkliste

Lawrence Abu Hamdan

The Whole Truth, 2012
Reverse engineered lie detector, 3-channel
video, stereo sound, desk, 2 chairs,
3 artificial plants / reprogrammierter
Lügendetektor, 3-Kanal-Video,
Ton (Stereo), Schreibtisch, 2 Stühle,
3 künstliche Pflanzen
24:00 min. (video), 612×435×190 cm
Courtesy the artist and Sfeir-Semler
Gallery Beirut / Hamburg

Maja Bajevic

How to Explain the World to the Martians,
2017
Series / Serie
Ink, print, collage on paper / Tinte,
Druck, Collage auf Papier
Each / je 78×57 cm

Just the Commercial, 2017
Video collage, color, sound / Videocollage,
Farbe, Sound
13:15 min. (loop)

All / alle: Courtesy the artist and Galerie
Kilchmann, Zurich / Zürich

Jean-Luc Blanc

Jeanne Angkor, 2020
Oil on canvas / Öl auf Leinwand
150×120 cm
Courtesy the artist

Nina Childress

Hedy, 2012
Oil on canvas / Öl auf Leinwand
250×200 cm
Courtesy the artist and Galerie Bernard
Jordan, Paris

Guy de Cointet

Enjoy the Commercials, 1971
Ink and pencil on paper / Tinte und
Bleistift auf Papier
47.8×60.5 cm
Private collection, courtesy Air de Paris

Remember the Stories About..., 1971
Ink and pencil on paper / Tinte und
Bleistift auf Papier
47.8×60.5 cm
Private collection, courtesy Air de Paris

When Radar Was New..., 1971
Felt-tip pen and pencil on paper /
Filzstift und Bleistift auf Papier
58.5×89 cm
Private collection, courtesy Air de Paris

Untitled (I Lovjad), ca. 1971
Polyptych (3 drawings) / Polyptychon
(3 Zeichnungen)
Felt-tip pen and pencil on paper /
Filzstift und Bleistift auf Papier
Each / je 27×38 cm
Private collection, courtesy Air de Paris

Untitled, ca. 1971
Polyptych (6 drawings) / Polyptychon
(6 Zeichnungen)
Felt-tip pen on thin paper / Filzstift auf
dünnem Papier
Each / je 28×21.5 cm
Private collection, courtesy Air de Paris

Sand Into Our..., 1972
Pencil on paper / Bleistift auf Papier
60.5×47.8 cm
Courtesy Guy de Cointet Society and
Air de Paris

...the..., 1976
Red ink on paper / rote Tinte auf Papier
48×61 cm
Private collection, courtesy Air de Paris

*The Medieval Painters Were Accustomed to
Prepare a Red Color*, ca. 1982
Ink and pencil on Arches paper / Tinte
und Bleistift auf Arches Papier
37.5×53.5 cm
Private collection, courtesy Air de Paris

Thomas Demand

Badezimmer, 1997
C-print / Diasec
160×122 cm
Courtesy the artist

Simon Denny

*Modded Server-Rack Display with David
Darchicourt Commissioned Map of
Aotearoa New Zealand*, 2015
Mixed media / verschiedene Materialien
254×350×313.5 cm
Courtesy the artist and Galerie
Buchholz, Berlin / Cologne / Hamburg

Dias & Riedweg

Cold Stories, 2010
Video installation, 4 puppets /
Videoinstallation, 4 Marionetten
Dimensions variable / Größe variabel
Puppets / Marionetten: 25×5×5 cm
Courtesy Galeria Vermelho, São Paulo

Stan Douglas

The Secret Agent, 2015 (adapted version
2020 / adaptierte Version 2020)
2-channel video installation, 4 audio
channels, 6 musical variations, color,
sound / 2-Kanal-Videoinstallation,
4 Audiokanäle, 6 musikalische
Variationen, Farbe, Sound
53:35 min. (loop)
Courtesy the artist, Victoria Miro and
David Zwirner

Charles and Ray Eames

Glimpses of the USA, 1959
Video installation / Videoinstallation
16:9 projection / Projektion
4:3 image pillarboxed / Bild mit Pillarbox
12:56 min. (loop)
Courtesy Eames Office LLC

Forensic Architecture

The Killing of Óscar Pérez, 2018
2:19 min. (video)
El Junquito Platform
Courtesy the artists

Dora García

The Romeos, 2018
Performance
Courtesy the artist

Mathis Gasser

Council / Burial, 2016
Collage and acrylic on paper /
Collage und Acryl auf Papier
59×42 cm

Disaster, 2016
Collage on paper / Collage auf Papier
59×42 cm

Disaster in Space, 2016
Collage on paper / Collage auf Papier
59×41.5 cm

Laboratories, 2016
Collage on paper / Collage auf Papier
59×40 cm

*Sculpture Garden
(Sparth / UN / McCracken)*, 2014
Collage and acrylic on paper /
Collage und Acryl auf Papier
59.5×42 cm

Space Jockey / United Nations, 2016
Collage on paper / Collage auf Papier
59×42 cm

All / alle: Courtesy the artist and
Weiss Falk, Basel

Rodney Graham

Newspaper Man, 2017
Painted aluminum light box with
transmounted chromogenic transparency / bemalter Aluminiumleucht-
kasten mit übertragenem chromogenem
Diapositiv
181.9×136.2×17.8 cm
Courtesy Museum Voorlinden, Wassenaar (The Netherlands / Niederlande)

Eva Grubinger

Control Tower (Dark Matter), 2003
Plywood, plexiglass, paint / Furnier-
platten, Plexiglas, Farbe
226×60×60 cm
Courtesy the artist

Humans since 1982

Surveillance Chandelier, 2011
Powder-coated aluminum, electronic
components / pulverbeschichtetes
Aluminium, elektronische Teile
100×90×75 cm
Courtesy Art Studio Humans since 1982,
founded by Bastian Bischoff and
Per Manuelsson

Alfredo Jaar

Searching for K, 1984
Photograph / Fotografie
18 panels and 1 pigment print / 18 Paneele
und 1 Pigmentdruck
Panels / Paneele: 34×81.6×35 cm
Pigment print / Pigmentdruck:
35.6×40.6 cm
Courtesy the artist, New York

Kiluanji Kia Henda

Under the Silent Eye of Lenin, 2017
Series of 20 posters / Serie mit 20 Postern
Mixed media, silkscreen, and inkjet print /
verschiedene Materialien, Siebdruck
und Tintenstrahldruck
84×60 cm
Courtesy the artist

Gabriel Lester

Collaboration with Monadnock
Architects
The Third Degree, 2020
Installation with sound / Installation
mit Ton
Dimensions variable / Größe variabel
Courtesy the artist, comissioned by
Schirn Kunsthalle Frankfurt

The Uninivited Guest 1, 2017
Photograph / Fotografie
80×60 cm
Courtesy the artist

The Uninivited Guest 2, 2017
Photograph / Fotografie
80×60 cm
Courtesy the artist

Lim Minouk

FireCliff2_Seoul, 2011
Video documentation / Videodokumen-
tation
Baek and Jang Theater of National
Theater Company of Korea
30:25 min. (adapted version, 2020 /
adaptierte Version 2020)
Courtesy the artist

Dora Longo Bahia

*Alice Marble / Switzerland, Germany / 1945–
1945 / M1 Carbine / Lee Miller 1945*, 2020
Water-based pen, acrylic paint on paper,
silkscreen on iron, iron frames, acrylic
on map mounted on foam board / Stift auf
Wasserbasis, Acryl auf Papier, Siebdruck
auf Eisen, Eisenrahmen, Acryl auf Land-
karte auf Schaumstoffplatte montiert
125×95 cm

*Coco Chanel / Germany, France, Spain,
Britain / 1941–1944 / StG44 / Unknown
1941*, 2020
Water-based pen, acrylic paint on paper,
silkscreen on iron, iron frames, acrylic on
map mounted on foam board / Stift auf
Wasserbasis, Acryl auf Papier, Siebdruck
auf Eisen, Eisenrahmen, Acryl auf Land-
karte auf Schaumstoffplatte montiert
105×115 cm

*Greta Garbo / Sweden, Britain, Germany,
Denmark, US, Bahamas / 1939–1945 /
Thompson Submachine Gun / Margaret
Bourke-White 1944*, 2020
Water-based pen, acrylic paint on paper,
silkscreen on iron, iron frames, acrylic
on map mounted on foam board / Stift auf
Wasserbasis, Acryl auf Papier, Siebdruck
auf Eisen, Eisenrahmen, Acryl auf Land-
karte auf Schaumstoffplatte montiert
150×100 cm

*Sonja Wigert / Sweden, Norway, Germany /
1942–1945 / Automatgevär m/42 /
Margaret Bourke-White 1945*, 2020
Water-based pen, acrylic paint on paper,
silkscreen on iron, iron frames, acrylic
on map mounted on foam board / Stift auf
Wasserbasis, Acryl auf Papier, Siebdruck
auf Eisen, Eisenrahmen, Acryl auf Land-
karte auf Schaumstoffplatte montiert
100×110 cm

All / alle: Courtesy the artist

Jill Magid

Becoming Tarden, 2010
Softcover book / Taschenbuch,
184 pages / Seiten,
13.4×21 cm, 1250 copies / Ausgaben

I Can Burn Your Face: Miranda IV, 2019
7 mm neon, transformers and wires /
7 mm Neon, Transformatoren und Kabel
Dimensions variable / Größe variabel

18 Spies, 2008
18 letterpress prints / 18 Hochdrucke
Each / je 43.2×27.9 cm

The Kosinski Quotes, 2007
9 four color silkscreen prints on Rives
BFK paper / 9 vierfarbige Siebdrucke auf
Rives BFK Papier
Each / je 69.9×111.8 cm

All / alle: Courtesy the artist and
LABOR, Mexico City

Fabian Marti

*3LvGvkLu98od9EugTPiRTKpXzagXBT
z3Wi*, 2020
Reduction-fired ceramics / reduktions-
gebrannte Keramik
25×26 cm

*36ByutkFwsdqjHPgWHEhQ6AEtzrq7W
Tx2Z*, 2020
Reduction-fired ceramics / reduktions-
gebrannte Keramik
37×31 cm

3Na2qeeZ6x3oHnjArdzKbdYRiX6TyspDf7,
2020
Reduction-fired ceramics / reduktions-
gebrannte Keramik
40×26 cm

37L7EL37q6q5SjDgicERnit8YVcz6Jizko,
2020
Reduction-fired ceramics / reduktions-
gebrannte Keramik
15.5×46 cm

*35sXKoqWSkWMPee7QFicNNnPik7fd3x
4cp*, 2020
Reduction-fired ceramics / reduktions-
gebrannte Keramik
27×27 cm

*352UKJPSAsg7m1Xwxo49gKw4XJMQNy
Q4KV*, 2020
Reduction-fired ceramics / reduktions-
gebrannte Keramik
33×32.5 cm

*34fUY8hYGGSFyNhQ2bKPaoeeEkqS17jC
Mj*, 2020
Reduction-fired ceramics / reduktions-
gebrannte Keramik
18×44 cm

*3KX2eaDFK7oDZ5kAgCqzJSX9s92xdKZ
k6B*, 2020
Reduction-fired ceramics / reduktions-
gebrannte Keramik
48×26 cm

*3Qu1gVwGDTD3jdJUZPHtrJeTwFZBKU
9woi*, 2020
Reduction-fired ceramics / reduktions-
gebrannte Keramik
36.5×31 cm

*32rJXFMzdZT79eiwB9MLVVW9yHsg1i
7ezJ*, 2020
Reduction-fired ceramics / reduktions-
gebrannte Keramik
18×42.5 cm

All / alle: Courtesy the artist

Josephine Meckseper

The Story of Mankind, 2014
Mixed media in a stainless steel and glass
vitrine with fluorescent lights and
acrylic sheeting / Verschiedene Materialien in einer Edelstahl-Glasvitrine
mit fluoreszierenden Lichtern und Acryl-
platten
203.2×203.2×50.8 cm
Courtesy the artist and Timothy Taylor,
London / New York

Mieko Meguro

Josephine Baker, 2020
Series of 9 paintings / Serie mit
9 Gemälden
Oil paint, charcoal, pencil, and colored
pencil on canvas / Öl, Kohle, Blei- und
Buntstift auf Leinwand
Each / je 35×28 cm
Courtesy the artist

Mathilda Carré, 2020
Series of 5 paintings / Serie mit
5 Gemälden
Oil paint, charcoal, pencil, and colored
pencil on canvas / Öl, Kohle, Blei- und
Buntstift auf Leinwand
Each / je 35×28 cm
Courtesy the artist

Metahaven

*The Sprawl (Propaganda about
Propaganda)*, 2016
Multiscreen video installation /
Multiscreen-Videoinstallation
Dimensions variable / Größe variabel
Courtesy the artists

Aleksandra Mir

Cold War, 2005
Felt-tip pen on paper / Filzstift auf
Papier, 8 sheets / Blätter
Each / je 152×177 cm
Total / insgesamt 302×469 cm
Courtesy the artist and Saatchi Gallery,
London

Henrike Naumann

Tag X, 2019
Installation with sound and video /
Installation mit Ton und Video
Dimensions variable / Größe variabel
Archive material of / Archivmaterial des
BStU, Narrator / Erzähler: Andreas Enke
Dramaturgy / Dramaturgie: Aljoscha
Begerich, Montage: Ekaterina Reinbold,
Sound design / Tongestaltung: Bastian
Hagedorn, Studio Henrike Naumann:
Carlo Bernhardt, Nik Mantilla, Christin
Rothe, Lara Wehrs
Courtesy the artist and KOW Berlin

Trevor Paglen

*Control Tower (Area 52); Tonopah Test
Range, NV; Distance ~ 20 miles; 11:55 a.m.*,
2006
C-print
76.2×91.4 cm

*Canyon Hangars and Unidentified Vehicle;
Tonopah Test Range, NV; Distance approx.
18 miles; 12:45 pm*, 2006
C-print
76.2×91.4 cm

*Code Names: Classified Military and
Intelligence Programs (2001–2007)*, 2009
Installation, vinyl / Installation, Vinyl
Dimensions variable / Größe variabel

They Watch the Moon, 2010
C-print
91.4×121.9 cm

*Reaper Drone; Indian Springs, NV;
Distance ~ 2 miles*, 2010
C-print
76.2×91.4 cm

*National Security Agency, Ft. Meade,
Maryland; National Reconnaissance
Office, Chantilly, Virginia; National
Geospatial-Intelligence Agency,
Springfield, Virginia*, 2014
Triptych / Triptychon, 3 C-prints
Each / je 45.7×68.6 cm

All / alle: Courtesy the artist and
Metro Pictures, New York

Park Chan-Kyong and
Park Chan-Wook

Believe It Or Not, 2018
Film
31:33 min.
Comissioned by Asia Culture Center
Moho Film Production
Courtesy the artists

Cornelia Schleime

Auf weitere gute Zusammenarbeit, 1993
Series of 14 / Serie von 14
Photograph on silkscreen / Fotografie
auf Siebdruck
Each / je 100×70 cm
Courtesy the artist and Deutsche Bank
Collection

Ich halte doch nicht die Luft an, 1982
Body performance / Körperaktion in
Hüpstedt
3 photographs by / 3 Fotografien von
Bernd Hiepe
Each / je 29.8×42 cm
Courtesy the artist

Jim Shaw

The Checkers Speech, 2019
Acrylic on muslin fabric / Acryl auf
Musselinstoff
96.5×132.1 cm

Mr. Hotdog, 2019
Acrylic on muslin fabric / Acryl auf
Musselinstoff
111.8×71.1×4.4 cm

Fighting On the Plain Of Jars, 2015
Acrylic on muslin fabric / Acryl auf
Musselinstoff
91.4×152.4 cm

*Study for the Liver is the Cocks Comb /
Prometheus*, 2015
Ink on paper / Tinte auf Papier
35.6×43.2 cm

*Study for the Wig Museum Installation
Elements*, 2017
Graphite on paper / Bleistift auf Papier
30.5×22.9 cm

Studies for Dreamt of Paperback Covers,
2013
Graphite on paper / Bleistift auf Papier
30.5×22.9 cm

Study for the Bay of Pigs Thing, 2019
Graphite on paper, Xerox copy / Bleistift
auf Papier, Fotokopie
47×81.3 cm

Study for Nazi Disinformation Piglets,
2018
Ink on paper / Tinte auf Papier
35.6×17.8 cm

All / alle: Courtesy the artist and
Praz-Delavallade, Paris / Los Angeles

Taryn Simon

*American Index, Transatlantic
Sub-Marine Cables Reaching Land, VSNL
International, Avon, New Jersey*, 2007
Chromogenic color print / Chromogen-
druck
113×94.6 cm
Courtesy the artist and Collection von
Kelterborn, Frankfurt am Main

*American Index, The Central Intelligence
Agency Main Entrance Hall, CIA Original
Headquarters Building*, 2007
Chromogenic color print / Chromogen-
druck
113×94.6 cm
Courtesy the artist and Collection von
Kelterborn, Frankfurt am Main

Jonas Staal

*Steve Bannon: A Propaganda
Retrospective, Model*, 2019
Video installation / Videoinstallation
4 tables with monitors / 4 Tische mit
Monitoren
Each / je 71.8×55 cm
Courtesy the artist

Noam Toran

If We Never Meet Again, 2010
Film with sound
Two 4:3 cube monitors / zwei tragbare
4:3-Monitore
7:25 min.
Courtesy the artist

Polygraph (from / aus Après-Coup), 2011
Vintage polygraph, custom electronics,
polygraph paper / Vintage Polygraph,
sonderangefertigte Elektronik, Poly-
graphenpapier
68×54 cm
Courtesy the artist

Suzanne Treister

*Tarot / Five of Swords – Google (from / aus
HEXEN 2.0)*, 2009–11
Archival giclée print with watercolor on
Hahnemühle Bamboo paper / archivali-
scher Gicléedruck und Wasserfarben auf
Hahnemühle Bambuspapier
21×29.7 cm

*Tarot / Three of Swords – MK ULTRA
(from / aus HEXEN 2.0)*, 2009–11
Archival giclée print with watercolor on
Hahnemühle Bamboo paper / archivalischer Gicléedruck und Wasserfarben auf
Hahnemühle Bambuspapier
21×29.7 cm

*CIA/Cruiser, AlienEyeExtended, Bubble-
Soft, Creeper, Flashback, Berliner,
SandCastles, LushlifeExtended, Tahoma,
Courier New, Haight, Chainlink, Enchant-
ment, Gravure-Plain, Copperplate, Impact,
Hobo Std, Sixties Vibe, LibertySpike,
MKUltra, Rosewood Std, Neon, Gill Sans,
Slasher, SwampTerror, WavyOrnamental,
VanVeen, DigitalMachineExtended,
BlackOak Std, Times New Roman*, 2017
30 archival giclée prints / 30 archivali-
sche Gicléedrucke
Each / je 42×29.7 cm
Total / insgesamt 148.5×252 cm

*POST-SURVEILLANCE ART POSTER /
NSA SEX BOMB*, 2014
Archival giclée print on Hahnemühle
Bamboo paper / archivalischer Gicléе-
druck und Wasserfarben auf Hahnemühle Bambuspapier
42×29.7 cm

*POST-SURVEILLANCE ART POSTER /
NSA ON DRUGS*, 2014
Archival giclée print on Hahnemühle
Bamboo paper / archivalischer Gicléе-
druck und Wasserfarben auf Hahnemühle Bambuspapier
29.7×42 cm

CAMOUFLAGE / NetOpsSV_2008_P1,
2013
Inkjet and watercolor on Hahnemühle
Bamboo paper / Tintenstrahldruck und
Wasserfarben auf Hahnemühle Bambuspapier
29.7×21 cm

CAMOUFLAGE / GIG-AV_V1_2007_P29,
2013
Inkjet and watercolor on Hahnemühle
Bamboo paper / Tintenstrahldruck und
Wasserfarben auf Hahnemühle Bambuspapier
29.7×21 cm

CAMOUFLAGE / GIG-AV_V1_2007_P12,
2013
Inkjet and watercolor on Hahnemühle
Bamboo paper / Tintenstrahldruck und
Wasserfarben auf Hahnemühle Bambuspapier
29.7×21 cm

CIA, 2011
Ink and watercolor on paper / Tinte und
Wasserfarben auf Papier
152×244 cm

HEXEN 2.0, 2009–11
Tarot deck / Tarotkarten
Box of 78 cards / Schachtel mit 78 Karten
Each card / jede Karte 9×15 cm

The U.S. National Security Agency on Fire,
2010
Pencil on watercolor paper / Bleistift auf
Aquarellpapier
63×122 cm

*HEXEN 2.0 / Historical Diagrams / From
ARPANET to DARWARS via the Internet*,
2009–11
Ink and watercolor on paper / Tinte und
Wasserfarben auf Papier
122×152 cm

HEXEN 2039 / DVD, 2006
Film
45:00 min.

All / alle: Courtesy the artist and Annely
Juda Fine Art, London

Nomeda & Gediminas Urbonas

TRANSmutation, 2018
Video installation / Videoinstallation
Dimensions variable / Größe variabel
Courtesy the artists

Jane and Louise Wilson

Stasi City, 1997
4-channel video installation / 4-Kanal-
Videoinstallation
4:50 min. (loop)
Courtesy the artists and 303 Gallery,
New York

Liam Young

Written by / geschrieben von Tim
Maughan
Where the City Can't See, 2012
Film
Shot entirely with laser scanners /
Komplett mit Laserscannern gedreht
11:00 min.
Courtesy the artist

Tamir Zadok

Art Undercover, 2017
Film
27:00 min.
Courtesy the artist and Rosenfeld
Gallery

We extend our thanks to Deutsches
Filmmuseum in Frankfurt am Main,
Deutsche Kinemathek in Berlin, and
La Cinémathèque Française in Paris for
generously providing all film posters. /
Wir danken dem Deutschen Filmmuseum
in Frankfurt am Main, der Deutschen
Kinemathek in Berlin und der Cinéma-
thèque française in Paris für die groß-
zügige Bereitstellung aller Filmplakate.

We also thank the following organiza-
tions for generously providing all
historical objects: Heinz Nixdorf
MuseumsForum in Paderborn,
Deutsches Spionagemuseum in Berlin,
Stasimuseum in Berlin, Combined
Military Services Museum in Maldon,
Essex, Musée de l'Armée in Paris,
Archives nationales in Paris, and Bürger-
komitee Leipzig e. V. für die Auflösung
der ehemaligen Staatssicherheit (MfS). /
Wir danken dem Heinz Nixdorf
MuseumsForum in Paderborn, dem
Deutschen Spionagemuseum in Berlin,
dem Stasimuseum in Berlin, dem
Combined Military Services Museum
in Maldon, Essex, dem Musée de l'Armée
und den Archives nationales in Paris
sowie dem Bürgerkomitee Leipzig e. V.
für die Auflösung der ehemaligen
Staatssicherheit (MfS) für die großzügige
Bereitstellung aller historischen
Objekte.

Images / Abbildungen

Gabriel Lester, Double Crossed, 2020, pp. / S. 14, 28, 60, 99f.; Simon Menner, Images from the Secret Stasi Archives or: what does Big Brother see, while he is watching? / 2019, pp. / S. 38, 109, 119, 124, 135, 165f., 171f., 175; Noam Toran, Camp 33, 2020, pp. / S. 33f., 55; Promotional photograph with Jack Palance for the film / Werbefoto mit Jack Palance für den Film Man in the Attic, 1953, 20th Century Fox, p. / S. 2; Barbara Feldon as Agent 99 in the television series / Barbara Feldon als Agent 99 aus der Fernsehserie Get Smart, 1966, NBC Television, p. / S. 2; Appaloosa, State Security Camera from the GDR / Kamera der Stasi aus der DDR, 2008, p. / S. 2; Lockheed USAF SR-71 Blackbird, 1994, U. S. Air Force, p. / S. 3; Demonstration of a polygraph / Vorführung eines Polygraphentests, 1970, U. S. Federal Bureau of Investigation, p. / S. 3; Headquarters of the / Hauptquartier der National Security Agency in Fort Meade, Maryland, 2006, U. S. National Security Agency, p. / S. 4; Ethel Rosenberg Arrest Photograph, 1950, U. S. National Archives and Records Administration, p. / S. 4; Al-Qaida training manual/ al-Qaida Trainingshandbuch, 2001, U. S. Central Intelligence Agency, p. / S. 4; Film still from the trailer for / Filmstill aus dem Trailer für Alfred Hitchcocks Foreign Correspondent, 1944, Walter Wanger Productions, p. / S. 5; David McCullum playing Illya Kuryakin in the film / David McCullum als Illya Kuryakin aus dem Film The Man from U.N.C.L.E., 1965, McDermott Company, p. / S. 5; Tom Tschida, MQ-9 Reaper Satcom, 2005, NASA, p. / S. 5; Glove gun / Handschuhpistole, 2017, Joy of Museums / International Spy Museum, Washington, DC, p. / S. 6; Training of special agents / Training von Spezialagenten in Fort Meade, 1949, U. S. Air Force, p. / S. 6; Promotional photograph with Hedy Lamarr for the film / Werbefoto mit Hedy Lamarr für den Film Heavenly Body, MGM, 1944, p. / S. 6; AntanO, Lens of a Mini-Camcorder / Linse eines Mini-Camcorders, 2015, p. / S. 6; Insect drone / Insektendrohne, 2011, U. S. Central Intelligence Agency, p. / S. 8; Dynazoom, 2008, U. S. Central Intelligence Agency, p. / S. 8; USS West Mahomet, 1918, U. S. Navy, p. / S. 8; Underwater Ice Station Zebra, U. S. Central Intelligence Agency, 2012, p. / S. 23; "Dead" drop spike / Briefstift, 2011, U. S. Central intelligence Agency, p. / S. 23; Dancer and Espionage Agent / Tänzerin und Spionin Mata Hari, 1906, Bettmann-Archiv, p. / S. 23; Golden cigarette lighter from the U.S. Embassy in Moscow / Goldener Zigarettenanzünder aus US-Botschaft in Moskau, 2012, U. S. Central Intelligence Agency, p. / S. 23; Elvis Presley and / und Richard Nixon, 1970, Executive Office of the President of the United States, p. / S. 24; Tessina camera hidden in a package of cigarettes / Tessina Kamera versteckt in Zigarettenpackung, 2011, U. S. Central Intelligence Agency, p. / S. 24; Promotional photograph with Barbara Feldon as Agent 99 and Joseph Ruskin for the series / Werbefoto mit Barbara Feldon als Agent 99 und Joseph Ruskin für die Serie Get Smart, 1965, NBC Television, p. / S. 24; Manuel Noriega with agents from the / Manuel Noriega mit Agenten der U. S. Drug Enforcement Administration, 1990, U. S. Air Force, p. / S. 44; Daan Noske / Anefo, Captain Idenek Jansen at Bromma Airport in Sweden / Kapitän Idenek Jansen am Flughafen Bromma in Schweden, 1955, p. / S. 44; Andrew Harnik / AP, Lawyer and former CIA employee / Anwalt und ehemaliger CIA-Mitarbeiter Jeffrey Alexander Sterling, 2015, p. / S. 45; Payment to an informant in the Philippines / Bezahlung eines Informanten auf den Philippinen, 2007, U. S. Navy, p. / S. 45; Flag design for / Graphic Tribe, Entwurf für eine Flagge für WikiLeaks, 2010, p. / S. 45; Bradley Manning, 2012, U. S. Army, p. / S. 45; Dmitry Rozhkov, Russian model and former agent / Russisches Model und ehemalige Agentin Anna Chapman, 2019, p. / S. 131; Espen Moe, Julian Assange, 2010, p. / S. 131; The "Spirit of the Missouri" on its maiden flight / Die „Spirit of Missouri" bei ihrem Erstflug, 2007, U. S. Air Force, p. / S. 131; Robert Hanssen, 2001, U. S. Federal Bureau of Investigation, p. / S. 131; FNMMP dolphin with locator / Delfin mit Ortungsgerät, 2003, U. S. Navy, p. / S. 148; Chinese opera singer and spy / Chinesischer Opernsänger und Spion Shi Pei Pu, ca. 1965, p. / S. 148; Radio hidden in a tobacco pipe / In einer Tabakpfeife verstecktes Funkgerät, 2011, U. S. Central Intelligence Agency, p. / S. 148; Host gift from / Gastgeschenk der Civil Air Transport, 2011, U. S. Central Intelligence Agency, p. / S. 148; Jason Rogers, Cap Gun / Spielzeugpistole, 2008, p. / S. 149; Letter remover / Briefentferner, 2011, U. S. Central Intelligence Agency, p. / S. 149; Team of agents for tracking down Soviet double agents / Agententeam zur Aufspürung sowjetischer Doppelagenten, 1990, U. S. Central Intelligence Agency, p. / S. 149; Agent / Agentin Noor Inayat Khan, 1943, Government of the United Kingdom, p. / S. 149

Back flap / Umschlagklappe: An owl illustrates the slogan "We never sleep" / Eine Eule illustriert den Slogan „We never sleep", Eighth Annual Convention of the United Typothetae of America, 1894

Image Credits / Bildnachweise

© Bettmann Archiv, p. / S. 23; © culture-images/fai, p. / S. 41; © Photo / Foto: Embassy of Saudi Arabia, p. / S. 46; © Executive Office of the President of the United States, p. / S. 24; © Photo / Foto: Alexander Demianchuk / Reuters, p. / S. 104; © Photo / Foto: Andrew Harnik/ AP, p. / S. 45; © Photo / Foto: AntanO, p. / S. 6; © Photo / Foto: Appaloosa, p. / S. 2; © Photo / Foto: Daan Noske / Anefo, p. / S. 44; © Photo / Foto: Dmitry Rozhkov, p. / S. 131; © Photo / Foto: Espen Moe, p. / S. 131; © Photo / Foto: Jason Rogers, p. / S. 149; © Photo / Foto: Joy of Museums, p. / S. 6; © Photo / Foto: Lee / Getty Images, p. / S. 42; © Photo / Foto: Nigina Beroeva, p. / S. 48; © Photo/ Foto: Yuri Kochetkov / epa, p. / S.105; © NASA, Photo / Foto: Tom Tschida, p. / S. 5; © New York Public Library, p. / S. 108; © Government of the United Kingdom, p. / S. 149; © U. S. Air Force, pp. / S. 3, 6, 44, 131; © U. S. Army, p. / S. 45; © U. S. Central Intelligence Agency, pp. / S. 4, 8, 23, 24, 148, 149; © U. S. Federal Bureau of Investigation, pp. / S. 3, 131; © U. S. National Archives and Records Administration, p. / S. 4; © U. S. National Security Agency, p. / S. 4; © U. S. Navy, pp. / S. 8, 45, 148

In spite of our best efforts, it has not always been possible to discover the owners of the rights to the pictures. Any justified claims in this regard will of course be recompensed under the usual agreements. / Trotz sorgfältiger Recherche war es nicht in allen Fällen möglich, die Rechteinhaber zu ermitteln. Berechtigte Ansprüche werden selbstverständlich im Rahmen der üblichen Vereinbarungen abgegolten.

Text Credits / Textnachweise

P. / S. 137: Jonas Staal, "Propaganda (Art) Struggle," *e-flux journal* #94 (October / Oktober 2018).
P. / S. 151: Metahaven, "Captives of the Cloud: Part I," *e-flux journal* #37 (September 2012).
P. / S. 167: Joanna Moorhead, "The artist who spied on MI6," *The Guardian* (February 14 / 14. Februar 2011).
P. / S. 173: Ulrike Knöfel, "Der Spion, der sich als Künstler tarnte," *DER SPIEGEL* 43 (2016), pp. / S. 118f.

Back flap / Umschlagklappe: "Language of Espionage," Courtesy of the International Spy Museum, © 2020 International Spy Museum, All Rights Reserved.

Colophon / Impressum

This catalogue is published in conjunction with the exhibition / Dieser Katalog erscheint anlässlich der Ausstellung

We Never Sleep

An exhibition project initiated and conceived by / Die Ausstellung wurde initiiert und konzipiert von Alexandra Midal and / und Cristina Ricupero

Schirn Kunsthalle Frankfurt September 24, 2020 - January 10, 2021 / 24. September 2020 - 10. Januar 2021

Editors / Herausgeberinnen Cristina Ricupero, Alexandra Midal, Katharina Dohm (Schirn)

Schirn Publication Management / Publikationsmanagement Schirn Antonia Lagemann, Anuschka Berthelius

Copyediting / Lektorat Dawn Michelle d'Atri (English / Englisch) Snoeck Verlag (German / Deutsch)

Translations / Übersetzung Susie Hondl (German-English / Deutsch-Englisch) Stefan Barmann (English-German / Englisch-Deutsch)

Graphic Design / Gestaltung Image collages / Bildcollagen NODE Berlin Oslo Serge Rompza, Lea Sievertsen

Production / Gesamtherstellung Snoeck Verlagsgesellschaft mbH, Cologne / Köln

© 2020 Schirn Kunsthalle Frankfurt, Snoeck Verlagsgesellschaft mbH, authors and artists / Autoren und Künstler

© 2020 for the reproduced works by / für die abgebildeten Werke von Gabriel Lester: © Gabriel Lester; Simon Menner: © Simon Menner and / und BStU; Viktor Pivovarov: © Viktor Pivovarov; Noam Toran: © Noam Toran

The assertion of all claims according to Article 60h UrhG (Copyright Act) for the reproduction of exhibition/collection objects is carried out by VG Bild-Kunst. / Die Geltendmachung der Ansprüche gem. § 60h UrhG für die Wiedergabe von Abbildungen der Exponate/Bestandswerke erfolgt durch die VG Bild-Kunst.

Published by / Erschienen im Snoeck Verlagsgesellschaft mbH Nievenheimer Str. 18 50739 Cologne / Köln www.snoeck.de

ISBN 978-3-86442-318-5

Printed in Germany

Exhibition / Ausstellung Schirn Kunsthalle Frankfurt

Director / Direktor Philipp Demandt

Deputy Director & Head of Exhibitions / Stellvertretende Direktorin & Ausstellungsleitung Esther Schlicht

Curators / Kuratorinnen Cristina Ricupero in collaboration with / in Zusammenarbeit mit Katharina Dohm (Schirn)

Student Assistant / Studentische Hilfskraft Alica Sänger

Registrars / Organisation Karin Grüning, Elke Walter, Luise Leyer

Supervision of Installation Crew / Leitung Hängeteam Andreas Gundermann

Conservators / Restaurierung Stefanie Gundermann, Susanne Silbernagel

Technical Services / Technische Leitung Christian Teltz, Oliver Taschke

Exhibition Architecture / Ausstellungsarchitektur Adrien Rovero

Exhibition Design / Ausstellungsgrafik VERY, Frankfurt

Press / Presse Johanna Pulz, Julia Bastian, Elisabeth Pallentin, Isabelle Hammer

Schirn Magazine / Schirn Magazin Antonia Lagemann, Anuschka Berthelius

Marketing Luise Bachmann, Heike Stumpf, Isabel Reiche, Elena Schmidt

Sponsoring Julia Lange, Hannah Ruiz

Education / Pädagogik
Chantal Eschenfelder, Simone
Boscheinen, Laura Heeg, Olga
Schaetz, Anna Haag

Events & Visitor Management /
Veranstaltungen &
Besuchermanagement
Ute Seiffert, Lena Sobczinski

Administration / Verwaltung
Heike Berndt, Tanja Mayer, Boris
Deckelmann

Assistant Head of Exhibitions /
Assistenz Ausstellungsleitung
Anna Noll

Assistant to the Director /
Assistenz Direktion
Andrea Canthal

Cleaning Supervision / Leitung
Gebäudereinigung
Rosaria La Tona

Reception / Empfang
Bettina Beyermann, Vilizara
Antalavicheva, Josef Härig

FRIENDS OF THE SCHIRN
KUNSTHALLE E. V. / VEREIN
DER FREUNDE DER SCHIRN
KUNSTHALLE E. V.

Executive Board / Vorstand

Christian Strenger (Chairman /
Vorsitzender)
Antje Conzelmann
Philipp Demandt
Hartmuth Jung
Sylvia von Metzler
Shahpar Oschmann
Ulrike von der Recke

Board of Trustees / Kuratorium

Rolf-E. Breuer (Chairman /
Vorsitzender)
Uwe Bicker
Clemens Börsig
Andreas Dombret
Armin von Falkenhayn
Diego Fernández-Reumann
Jürgen Fitschen
Peter Gatzemeier
Joachim Häger
Helmut Häuser
Elisabeth Haindl

Gerhard Hess
Marli Hoppe-Ritter
Gisela von Klot-Heydenfeldt
Jessica Köhler
Salomon Korn
Renate Küchler
Jörg Kukies
Simone Menne
Andreas Muschter
Lutz R. Raettig
Tobias Rehberger
Horst Reinhardt
Michael Riedel
Petra Roth
Florian Schilling
Martin Scholich
Willi Schoppen
Doris Maria Schuster
Nikolaus Schweickart
Wolf Singer
Claudia Steigenberger
Bettina Volkens
Eberhard Weiershäuser
Susanne Zeidler
Matthias Zieschang

Schirn Contemporaries / Schirn
Zeitgenossen

Jan Bauer and / und
Lena Wallenhorst
Oliver and / und Nicole Behrens
Olaf Gerber and / und
Nicole Emmerling de Oliveira
Markus Hammer and / und
Birgit Heller
Hartmuth and / und Lilia Jung
Shahpar Oschmann
Björn and / und Kim Robens
Jörg Rockenhäuser and / und
Vasiliki Basia
Reiner Sachs and / und
Brigitta Bailly
Julia Schönbohm and / und
Ralf Böckle

Corporate Members / Fördernde
Firmenmitglieder

Deutsche Bank AG
Deutsche Beteiligungs AG
Deutsche Börse AG
DWS Investments GmbH
Europäische Zentralbank
Fraport AG
Gemeinnützige Hertie-Stiftung
Landwirtschaftliche Rentenbank
Lufthansa Group
Morgan Stanley Bank AG
Nomura Bank (Deutschland)
GmbH

ODDO BHF AG
UBS Europe SE
Verianos AG

Managemant / Geschäftsführung
Tamara Fürstin von Clary

PARTNERS / PARTNER

Corporate Partners of the
Schirn Kunsthalle Frankfurt /
Corporate Partner der
Schirn Kunsthalle Frankfurt

Bank of America
Bloomberg L.P.
Commerz Real AG
HEUSSEN
Rechtsanwaltsgesellschaft mbH
Le Méridien Frankfurt
Messe Frankfurt GmbH
Oliver Wyman GmbH
PPI AG
PwC

Partners of the Schirn
Kunsthalle Frankfurt, the Städel
Museum, and the Liebieghaus
Skulpturensammlung / Partner
der Schirn Kunsthalle Frankfurt,
des Städel Museums und der
Liebieghaus Skulpturensammlung

Allianz Global Investors
Fraport AG
Samsung Electronics

Cultural Partner / Kulturpartner

hr2-kultur

Cristina Ricupero would like to
especially thank / Ein besonderer
Dank von Cristina Ricupero
an: Alexandra Midal, Véronique
Bacchetta, Francisca Bagulho,
Florence Bonnefous, Dora Longo
Bahia, Ina Blom, Giangi Fonti,
Eva Grubinger, Jörg Heiser,
Gabriel Lester, Fabian Marti,
Rubens Ricupero, Adrien Rovero,
Nicolaus Schafhausen, Caroline
Schneider, Noam Toran, Gabriela
Trujillo, Nomeda & Gediminas
Urbonas, Christine Van Assche,
Sophie Vianey